CLEARED FOR TAKE-OFF

In memory of Donal Griffin, S.C.

Cleared for Take-Off

Structure and strategy in the low fare airline business

THOMAS C. LAWTON
Imperial College London

ASHGATE

Published by
Ashgate Publishing Limited
Gower House
Croft Road
Aldershot
Hants GU11 3HR
England

Ashgate Publishing Company
Suite 420
101 Cherry Street
Burlington, VT 05401-4405
USA

Ashgate website:http://www.ashgate.com

British Library Cataloguing in Publication Data
Cleared for take-off : structure and strategy in the low
    fare airline business. - (Ashgate studies in aviation
    economics and management)
    1.Airlines - Europe - Management 2.Aeronautics, Commercial
    - Europe - Deregulation 3.Competition - Europe
    I.Lawton, Thomas C.
    387.7'068

Library of Congress Control Number: 2001099943

ISBN 0 7546 1269 4

Reprinted 2003, 2004

Printed and bound in Great Britain by MPG Books Ltd, Bodmin, Cornwall

Contents

List of Tables

List of Figures

Acknowledgements

As with every undertaking of this magnitude, I am beholden to many people for their occasional or ongoing support. At the risk of omission, permit me to thank those individuals who proved particularly helpful.

Within the low fare airline sector, my thanks to Sean Coyle and Jim Callaghan of Ryanair, Toby Nicol of easyJet, Tony Camacho of Buzz and representatives of Go and Virgin Express who would prefer to remain anonymous. I am grateful to both easyJet and Southwest Airlines for permission to reproduce images of their aircraft on the front cover of this book. A number of people were of assistance in this matter: Dr Thomas Seamster, Cognitive and Human Factors, New Mexico, USA; Linda Rutherford, Director of PR, Southwest Airlines; Dr Nawal Taneja, Ohio State University, USA; John Jamotta, Senior Director for Airline Planning, Southwest Airlines.

A number of other industry executives were very helpful, most notably Stanislav Solomko and Lian Qiu of Air Canada. Emy Lin, formerly of EVA Airlines, was kind enough to provide me with numerous industry publications during 2000/2001. Among industry associations, a note of thanks to Andrew Clarke, Director of Air Transport Policy at the European Regions Airline Association. In airport authorities, I am grateful to John Burke, Chief Executive and Tom Haughey, Director of Market Development and Strategy at Aer Rianta for their time and contribution.

In the realm of aviation consultants, Conor McCarthy, Managing Director of PlaneConsult.com and David Stewart, Principal of AeroStrategy, were especially authoritative and consistently obliging. My thanks also to David Feldman, Vice President of Mercer Consulting (France) for his input.

Managers at the UK Civil Aviation Authority's Economic Regulation Group proved particularly accommodating. In addition to Trevor Smedley, Head of Policy and Strategy, I am especially grateful to Trevor Metson, Fares Manager, who provided much needed data and feedback.

Within government, thanks go to Matt Benville and Roger Harrington at the Aviation and Airports Division of the Irish Department of Public Enterprise and Tim May, Aviation Directorate, UK Department of the Environment, Transport and the Regions.

A number of scholars have also given of their time to provide verbal comments or to read chapter drafts. These include Professor Dean Headley of the W. Frank Barton School of Business, Wichita State University, Kansas and Dr Steven McGuire of the University of Bath School of Management. In addition, my thanks to both Professor Headley and Professor Brent Bowen of the Aviation Institute at the University of Nebraska, Omaha, for permitting me to reproduce their AQR model in Chapter 5. I am also grateful to participants at the July 2001 AMERC conference organised by the John Molson School of Business at Concordia University, Montreal, in collaboration with IATA, for useful feedback on my conference paper derived from sections of this book. Philippe Albe deserves a mention at this point for his research support in gathering data for the AMERC conference paper and the related Chapters 3 and 4 of this work.

I have profited from discussions with numerous knowledgeable friends. A special thank you to Dr Kevin Michaels, Principal of AeroStrategy, for his constant help, keen insights and critical eye.

My publisher, John Hindley, deserves a mention for encouraging me to undertake this project and for his ongoing promotional efforts. Thank you also to Cambridge University Press, Elsevier Science and the Journal of Air Transportation (formerly the JATWW) for allowing me to reproduce sections of papers that I previously published in their respective periodicals.

I would like to convey my appreciation to my father, James Lawton, for his research support throughout this venture. He was assiduous in keeping a watchful eye on the Irish press and ensuring that I received copies of all newspaper reports on Ryanair in particular and the aviation business more generally.

As ever, Kirstin was the main source of editorial assistance and support throughout. I should also spare a thought for her having to endure many years of my plane spotting. It must be rather tedious to listen to endless turnaround time comparisons and comments on service quality on every air journey!

Finally, this book is dedicated to my uncle, Fr Donal Griffin, who died shortly before its completion. A professor of English literature, scholar of Irish ecclesiastical history and priest in the Missionary Society of St. Columban, he spent almost fifty years of his life ministering to spiritual and educational needs in East Asia. *Requiescat in pace*.

Thomas C. Lawton
London, England

Abbreviations

AEA	Association of European Airlines
ANZ	Air New Zealand
ASK	available seat-kilometre
ASM	available seat-mile
ATK	available tonne-kilometre
ATM	available ton-mile
AQR	Airline Quality Ranking
AUT	Air Transport Users Council
BA	British Airways
BELF	breakeven load factor
CAA	Civil Aviation Authority (UK)
COREPER	Committee of Permanent Representatives
CRS	computer(ised) reservations system
DoT	Department of Transportation (USA)
ECAC	European Civil Aviation Conference
EC	European Community
ERA	European Regions Airline Association
EU	European Union
FAA	Federal Aviation Administration (USA)
GDP	gross domestic product
GPS	global positioning system
IATA	International Air Transport Association
ICAO	International Civil Aviation Organisation
LFA	low fare airline
RAA	Regional Airlines Association (US)
RPK	revenue passenger-kilometre
RPM	revenue passenger-mile
RTK	revenue tonne-kilometre
RTM	revenue ton-mile
SEA	Single European Act
SIA	Singapore Airlines
SKA	seat-kilometre available
TCAA	Transatlantic Common Aviation Area
TAESA	Transportes Aeroes Ejecutivos (Mexico)

TKA	tonne-kilometre available
VFR	visiting friends and relatives
WTO	World Trade Organisation
YMS	yield management system

Chapter 1

Prologue:
Setting the Scene

Shake-ups and shakeouts

The decade spanning the second and third millennia proved a tumultuous time for world airline business. The globalisation of the industry, accompanied by market deregulation in Europe and parts of Asia, encouraged a newfound vigour in a relatively staid industry.[1] These dynamics prompted the emergence of a multitude of price-based competitors, together with a fundamental restructuring of most existing airline companies and a consolidation of the airline industry. Consolidation was symbolised by first, a wave of mergers and acquisitions, particularly in the United States (US); and second, the emergence of a number of competing global alliance groups. These two phenomena are interrelated, with the largest survivors of US industry consolidation spearheading the formation of global alliance clusters. As Friedel Rödig, former Star Alliance chief executive, commented:

> the number of alliances will be as many as there are large US partners…it is vital for each alliance to have a footing in the US.[2]

Most of the world airline industry therefore consolidated around a number of strategic 'families' of airlines, each one led by a large US – and European – airline. By early 2001, five such strategic families existed in global aviation. The Star Alliance had 15 member airlines and included large carriers like United Airlines, Air Canada, Singapore Airlines and Lufthansa. Oneworld had eight members and was headed by large carriers such as American Airlines, British Airways (BA), Cathay Pacific and Quantas. The Qualiflyer Group had 11 participants, including Swissair, Air Portugal and LOT Polish Airlines, but did not include any of the largest airlines and lacked a US member. Skyteam was smaller, having five associates, but did count major carriers such as Delta Airlines and Air France amongst its numbers. The final grouping had the fewest number of member airlines and was a more integrated coalition between Northwest Airlines, KLM and Alitalia. In terms of share of the world air passenger market, figures for 2000 ranked the Star Alliance first (19 per cent), followed by Oneworld (13 per cent), Skyteam (10 per cent), Northwest/KLM/Alitalia (nine per cent) and Qualiflyer trailed with three per cent.[3] Overall, alliance groups constitute well in excess of 50 per cent of the total world air passenger market. These alliances offer numerous benefits to participating airlines such as cost savings, improved interlining service for customers and transcontinental hub-and-spoke networks. The downside is the impact on competition and therefore on the consumer, with at least the symbolic, if not actual, entrenchment of an oligopolistic structure in world aviation. It also indicates a return to pre-deregulation norms in the US and in the EU. However, there is one fundamental difference between the airline market of today and that of Europe in the 1980s or the US in the 1970s: alongside the large traditional airlines and their strategic partners are well-established, low price alternatives. Companies such as Southwest Airlines and JetBlue in the US and Ryanair and easyJet in Europe offer a clear and proven alternative model of air transport. Their profit margins and return on assets are among the highest in the industry and their cost structures and fare prices are forcing larger airlines to restructure and rethink their value proposition. It is these low cost/low price carriers that represent the emphasis of our study.

Purpose and parameters

This book is a general introduction to and overview of the low fare airline (LFA) sector, its market and competitor context and the structures and strategies of its main protagonists. It is not intended as a comprehensive economic or managerial study. We examine the industry structure and market conditions of the European airline sector, identify the main low fare carriers and comment on the impact that low fare operators have had on stimulating competition within the European air transport market. Significant attention is also given to the low fare experience elsewhere in the world, particularly in the US but also in Canada and Australia and to a lesser extent, Japan and Latin America. The competitive strategies of the main LFAs are compared and their limitations are highlighted. The US deregulation experience indicates that the large number of low fare carriers which emerge in the wake of market deregulation will dwindle over time and that only a handful will ultimately survive. Many are driven out of business by insufficient access to landing slots or by predatory activity on the part of larger airlines. Others simply cut prices further than they can afford, effectively pricing themselves out of the market. We determine the conditions and strategies that shape sustainable advantage for LFAs in highly competitive deregulated markets where established airlines seek to force out new entrants and considerable political interference remains. Despite the inevitability of a shakeout reminiscent of early 1980s America, Europe's LFA sector is here to stay. Ever increasing industry liberalisation, together with customer demand, will guarantee a place in the market for cost efficient and reliable low fare carriers.

The cult of cost reduction

Constant and ever improving methods of operational cost reduction are *de rigueur* for any organisation. Ames and Hlavacek (1990) argue that managing costs is at the heart of every successful company and that four related cost truisms apply universally to every business situation. These are first, over the long term, it is essential to be a lower cost supplier; second, to maintain a competitive position, the inflation-adjusted costs of producing and supplying any product or service must continuously decrease; third, the true cost and profit of each product or service and every customer segment must always be transparent; and fourth, a company should focus on cash flow as much as on profit generation. Market deregulation and industry globalisation have increased the competitive pressures on companies, reducing the margin for error and rendering the 'cult of cost reduction' indispensable. Nowhere is this more apparent than in the commercial air transport business. For airline companies, successful and constant cost control is essential and cannot be neglected, even temporarily. SAS learned this lesson during the 1980s when their market driven philosophy caused their costs to escalate unchecked (Robertson 1995, p. 29). The margin of profit for most airline companies is minimal. There is little difference between the average total cost of any given flight and the number of passengers and yield per passenger needed on that flight to turn a profit. For traditional full fare airlines, the difference is normally only a few percentage points. This means that airlines are highly susceptible to market fluctuations and any related fall in traffic. The obvious way to safeguard a company against this acute market vulnerability is to decrease operational expenses and increase employee and aircraft productivity. By suppressing the breakeven load factor figure, an airline can ensure that any drop in the average passenger load factor figure will still reap a profit – albeit reduced – for the company. The key factors affecting indirect costs for an airline are fleet structure, route network and company policies on remuneration and work rules (Seristö and Vepsäläinen 1997, p. 11). Together, these determine the total cost differences between airlines and the primary ways in which an airline can reduce its costs relative to competitors. Uniform fleet structures, flexible work rules, performance-related pay schemes and point-to-point services operating between lower cost and less congested secondary airports, are all examples of ways in which a carrier can reduce its costs and improve its relative competitiveness. As we will illustrate throughout this book, all of these cost reduction techniques are fundamental elements of the LFA business model.

The 1990s witnessed substantial improvements in productivity and costs in the airline industry but the gains were not uniform (Morrell and Lu 2000, p. 80). Studies[4] show that during the 1993-8 period, average European available tonne-kilometre (ATK) per employee increased by 31 per cent to 380,000 and unit costs decreased by 15 per cent to 58 US cents per ATK. Improvements also occurred in other areas of productivity and cost reduction. The North American and Asia Pacific regions experienced similar improvements. These were usually not as considerable as in Europe because most European carriers lagged behind their North American and Asian counterparts and were going through a process of 'catch-up'. These gains were not uniform within Europe either, as measures of productivity and cost differ according to the nature and strategic objectives of an airline. For instance, costs are lower for a carrier heavily involved in the charter and cargo markets. Similarly, long haul carriers have a per unit cost advantage over short haul carriers (Morrell and Lu 2000, p. 81). Likewise, short haul carriers experience higher aircraft utilisation and greater yields than their long haul counterparts.

In the airline business, the contest to lower costs, increase productivity and gain market advantage is often accompanied by price-based competition. Demand for air travel is highly elastic: reduce the price and sales rise sharply. However, reducing prices to gain market share is not usually a sound business strategy. Unless a company has a significant cost advantage of at least 30 per cent, reducing prices can trigger a suicidal price war (Garda and Marn 1993, p. 87). Price wars are common in the airline industry, where the commodity is largely undifferentiated, customers are highly concentrated and many are very price sensitive, and switching costs for consumers are very low (Garda and Marn 1993, p. 94). This scenario is accentuated in markets where many competitors co-exist. In essence, a company that competes on price must ensure that it has the cost base and cash resources to be the low price leader and not just a low price competitor. In operational terms, cash resources are vital to ensure a new entrant's survival in the face of predatory pricing by established carriers – a customary reaction by many existing large airlines. Cash also enables the airline to defer any downsizing measures during periods of market stagnation or decline. Low price market leaders such as Southwest Airlines in the US and Ryanair in Europe have developed business models that place constant cost reduction and cash accumulation at their core. These companies have emerged as the most effective cost and price competitors in the business. They are also the most consistently profitable airlines in the world. In addition, companies such as Southwest and Ryanair are extremely robust during times of economic crisis and market decline. For these reasons, we have chosen to study the structures, strategies and contexts (market and industry) of LFAs. Many invaluable lessons emerge both for other airline companies and for all companies struggling to compete in highly competitive international markets.

An introduction to Europe's low price players

As of 2001, five scheduled European airlines had established proven track records as LFAs[5] (Table 1.1). This group represented the most visible and clearly identifiable low fare players in Europe. Basiq Air is not included, as it had not established a clear market profile by the time of writing.[6] Other airlines, such as Air One in Italy or Deutsche BA in Germany, are occasionally referred to in trade publications and the media as low cost/low fare players. Although they have slightly lower costs than larger rivals, their fares are not low in the Ryanair or easyJet sense, nor do they adhere to many of the basic elements of the low fare model outlined in subsequent chapters. Such airlines are more accurately classed as regional carriers and do not meet the requirements set out in this book to be classified as LFAs.

Table 1.1 Europe's low fare airlines in 2000

Airline (& Home Country)	At a glance	Turn over (£m)	Net profit (£m)	Load factor (%)	Passenger No.
Ryanair (Ireland)	Largest fleet, most extensive route network, highest profits. Develop-ing European multi-hub approach.	304. 6	65.3	72.5	7.4 million

easyJet (UK)	Second largest fleet and network, strong profit and revenue growth. 90% sales online. Existing European multi-hub approach.	263	22	80.8	6 million
Go (UK)	BA spin-off, third largest fleet and rapidly expanding network. UK multi-hub approach.	159.7	4	72.5	2.8 million
Buzz (UK)	UK low fare arm of KLM. Higher operating costs than other LFAs. Growing route network.	n/a	n/a	n/a	n/a
Virgin Express (Belgium)	Loss-maker. Network restructuring – sale of Irish subsidiary. Fleet reduction. Small Brussels based fleet and route network.	181.4	-29.2	69	3.8 million

The airlines are ranked according to aircraft fleet size (see Figure 7.1) and net profit margins (1999-2001). A point worth noting from the above table is the degree of market penetration and saturation in the UK and Ireland. It is unlikely that these markets will experience any further growth or new entrants. This fact is acknowledged by Ryanair in its efforts to grow mainland European markets through establishing a hub in Belgium (due to be followed by hubs elsewhere – probably in Italy, Germany and Sweden). The market potential across Europe is enormous, with an EU population base alone that is close to 100 million more people than in the US. Statistics already indicate that this potential is being exploited, as the low fares market is the fastest growing segment of the European air industry. The number of LFA passengers increased from 10.5 million in 1998 to 14 million in 1999 and is predicted to grow to 19 million in 2001.[7]

Overview and arguments

The book is divided into ten chapters, with a number of common issues and ideas permeating each and creating a follow-on from one to the next.

Chapter 1 establishes the book's context, objectives and structure and introduces us to the low fare players in European aviation.

Chapter 2 details the global and European policy shift towards a more liberalised airline industry and devotes particular attention to the EU's three phases of market deregulation. The conflict between national governments and the European Commission over state aid transfers to national carriers is also discussed, as are more recent developments in the EU-nation state-firm policy interplay.

In Chapter 3 we examine the impact that LFAs have had on the European air transport industry and market. We also define and discuss LFAs and place them in the wider context of the European airline industry. This leads us into a consideration of the similarities and differences between low fare, charter and regional airlines in Europe. This is followed by a brief comparison of the point-to-point and 'hub-and-spoke' systems and a review of route networks in the European LFA sector.

Chapter 4 begins by charting the evolution and dynamics of the European airline industry during and immediately after the deregulation process. This leads into an assessment of the widely cited barriers to airline competition in Europe. We examine a number of these in detail, consider their impact on LFA expansion strategies and comment on the extent to which there are limits to the liberalisation of Europe's airline market.

Chapter 5 considers how to best define and measure customer service for airlines and considers whether customer satisfaction and service quality are interchangeable or distinct concepts. We argue in this chapter that the price to service equation does not need to be a zero-sum game. You can have a win-win situation, with low prices and high quality service.

In Chapter 6, we examine the business model and cost reduction techniques of the European low fare leader, Ryanair. Ryanair's operational structure and corporate strategy are placed in the context of Porter's strategic positioning framework and strengths and weaknesses are assessed. We propose that through emulating Ryanair's best practices, European low fare and regional airlines can strengthen their market position and remain a viable competitive challenge to the larger, more established airlines.

Chapter 7 considers alternative low price models to the Ryanair approach. We examine each of Europe's other LFAs, evaluating and comparing their respective business models. Particular attention is given to Europe's second largest LFA, easyJet, and to the financial soundness and strategic logic of its particular business model. Attention is also given to the reasons for the failure of low fare carrier Debonair at the close of the 1990s and the lessons that other low price carriers can learn from Debonair's demise.

Chapter 8 studies the development of the US airline industry in the post-deregulation era. Specific consideration is given to the archetypal LFA model, Southwest Airlines, and the essence of its success. This is followed by a discussion of the strategies, structures and competitive challenges of more recent, prominent market entrants such as JetBlue, Vanguard and AirTran.

In Chapter 9, we move into the wider world, beginning with an examination of low price competition in Canadian and Australia. This involves charting the structures and strategies of companies like WestJet, Impulse and Virgin Blue and examining the response of incumbent airlines to these market entrants. The chapter concludes by looking briefly at some of the other countries around the world – particularly Latin America – where LFAs have emerged.

Chapter 10 brings together and summarises the book's main arguments and findings and reflects on key issues raised. Price leadership strategy is also revisited and a number of lessons from the LFA experience are advanced for other airlines and industries. Finally, we undertake an assessment of LFAs in times of crisis and an explanation of why leading LFAs such as Southwest and Ryanair fared so well relative to traditional carriers during and following the world airline crisis of September 2001.

Notes

1   In saying that the industry was relatively staid, we are referring to the industry outside of the US, long dominated by over-priced, oligopolistic markets. It is acknowledged that the US industry had experienced considerable change and dynamism since market deregulation in 1978.

2   Quoted in The Economist, 'The Sky's the Limit: a survey of air travel', 10 March, 2001, p.6.

3   This data is derived from the EU's 2000 Annual Report on the European air travel industry, July 2001, pp. 66-7.

4   These include Cranfield University's Air Transport Group's 2000 study of productivity, costs and yields in 24 of the world's airlines, titled 'Measures of strategic success: the evidence over ten years'.

5   This was confirmed in discussions with leading LFA analysts such as Mr Conor McCarthy, Ryanair's former Director of Operations and now an independent aviation consultant, 9 March 2001.

6   Basiq Air is however discussed in Chapters 4 and 7 and is best described as a 'quasi LFA', given its clear emphasis on low prices for scheduled flights but ambiguous relationship with Transavia/KLM and very limited route network and fleet numbers.

7   As argued by Barry Zorn, Managing Director, European Air Express, in a paper titled 'Comparing low cost markets in the USA, UK and Europe', presented at an aviation conference in Amsterdam, 27 February 2001.

Chapter 2

Liberalising Europe's Air Ways[1]

Introduction

When the European project was first initiated, the transport sector may
logically have been envisaged as a key component of the integration process.
The post-World War Two period heralded faster and cheaper modes of mass
transport. For the first time, air, sea, rail, and road transport were accessible
to everyone. Routes multiplied, travel time plummeted, and Europe became a
much smaller and more harmonised place. A core aim of the European plan –
the free (and increased) movement of people – appeared to hinge upon
developments in the transport arena. Air transport was at the vanguard of this
sector as it was here that some of the greatest developments were occurring.
Thus, civil aviation had the potential to play an integral part in the political
integration of Western Europe. Walter Hallstein, the European
Commission's first president noted that European transport was paradoxical
in nature, having the potential to be a motor of integration through increasing
the mobility of European citizens but, at the same time, proving to be a major
obstacle to greater unity, due to its politicised, nationalist persona.[2] States
were not as willing to pool authority for transport (particularly civil aviation)
as they were for other areas of economic activity (Sochor 1991, p.186).

This chapter examines the process that led to the deregulation of
commercial air transport in Europe and has witnessed a significant
transference of aviation policy authority from the national to the European
Union (EU) level. Particular attention is given to the controversial issue of
state aid[3] to airlines and the extent to which free and fair competition is
enforced and enforceable across Europe.

A history of intergovernmental regulation

The jealous guarding of national autonomy in air transport matters was not
an attitude that existed from the industry's inception. During its formative

years, global idealism had permeated the realm of air transport. Evidence of this spirit was visible even at the 1944 Chicago Convention, which granted governments supreme authority over their national aviation arenas (Kassim 1995, p.191). The United States expressed their wish for 'open skies', not subject to any national sovereignty. In his opening address to the Chicago conference, Franklin D. Roosevelt pronounced:

> Let us rather, in full acknowledgement of the sovereign rights of all nations and the legal equality of all peoples, work together in order that the skies of the world can be exploited by man for all mankind (Sampson 1984, p.66).

Such high ideals were soon replaced by the horse-trading that, throughout history, accompanied all new vehicles of commercial and societal change. States agreed in Chicago that governments would bargain bilaterally over airline access to their respective national markets. The subsequent Anglo-American Bermuda Bargain of 1946 set a precedent for such air transport deals and served as the blueprint for most bilateral international agreements during the ensuing decades (Sampson 1984, p.72). The idealism of free and equal access to air transport was thus replaced by hard reality, as national governments realised the economic and political significance of the air transport industry. A limited form of global co-operation did develop in the area of price setting. Most governments acknowledged the difficulties involved in fixing seat prices unilaterally or bilaterally and thus accepted the creation of an international body to deal with this matter. As part of the 1946 Bermuda Bargain, the contentious issue of whether and how to fix fares was ceded by governments to the airline firms themselves, represented by the International Air Transport Association (IATA). IATA's dominant ethos through until the late 1970s was based on the belief in firm regulation and controls of air transport (Sampson 1984, p.73). This mindset amongst the corporate actors thus handed ultimate authority back to the nation state.

Despite this limited multilateral co-operation, the linchpins of national aviation policy – market and industry regulation, aid, traffic rights, and international market access – were jealously guarded by all governments. The idea of pooling authority in these areas or of transferring power to a supranational body did not appeal to most nations.

Despite this fact, efforts to develop a European policy for civil aviation have been ongoing since the late 1940s. As early as 1949, when the Council of Europe was established, talks developed within that forum as to the possibility of establishing regional co-operation in the sphere of air transport (Sochor 1991, p.187). Efforts to create an acceptable blueprint for European air transport policy continued throughout the subsequent decades, both at an intergovernmental and a supranational level.[4] One significant achievement was the 1954 creation of the European Civil Aviation Conference (ECAC), a permanent regional air transport consultative organisation. Progress towards the development of a fully-fledged European air transport policy was however constantly stymied by national governments. An attempt in the 1950s to establish a homogenous air traffic control system (Eurocontrol) failed due to national opposition to the plan (Scharpf 1994, p.231). In 1964, the European Commission pressed for extending the application of the Rome Treaty's provision for a common transport policy to include both air and sea transport. European governments had no desire to upset the status quo however, and the Commission's plan failed to secure the approval of the Council of Ministers (Sampson 1984, p.98). As we will see later, it was not until the early 1980s, in the wake of liberalisation in the United States, that Europe eventually began moving towards a common air transport policy which more closely resembled the multi-faceted policies found at a national level.

Supranationalism versus intergovernmentalism: where does power reside in Europe?

Any study of the EU inevitably confronts the question of where political authority resides. As Mazey (1996) points out, the key issue in all EU treaty negotiations from Rome to Amsterdam has been what kind of Europe will emerge – intergovernmental or supranational? The term 'supranational' derives from the seminal work of Haas (1958) and refers to a body whose laws are above those of the nation state in the area of its competence (Archer and Butler 1996, p.36). Contrary to subsequent misinterpretation, Haas did not interpret supranationality as the subservience of nation states to Community institutions. Instead, he viewed it as an inclusive style of political behaviour through which political interest would be realised, not as a depoliticised form of technical decision-making (Keohane and Hoffman 1991, p.15).

Keohane and Hoffman (1991) argue that although the process of EU policy making is supranational, all of the negotiation and coalition building takes place between governments. Moravcsik (1991) illustrates this through his study of the process that led to the Single European Act (SEA). He contends that any attempt to understand the Single European Act must begin with a recognition that *governments* ultimately struck the bargain and ratified the accord. The concept of 'intergovernmentalism' therefore assumes that states are the primary (albeit not exclusive) actors in any integration process.

When examining specific policy areas, identifying the source of political authority often supplants the identification of legal authority. Within the EU, legal control does not always translate into actual power. EU competition policy is a prime example of this apparent contradiction: the EU's legal authority has, since the 1950s, frequently been eclipsed by national governments political or popular mandate. During the European Community's (EC) first 25 years of existence, the European Commission and European Court of Justice rarely challenged Member States on competition policy matters. In a widely publicised and politically charged area such as air transport policy, this issue is of central importance. Europe's supranational institutions were virtually uninvolved in air transport policy until the mid-1980s. Spurred on by the Single Market inspired drive towards deregulation, Europe's supranational bodies gradually increased their involvement in the regulation of air transport. The leadership role of the European Commission has been an important factor in this gradual shift away from a wholly intergovernmental regime for European air transport.

The Europeanisation of airline policy: conditions for change

Efforts to create a common European civil aviation policy were set in motion in 1974 when the European Court of Justice ruled that the general principles on a common transport policy, outlined in Article 84(2) of the Treaty of Rome, apply to air transport (CEC 1994, p.1). However, a majority of EU Member States chose to block the legislative development and enactment of this ruling prior to its inclusion on the Single Market agenda (Kassim 1995, p.196).

During the first half of the 1980s, a global trend emerged towards greater economic liberalisation, championed by the United States and the United Kingdom. The United States led the way in world airline liberalisation. Passenger services within the US experienced rapid and far-reaching deregulation. This trend was transferred across the Atlantic as the decade progressed. From the mid-1980s on, Europe began the tumultuous and often painful process of liberalising its airline industry. Doganis argues that this process was precipitated by mounting pressures emanating from consumer groups, the European Parliament, and the European Commission (1991, p.79). The European airline industry's regulatory framework was transformed in two ways:

...first, bilaterally through the renegotiation of air services agreements between pairs of countries; secondly, multilaterally, through actions initiated by the European Commission in Brussels or the European Court of Justice (Doganis 1991, p.79).

Working in parallel with national governments, and in alliance with the Court of Justice, the European Parliament, and industry pressure groups, the Commission thus acted as a policy leader in the field of airline liberalisation (Doganis 1991, p.79; Button 1991, p.114-115; Sochor 1991, p.189).

The move towards a more liberal European policy for airlines began with the 1984 British and Dutch renegotiation of their respective bilateral agreements (Button and Swann 1989, p.262). In fact, the deregulation of air services between these two countries[5] may be seen as a significant break with the past and one of the first major steps towards European-wide airline deregulation. It was followed by similar agreements between the UK and Germany (1984), Luxembourg (1985), Belgium (1985) and Ireland (1988). The British Government clearly perceived these agreements as setting the scene for multilateral liberalisation at an EC level.[6]

At the same time, EU institutions (primarily the Commission), in association with air carrier interest groups such as the International Air Transport Association (IATA), the Association of European Airlines (AEA) and the European Regions Airlines Association (ERA), began constructing a new multilateral European airline policy.[7] As Doganis points out, the Commission's Directorate General for Transport was an early advocate of liberalisation (1991, p.82). As early as 1972, the Commission advanced some suggestions concerning airline deregulation. The first significant proposals came in 1978, when the Commission issued a memorandum on civil aviation (CEC 1994, 1). The proposals contained within this memorandum were relatively moderate however, emphasising such needs as the introduction of cheaper fares, increased possibilities for market entry, and developing a policy to monitor state aid to airlines.[8] The first tangible EC-level initiative to result from this Commission activism was the Council Directive on Inter-Regional Air Services of July 1983, allowing air carriers using small seventy seat or less planes to freely develop air routes between EC regional airports (Doganis 1991, p.82). This was followed in 1984 by the Commission's own air transport objectives, outlined in a memorandum to the Council of Ministers.[9] The proposals discussed in this document were much more robust and detailed than in its 1979 predecessor. In particular, the Commission called for the application of EC competition rules to the air transport sector. As the Economic and Social Committee response document noted:

...the Commission's Memorandum seeks to establish an overall framework for a Community air transport policy designed to improve the efficiency and profitability of the air transport industry as well as the quality and price of the product it offers (1985, p.3).

Overall, the Commission's objectives were twofold: to liberalise existing intra-Community air traffic, and to open up heavily protected national air transport markets (Doganis 1991, p.83). Both of these objectives were in harmony with the liberalisation principles of the Single Market Initiative. In fact, an important implication of the Single Market Programme was to deregulate the air transport sector and open the industry up to greater competition.[10] The deregulation and increased privatisation of this industry may thus be seen as a Single Market success story. With some notable exceptions,[11] European governments did not freely embark upon more liberal air transport policies. Although their Treaty obligations committed them to promoting and enforcing competition rules, their status as major stockholders did not dispose them towards increased competition against their national flag carriers (Sochor 1991, p.185). Instead, they were led along the path to more open markets by a coalition of interests. Williams argues that pressure was exerted on governments by consumer groups, air carrier associations, and the European Commission (1993, p.67). Governments gradually and reluctantly came to realise that they would have to give up control of regulation, one of the most important instruments of public policy (Williams 1993, p.67).

There is evidence to suggest that this concurrent national/EU liberalisation process was loosely co-ordinated. Van den Polder argues that there has been a fractious but single-minded coalition of actors actively involved in the EU legislative process for the airline industry. These consisted of the national ministries, parliamentary committees, and government advisory bodies of several Member States; the Council of Ministers and the Committee of Permanent Representatives (COREPER); a number of airport authorities; individual airline companies; organisations such as the Association of European Airlines, ECAC, and IATA; European consumer associations; the European Commission, particularly the Directorates for Transport, Competition, the Environment and External Relations; and the European Parliament, primarily through the Committee for Transport and Tourism (1994, p.108-9). As Figure 2.1 illustrates, a finite but nevertheless identifiable interest coalition formed around the specific issue of airline deregulation. This coalition's main players were the European Commission, consumer interest groups, individual airline carriers such as KLM, the

European Parliament, the Association of European Airlines, the European Regions Airlines Association and a limited number of member states – primarily the United Kingdom and the Netherlands.[12]

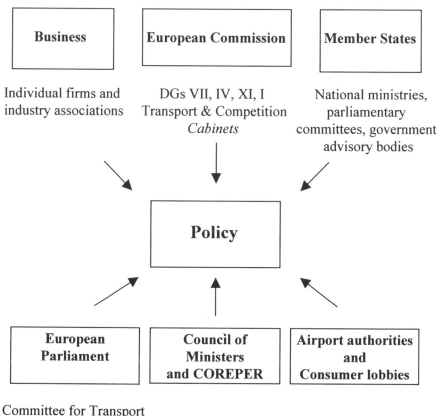

Figure 2.1 Interest coalition actors for European airline liberalisation

A significant juncture was reached in April 1986 when the European Court of Justice ruled on the *Nouvelles Frontières* case,[13] involving a dispute between the French regulatory authorities and a French travel agent over price-cutting activities:

> The court decided that the competition articles 85-90 of the Treaty of Rome do apply to air transport and that only a specific decision by the Council of Ministers could give exemptions for inter-airline agreements (Doganis 1991, p.83).

The travel agent initiated the case but the Commission quickly seized upon its wider implications. The judgement gave legal support to the Commission in its efforts to intervene when confronted with uncompetitive air transport practices such as fare fixing. Prior to this decision, the Commission lacked the legal power to directly apply competition rules to the air transport sector. This was due to Article 87 of the Rome Treaty, which enabled the Council of Ministers to confer implementing powers on the Commission. The Council did not do so in the case of air transport (Button and Swann 1989, p.272). The *Nouvelles Frontières* ruling provided the Commission with a way around Council intransigence. It illustrated how 'the Commission is able, on occasions, to take advantage of events to force the Council to act' (Button 1991, p.115). Hence, one may interpret the *Nouvelles Frontières* case as an example of the Court allying with the Commission to take power from the Council. The result for EU decision-making was supranationalism gaining at the expense of intergovernmentalism. Europe's transnational authorities increased their policy-making mandate, siphoning authority away from national governments. This ruling concretely established air transport within the legal jurisdiction of the Treaty of Rome, and thus guaranteed the European Commission at least partial competence in this sector. Moreover, it paved the way for the then Competition Commissioner, Peter Sutherland, to take a tough stance on uncompetitive practices in the airline industry. For instance, in the immediate wake of the *Nouvelles Frontières* judgement, the Commission formally charged ten airlines with infringement of competition rules (Sochor 1991, p.184). This led subsequently to the Community's introduction of a staged liberalisation programme, aimed at opening up the European airline market to greater internal competition.

The three packages

Doganis (1994) argues that controls on market access, frequencies, pricing and capacity serve to disadvantage the travelling public. In particular, such controls (i) limit the range and choice of service quality and airline; (ii) protect high cost inefficient carriers and result in higher fares; (iii) exclude start-up low price competitors or those willing to innovate; and (iv) limit international services to a few gateway cities (Doganis 1994, p.15). Liberalisation of the airline industry is therefore normally justified on the grounds that competition encourages the efficient provision of airline services, with carriers offering good quality services at the lowest possible cost and price. It was with this objective in mind that the European

Commission's twin objectives for the European airline industry – deregulating existing intra-EC routes and liberalising national markets – began to be realised with the introduction of a three-steps-to-liberalisation approach, approved by the Council of Ministers in December 1987. The EU introduced three legislative packages, in 1987, 1990, and 1992, which gradually eroded Member States' rights to regulate the airline industry and consolidated the emergence of a European policy for aviation. Despite Article 84 of the Rome Treaty explicitly advocating a common European transport policy, it was only with the introduction of these three legislative packages that liberalisation ensued (Kassim 1995, p.196). Consecutive cabotage[14] was subsequently established, with full cabotage in place by early 1997. The only exceptions are some public service obligation routes non-profitable but socially necessary flights to remote regions of a country. Although these routes remain sheltered from direct competition, the right to fly them is awarded through competitive tendering (Graham 1997, p.227). Consecutive cabotage has resulted in airlines being permitted to fly between destinations within another Member State, following or preceding a flight from their country of origin ('eighth freedom' rights). For example, in 1993, Lufthansa began operating a Rome-Bari service (as the second leg of a flight originating in Germany), signifying that the era of national monopolies was coming to an end. The eighth 'freedoms of the air' referred to here are elements of the eight global air transport principles that have evolved since the 1944 Chicago Convention. Together these symbolise the essence of airline market liberalisation and all eight are enshrined in the three packages of EU airline liberalisation (Table 2.1). The first four are generally accepted principles across the world. However, the other (four) freedoms are vigorously disputed and are seen by most countries as major infringements of national sovereignty (as well as unwanted mechanisms for introducing significant competition to a state's domestic carriers). For example, the US does not allow cabotage in even its most liberal air service agreements. In ensuring fifth, sixth, seventh and eighth freedom rights, the EU has gone much further than any other state or region in liberalising its air transport regime.

Table 2.1 Freedoms of the air

First freedom	To fly over another state
Second freedom	To land in another state in emergency or for refuelling
Third freedom	To put down revenue passengers and freight from state of registry
Fourth freedom	To take on revenue passengers and freight to state of registry
Fifth freedom	To take on revenue passengers and freight in a second state to a third state
Sixth freedom	To take on revenue passengers and freight in a second state and fly via state of registry to a third state
Seventh freedom	To take on revenue passengers and freight in a second state, to which the aircraft can be domiciled, to a destination in a third state
Eighth freedom	To take on revenue passengers and freight in a second state to a destination within that state

Source: Reproduced from Gudmundsson (1999) 'Airline alliances: consumer and policy issues', *European Business Journal,* p.140.

Moreover, a more liberal approach to fares has been established, with the removal of virtually all restrictions on low fares.[15] These pieces of legislation have together facilitated the proliferation of low-cost carriers, thus ensuring greater competition within the industry and cheaper flights for the consumer. The right to acquire landing slots at international airports is now also an established principle within the EU. The final package therefore consolidates full exercise of the freedoms of the air. All remaining restrictions on domestic air transport were removed as of 1 April 1997.

The air transport liberalisation programme has proven effective. The UK Department of Transport argued that EU liberalisation measures have promoted and increased competition and served to open up an assortment of new opportunities for EU airlines (1997, p.2). This is largely due to the decisive leadership shown by the Commission in pushing for a rapid and complete national implementation of the programme's measures. The UK Civil Aviation Authority (CAA) argued that:

Where member states have been slow to allow the new freedoms given by the Third Package, the Commission has intervened decisively and effectively (1995, p.v).

The CAA also concluded that the three packages have contributed significantly to the increased levels of competition in Europe. The dominance of national carriers has been shaken, price competition is growing, and competition on international routes is increasing (CAA 1995, p.v). In addition, through forcing several state airlines to adopt painful restructuring processes, it has launched them on the path to privatisation and won the grudging approval of previously sceptical governments.[16]

However, air transport best illustrates the remaining national interest instincts of some European governments: French authorities denied a foreign airline access to the Toulouse-Brussels route, on the grounds of airport congestion (Kassim 1995, p.203). Similarly, BA experienced enormous difficulties in its efforts to establish its subsidiary, Deutsche BA, in another EU country.

Undoubtedly, liberalisation is forcing many national governments towards privatisation of their national airline carriers.[17] Wright argued that the firm-state relationship has been fundamentally transformed as a result of such initiatives as the EU's air transport liberalisation programme. He concluded that the days of the 'activist state', promoting and protecting national champions, are over (1995, p.352-3).

State aid and Commission power

Wright's conclusions warrant closer scrutiny. The activist state, although on the defensive, has not disappeared. The EU's programme for liberalising air transport continues to encounter the intransigence, if not the active opposition, of some Member States. Several European governments are still willing to confront the European Commission on behalf of their airlines. Nowhere has this been more evident than in the realm of state aid to national flag carriers. It is here that we may best assess the clash between national and supranational authority and comment on the extent to which the Europeanisation of airline policy is an ongoing process.

State aid involves the transfer of public resources to a private company or industrial sector. It may be used to assist or facilitate industrial restructuring or simply as a subsidy to prop up an uncompetitive firm or sector. By its very nature, state aid regulation or policy is somewhat of an anomaly, being distinctively supranational in nature and not existing in any national competition policy context. Within the EU, state aid policy is therefore the competence of the European Commission. The European Commission's role in policing state aid is central to the debate concerning the Europeanisation of industrial policy. As Cini and McGowan argue:

> In restricting the capacity of governments to support their national firms, the policy sounds the death knell of purely national industrial strategies by granting the Commission the task of ensuring that subsidies granted within the EU are compatible with single market objectives (1998, p.135).

The concept of state aid is much wider than the notion of 'subsidy'. It is a more inclusive term and can involve tax concessions, state guarantees and state participation in industry, as well as straightforward financial assistance (Cini and McGowan 1998, p.136). Its objectives are usually driven more by social concerns than by market forces. For instance, state aid can involve money to alleviate the social fall-out (redundancies) resulting from corporate or industry restructuring. State aid can also be employed in cases of perceived market failure. This is particularly relevant to air transport, as airlines do perform functions analogous to utility companies. Many European flag carriers receive government subsidies to provide services to remote regions of their countries where passenger numbers are low but where government is obliged to ensure a transport link. The logic behind this form of subsidy is often flawed as regional carriers can frequently provide a service to such regions without public support.

In general, as with most subsidies, state aid tends to distort the market. The airline industry is a very clear example of this actuality. The International Chamber of Commerce argues that 'state assistance to airlines, whether direct or indirect, should be deemed to distort the market and to be detrimental to airlines and users'.[18] The EU adopts the position that state aid adversely affects the competitiveness of firms within a specific industrial sector.[19] Within the EU, most cases of state aid have to be approved by the European Commission's Directorate for Competition. Transport is an exception: all issues of state aid to transport sectors (including airlines) are dealt with by the Transport Directorate General. The issue of state aid is fraught with problems. Hanlon argues that with the proliferation of privatisation within the airline industry, 'aid to state owned carriers is potentially a significant distortion of competition' (1996, p.25). On the other hand, the politics of state aid cannot be underestimated. Flag carriers are a vivid symbol of a country's international potency and governments generally acknowledge their emotive appeal.[20] Sir Michael Bishop, chief executive of Bmi British Midland, observed that:

> ...airlines have mainly been founded and expanded as a clone of the government – an unassailable symbol of prestige and sovereign virility...The intimacy of these airlines with their governments developed a long-standing acknowledgement that consumer and commercial considerations have been subordinated to national interest and political interference.[21]

Government support of these companies often defies economic logic and will frequently be more enduring than for firms in other, less symbolic sectors of an economy. Thus, state aid in general has proven to be one of the most consistent and intractable obstacles to the successful completion of the Single Market and to the further transference of aviation sovereignty to Brussels. State aid to airline flag carriers has proven particularly problematic for the achievement of a free and fair internal market, due to the perception of these companies as prestigious state assets. A protectionist regulatory regime, allowing governments to control and often subsidise their national flag carriers, was central to most countries' perceptions of the national interest (Sochor 1991, p.183).

Justifying state aid

The Commission generally identifies instances of state aid on the basis of its 'market economy investor principle'.[22] The rationale is simply that state aid is involved if a company is unable to raise the appropriate finances on private capital markets. Moreover, state aid is justified only if the return on investment is deemed adequate. This principle applies to all kinds of government financial investment. Under Article 92, paragraph 1 of the Rome Treaty, there are certain forms of state aid that are permissible outside of the scope of the market economy investment principle. Examples would include 'social aid' (subsidies to allow cheaper fares for disabled passengers for instance), 'disaster aid' (money to help firms recover from floods or earthquakes perhaps),[23] and 'regional aid' (public investment in companies which establish in poorer parts of a country).[24] The most interesting form of permissible state aid concerns 'restructuring aid'. The basic premise is that state aid to help restructure a particular firm or industry is acceptable if the aid facilitates the development of the economic sector and does not distort trade. It is here that national governments have the greatest opportunity to exploit EU state aid regulation to the benefit of their own firms. Two scenarios are likely in the event of the Commission sanctioning state aid activities under the restructuring umbrella. One is that restructuring works, whilst the other is that the return on investment is inadequate. Thus far, both of these scenarios have been manifest. In the case of Olympic Airways, the Greek flag carrier, aid was initially only approved under a strict set of twenty-three conditions. It has yet to show any measurable benefits in terms of making Olympic more competitive.[25] Another example, that of Aer Lingus, the Irish flag carrier, shows a different picture. In this case, state aid was approved in a staged fashion, with the stipulation that, at the same time, the company had to bring about a £50 million reduction in its cost base. Despite some initial problems, Aer Lingus subsequently underwent a successful restructuring programme.[26] Similarly, in spite of the lack of positive results from earlier infusions of state aid, Air France was eventually launched on the path to successful restructuring. Table 2.2 illustrates the overall number and financial scale of state aid investigations to national airlines during the 1990s.

Table 2.2 European state aid to national carriers

Year	Airline	Amount (st£m)	Commission Decision
1991	Sabena	584	approved
1991	Air France	665	approved
1992	Iberia	670	approved
1993	Air France	170	rejected
1993	Aer Lingus	170	approved
1994	TAP-Air Portugal	710	approved
1994	Olympic Airways	995	approved
1994	Air France	2.4 billion	approved
1996	Iberia	445	approved
1997	Alitalia	930	approved

Source: UK Department of Transport, International Aviation Directorate and the *Financial Times*.

These grants met with fierce criticism from several of the less interventionist European governments and from many of the smaller private air carriers within the EU – particularly the LFAs. The UK government challenged the Commission decision to grant such a large aid package to Air France and took the Commission to the European Court of Justice, seeking to get the decision reversed (Hanlon 1996, p.26). In addition, several airline companies also took legal action, both independently and collectively, arguing that Air France was using state aid money to fund cuts in airfares.[27]

State aid and market competition in the airline industry

During the 1991/2 period, the Commission undertook an inquiry, which resulted in an inventory of existing state aids in the air transport sector.[28] The report revealed that several airlines were benefiting from state intervention, often direct operating aids or aids aimed at improving the airline's financial structure. Several potential state aids in the form of exclusive rights concessions were also revealed. In response to these findings, and complaints by various Member State governments and airline companies, the Commission, in the summer of 1993, set up a committee of experts, the *Comité des Sages* for Air Transport, for the purpose of analysing the situation of Community civil aviation and making recommendations for future policy initiatives. Within this study, the group devoted some attention to the state aid issue. Its conclusions, released in a 1994 report to the Commission, were driven by principles of fair competition, rather than by notions of national prestige. The *Comité* argued that access to finance should be equal, regardless of an airline's size or ownership. Moreover, a state should not extend preferential treatment to a carrier that it owned or partly owned. All domestic-based airlines should be equal and none more than others. On this point, the *Comité* argued that the surest way to avoid preferential treatment would be to privatise national flag carriers. This would have the added benefit of enabling these companies to compete in what was becoming an increasingly global business (Hanlon 1996, p.25-6). Overall, the *Comité* stressed that the Single Market must be made to work by enforcing its rules and addressing sensitive issues such as state aid (1994, p.6). The *Comité* acknowledged that many of the national carriers were not in a position to compete unaided in a fair and open market. Thus, if privatisation were immediate and unconditional, a significant number of these companies ran the risk of bankruptcy (Hanlon 1996, p.26). The solution reached was the self explanatory 'one time, last time' principle.[29] The *Comité* reluctantly conceded that, for a brief transitionary period, some states would have to act to put airlines on a normal commercial footing. The group emphasised that the reasons for granting exceptions are essentially political (1994, p.21).

This principle was to provide governments with a short transition period, during which they were to launch their flag carriers on the path to market competitiveness and (preferably) private ownership. Approval of this transitional state aid was subject to several conditions. These included:

> ...the submission of a radical restructuring plan for commercial viability and ultimately privatization; a prohibition on the use of public money to buy or take over another carrier; and restrictions on the use of state aid in financing an increase in capacity (Hanlon 1996, p.26).

In addition, the recommendations made reference to some less tangible conditions such as proof that the competitive interests of other airlines are not negatively affected and a guarantee that the aid would genuinely be on a one time, last time basis (Comité des Sages 1994, p.22). The former condition may be violated through, for example, the use of state aid to cut prices on an airline's domestic routes, thus undermining the position of rival airlines.[30]

The clash between Commission authority and national preference

In general, the Commission welcomed the Comité's recommendations,[31] which, it argued, by and large confirmed current EU policy. Where it did not, the Commission agreed to follow the Comité's recommendations. A notable exception concerned the 'one time, last time' principle. Although agreeing to employ the principle, the Commission argues that the conditions that the aid is the last one have to be interpreted in conformity with Community law. This implies that such a condition does not prevent a Member State from notifying a further aid to a company that has already been granted aid.[32] According to Court of Justice case law, in such a case the Commission will take all the relevant elements into account. An important element in the Commission's assessment is of course the prior receipt of state aid. In this case, the Commission only permits the granting of further aid in 'exceptional circumstances, unforeseeable and external to the company' (European Communities Official Journal 1994, p.7). Such 'exceptional circumstances' are open to interpretation and the condition can be subject to abuse. In effect, here lies the loophole in EU state aid regulation and the crux of the Commission-Member State power struggle. Allowing a country to notify the Commission of further aid to a previous recipient provides states with an escape clause and gives them scope within which to construct a case for further aid. A case in point concerns Iberia. The Spanish national carrier did not restructure adequately, despite a capital injection of £455 million from the Spanish government.[33] The company continued to lose money. The

Spanish government persisted in arguing for aid, on the basis of factors beyond the control of Iberia ('exceptional circumstances'), such as the Spanish recession and the problems associated with privatising South American subsidiaries.

The issue of state aid is therefore a significant battleground between the EU's national and supranational regulatory authorities. Due to the politically sensitive nature of the airline industry, the European Commission traditionally tended to tread more softly than it has done in other sectors. In addition, the Commission's interpretation of the Treaties, allowing multiple applications for state aid, provides governments with a means of directly challenging the EU's 'one time, last time' principle. The result can be an impasse – such as in the Iberia case – where the grey notion of 'exceptional circumstances' is interpreted more loosely in Madrid than it is in Brussels. Moreover, the Commission has too often been seen to back down in the face of Member State intransigence. For instance, controversy arose over then Transport Commissioner Neil Kinnock's 1996 decision to grant Iberia a second cash injection.[34] Opponents argued that this might well lead to previous aid recipients such as Sabena or Olympic Airways demanding similar concessions again.

The appointment of Commissioner Loyola de Palacio as Mr Kinnock's successor precipitated a noticeable change in the Commission's attitude toward state aid. A new found willingness to apply the more watertight Comité des Sages rules governing state aid requests and a readiness to stand firm by these rules allowed the Commission to gradually assert its pre-eminence in European airline policy. However, as the industry crisis of late 2001 illustrated, numerous EU Member States continue to be reluctant exponents of edicts from Brussels that strive to prevent them from assisting troubled national champions. The Commission has dramatically increased its power in air transport policy since the mid-1980s. It is, *de jure*, the ultimate appraiser of state aid requests. Despite this fact, national sensitivities and governmental antipathy continue to hamper the absolute supranational control of state aid regulation.

EU aviation policy in the 21st century: setting a new agenda

Another top policy priority at a European level has been to tackle the air traffic delays caused by the region's creaking air traffic control system.[35] The approach is to tackle underlying causes of the problems such as the inefficiencies caused by the fragmented patchwork of national air traffic control regions within the EU. The creation of a collective management structure – the 'single skies' initiative – is viewed by the European Commission as an imperative. In a political context, the single skies initiative is simply a continuation of the European Commission's drive to further the integration process. Following on from the airline market liberalisation of the 1980s and 1990s, the effective management of a single European airspace is seen as an essential complement to the European single market.

A second major strand of EU airline policy in the early 21st century is the problematic issue of transatlantic bilateral negotiations. Transport Commissioner de Palacio's predecessor, Neil Kinnock, fought to hold US talks on behalf of the EU and opposed deals developing between the US and individual EU Member States. He failed to obtain a genuine mandate on this matter. The approach of Commissioner de Palacio has centred on the development of a Transatlantic Common Aviation Area (TCAA), an idea strongly advocated by the AEA (Association of European Airlines). The idea is to move away from the notion of exchanging bilateral rights and towards the creation of a single aviation market extending across the Atlantic, jointly managed by the EU and the US. This approach borrows from the EU's own single market model and also fits well with the World Trade Organisation's (WTO) open trade agenda. At the time of writing the EU was pressing ahead with its efforts in this area and looked likely to wrest control of open skies negotiations from individual national governments by late 2002.

Two other important areas where the EU perceives a role for central co-ordination include airline safety and environmental standards. For instance, the Commission favours the creation of a European safety agency for air transport. As O'Toole (2000a) points out, air traffic control, external relations, safety and the environment are the four themes that constitute the bedrock of the European Commission's air transport policy agenda. The restructuring of the EU Transport Directorate's air transport division along these lines is indicative of the new found focus of European aviation policy. This focus, together with the negotiating skill of the current Transport Commissioner and the more favourable political and regulatory environment surrounding air transport,[36] means that the EU may be well placed to realise its objectives. Relations with business have also improved. The Transport Directorate has been striving to establish good working relations with Europe's airlines, particularly those that it conflicted with during the state aid cases of the 1990s. The firms have been willing to reciprocate. Both sides are striving to respect each other's position and to be more constructive in their approaches, even on controversial issues such as the air passenger rights charter.

The state aid debate arose again in late 2001, following the US terrorist attacks. The US federal government provided financial assistance packages totalling $15 billion to American carriers in the wake of the New York and Washington D.C. bombings. This prompted calls for aid by some of Europe's flag carriers. Aer Lingus of Ireland claimed that government cash was needed as their ticket sales plummeted in the wake of the attacks on the US, particularly on lucrative transatlantic routes.[37] Other state-owned carriers – notably Air France, Sabena of Belgium and Olympic Airways of Greece, also planned to apply for state aid. European Transport Commissioner Loyola de Palacio responded to such appeals by arguing that consolidation was needed in European aviation and that the repercussions of the US attacks should not be used as an excuse for ailing airlines to delay the inevitable. Despite the sharp downturn in transatlantic traffic, there would be no relaxation of the strict state aid regime governing airlines.[38] Breaking from past experience, EU member state governments ultimately agreed with the strong stance taken by the European Commission. In a meeting in Luxembourg on 16th October 2001, the EU's Council of Ministers opposed extensive state aid for stricken airlines and broadly endorsed restrictions imposed by the Commission.[39] The final decision reached was to only provide direct financial compensation for loss of revenue incurred by European airlines during the four-day shutdown of US airspace following the attacks. Some horizontal measures that did not discriminate between airlines were also approved. This included the underwriting of airline insurance costs by certain governments, the sharing of routes for a limited time and the relaxation of rules on slot usage at busy airports.[40]

Conclusions and forecasts

During the four decades that followed the Chicago Convention of 1944, airline policy was purely national except for the realisation that co-operation was needed in the area of price setting for international routes. By the early 1980s, governments began to realise that this nationalistic, interventionist policy fashion was no longer tenable. Taking the lead from countries such as the UK that were undertaking dramatic internal liberalisation measures, governments began conforming to global economic reality and (often grudgingly) accepted the need for airline liberalisation. As Cram (1994) attests, many national governments were not willing participants in this transfer of authority to Brussels.[41] However, spurred on by international changes in air transport policy, a Commission-led interest coalition exerted pressure on intransigent national governments, which led to a change in policy substance within Europe, causing the gradual Europeanisation of air transport policy.

A partial transference of sovereignty has occurred in this area of policy. With reference to our earlier checklist of national aviation policy components, competence has moved to Brussels in a number of areas. Most notably, the EU now controls the instruments for regulating the airline market and industry. Moreover, financial aid to airline companies is within the legal competence of the European Commission and its willingness and ability to enforce this mandate has increased. However, despite these developments, the EU remains largely powerless in the areas of air traffic control, airline safety, third-country traffic rights and extra-EU market access. Moves are afoot to change this situation and to complete the transference of aviation policy authority from national capitals to Brussels. The policy agenda of Commissioner de Palacio focuses directly on EU-US air transport liberalisation and European-level management of air traffic control systems and safety standards. There is considerable opposition in national capitals to such a further erosion of national sovereignty and it thus remains to be seen whether such a complete power transferral will become an actuality, in law or in practice.

Europe's governments are reluctant to give up explicit control of external relations policy but have no difficulties with harmonising regulatory rules. As former EU Transport Commissioner Neil Kinnock acknowledged[42] and as the emphasis of Commissioner Loyola de Palacio illustrates, this is the way in which the Commission is most likely to wrest external relations authority from the Member States. If the Commission succeeds in negotiating an EU-US accord which focuses primarily on harmonising the airline regulatory regimes of the US and the EU, this may be the first step towards the creation of the transatlantic common aviation area that the EU now aspires to building.

Notes

1   This chapter is derived in large part from a paper published by the author in 1999 in the Journal of Public Policy. Sincere thanks to the journal editor, Professor Richard Rose of the University of Strathclyde, and to Cambridge University Press for granting reproduction permission. The full reference of the paper is Thomas C. Lawton (1999) 'Governing the skies: conditions for the Europeanization of airline policy', Journal of Public Policy, vol.19 no.1, pp. 91-112.

2   Walter Hallstein, paraphrased in Eugene Sochor, *The Politics of International Aviation,* 1991, p. 187.

3   I acknowledge that there are other important elements of an air transport policy, such as air traffic management and external relations. External relations competence in particular has become a highly contentious issue area between national governments and the European Commission. It remains too early to comment on the likely outcome of this power play. However, in the areas of regulatory/competition authority and state aid we may comment upon the transference of sovereignty within this policy sector. The Commission and national governments have been openly competing for influence in both of these spheres of aviation policy since the mid-1980s and there is a bountiful supply of empirical evidence with which to formulate an opinion on the outcome of this contest.

4   These efforts included the French-sponsored Bonnefous Plan to create a High Authority for Transport, in line with that created for coal and steel. The Italian government's so-called Sforza Plan sought to establish a single authority for airlines, in which influence depended upon factors such as national population, as was the case within the Council of Ministers. For further details see Eugene Sochor, *The Politics of International Aviation,* 1991, pp. 187-8.

5   The UK-Netherlands deregulation agreement centred on free entry of new carriers, access by designated airlines to any point in either country, no capacity controls, and a 'double disapproval' regime for fares – meaning that although one government may not like a particular tariff it cannot on its own prevent an airline from implementing it if the other government is prepared to approve it. On this last feature, what it meant in practical terms was the agreement of a government to give up its veto power on tariffs. This was a significant step on the part of governments (Doganis 1991, 56/80).

6   This was stated explicitly in a 1997 UK Department of Transport information pack on EC aviation liberalisation, p. 1.

7   This alliance between the Commission and the main air transport industry associations was brought to this author's attention during discussions with Mr Kees Veenstra, deputy secretary general of the Association of European Airlines, Brussels.

8   For further details on the Commission's *Civil Aviation Memorandum Number 1* (1979), see Button and Swann (1989), 'European Community Airlines – Deregulation and its Problems', p. 272.

9   Communication and Proposals by the Commission to the Council, *Civil Aviation Memorandum No.2 - Progress towards the development of a Community Air Transport Policy,* COM (84) 72 final.

10   This Single Market objective became evident during discussions with both Commission and national government air transport policy officials.

11   The governments of the United Kingdom, the Netherlands, and Germany, to varying extents, actively championed air transport liberalisation.

12   The composition of this coalition was substantiated during discussions with industry representatives, senior representatives of the AEA and the ERA and air transport officials from both national governments and the European Commission.

13   For further details of the *Nouvelles Frontières* case, see Button and Swann (1989), 'European Community Airlines - Deregulation and its Problems', pp. 273-4.

14   The 'consecutive cabotage' principle guarantees that an airline can, on the same flight, serve two airports in another state.

15 The word 'virtually' is used here because not all restrictions have been removed on low fares. There remains a safeguard against a 'downward' spiral of fares. However, the UK CAA believe that this is probably unworkable and has never been invoked.

16 This is particularly true in the Irish and French cases.

17 This fact was evident in interviews conducted with government transport officials in several European national capitals. In particular, in two of the countries where the privatisation of the national carrier is likely – Ireland and France – officials argued that EU liberalisation measures forced their hand on the issue of privatisation.

18 International Chamber of Commerce, policy statement, 'State Aid to Airlines', Commission on Air Transport, 13 June 1995.

19 This position was explicated in an interview conducted by this author with a European Commission official responsible for the regulation of state aid to airlines, Brussels.

20 This argument was sustained during discussions conducted by this author with air transport officials of the Irish, Dutch, British, and French governments.

21 Michael Bishop cited in Eugene Sochor, The Politics of International Aviation, 1991, p. 183.

22 The 'market economy investor principle' was outlined by Giuseppe Abbamonte, DG VII of the European Commission, in a lecture given at Nuffield College, Oxford, 22 November 1995.

23 The impact of the US terrorist attacks of September 2001 on the aviation industry prompted calls for state aid to many European flag carriers. Despite initial resistance on the part of the European Commission, limited state assistance was finally permitted under the aegis of 'disaster aid'.

24 These exceptions are deemed to be compatible with the common market, according to Article 92, section 2 of the Rome Treaty.

25 These arguments were advanced by a Commission official responsible for state aid to airlines, in an interview conducted by this author in Brussels.

26 Meetings with transport officials at the Irish Department of Transport and Tourism, as well as with Aer Lingus executives, sustain this argument.

27 British Midland lodged an independent complaint with the European Court of Justice over the Air France decision, whilst a number of other large and small airline firms filed a collective complaint with the European Court of First Instance. These include Lufthansa and KLM.

28 See Commission of the European Communities, 'Report by the Commission to the Council and the European Parliament on the evaluation of aid schemes established in favour of Community air carriers', Doc. SEC(92) 431 final, 19 March 1992.

29 The 'one time, last time principle' is strongly supported by liberal European governments such as the UK and the Netherlands.

30 In early 1998, the European Commission reopened an investigation into state aid paid to Alitalia, citing violation of this *Comité des Sages* condition. The Commission argued that Alitalia was using its approved L2,750 billion in state aid to cut prices on many of its domestic routes.

31 The Commission's support for the Comité's report was explicitly acknowledged in the EC's Official Journal (94/C 350/07) of 10 December 1994.

32 This issue was detailed in the Official Journal of the European Communities, ibid.

33 The Financial Times, 'Airlines may have breached Brussels terms', 23 February 1996.

34 The Financial Times, 13 February 1996.

35   European Transport Commissioner Loyola de Palacio quoted in an interview conducted by Kevin O'Toole, Airline Business, March 2000, p. 32.

36   The previous Transport Commissioner, Neil Kinnock, had to ensure the completion of the single aviation market in Europe and was also beset for much of his tenure with state aid controversies and an aggressive US approach to bilateral open skies deals. In addition, aviation slipped down the European policy agenda in the latter half of the 1990s. As such, it proved difficult to seize the policy initiative.

37   Conor Sweeney 'State aid to Aer Lingus ruled out', Sunday Independent, 7 October 2001, p. 17.

38   Conor Sweeney 'She holds the skies in her own two hands', Sunday Independent, 7 October 2001, p. 18.

39   Daniel Dombey 'Member states support EU restrictions on aid for stricken airlines', Financial Times, 17 October 2001.

40   Conor Sweeney, op cit.

41   Cram's 1994 work, 'The European Commission as a multi-organization: social policy and IT policy in the EU', substantiates this claim. She argues that in both social policy and policy for information technology, national governments strongly opposed the extension of Community competence (198).

42   Neil Kinnock, interviewed in Airline Business, May 1995.

Chapter 3

The Emergence of Low
Fare Competitors in Europe

Introduction

The European airline industry underwent a major competitive shake-up during the 1990s. With the advent of full European airline liberalisation, a wide array of new airline start-ups emerged within the EU, many of them competing on price with established carriers.

A 1998 study conducted by the UK Civil Aviation Authority (CAA) described the emergence in the 1990s of a 'third way' in European aviation. 'Third way' (low fare) airlines bring together costs at the charter level with the convenience (if not the comfort) of scheduled services (CAA 1998, p.125). The CAA contends that the spread of third way – low fare – airlines was one of the most striking developments in airline competition in Europe during the latter half of the 1990s and possibly one of the more significant for the longer term. The CAA further states that 'the entry of these airlines has generally led to substantial stimulation of new air traffic without serious detriment to incumbents' operations' (CAA 1998, p.ix). For instance, when easyJet and Debonair commenced operations on the London-Barcelona route, passenger numbers increased by a staggering 32 per cent in the first year alone (1996-7). This compared with growth of 7 per cent in the previous year (CAA 1998, p.136). Similarly, traffic growth on the London-Glasgow route was double the UK average in the twelve months following the entry of Ryanair and easyJet in late 1995. Just over 2.2 million people flew between London and Glasgow in the year ended October 1996, compared with 1.8 million in the year previous. This was a growth rate of 21 per cent, compared with a national average of 10 per cent. Such figures indicate that the entry of LFAs onto routes (both domestic and international) generally results in considerable market stimulation. This viewpoint equates with that offered by LFAs, who tend to argue that rather than winning market share from traditional scheduled airlines, they in fact create new market space. They do so by attracting people away from other modes of transport such as the train or ferryboat and by encouraging people who rarely or never fly to do so on a regular basis. The low price, high frequency service offered by the new entrants brings new customers into the airline market and increases the travel frequency of many existing air travellers. Much of the resultant market growth was captured by the LFAs. The LFAs have also put pressure on traditional airlines to lower their prices and on the charter airlines to sell 'seat only' tickets.

This chapter begins by examining the impact that LFAs have had on the European air transport industry and market. We then define and discuss LFAs and place them in the wider context of the European airline industry. This leads us into a consideration of the similarities and differences between low fare, charter and regional airlines in Europe. This is followed by a brief comparison of the point-to-point and hub-and-spoke systems and a review of route networks in the European LFA sector.

Developing the airline market: the role of LFAs

The airline industry depends primarily on two distinct market segments: business and leisure travellers. These markets have had fundamentally different needs and priorities. Time is uppermost in the minds of business travellers: maximising the working day, being on time for meetings, and getting home by the evening or weekend being more important than the subsequent cost incurred. Such customers want frequent departures, short check-in times, good onward connection options, and so forth. By comparison, price is generally of primary importance to the leisure traveller. Surveys[1] show that for the leisure traveller, price is more important than comfort or convenience and that such travellers shop for seats as a commodity. Late departures or obligatory Saturday night stop-overs are not usually of major inconvenience, given that the customers are in no real rush. Catering to these different markets is an essential feature of the contemporary global airline industry. Most airline companies try to attract both categories but many make the bulk of their profit from only one segment. For example, although business travellers fill only one fifth of the seats on conventional scheduled flights, they generate half the revenue, being charged up to five times as much as an economy class passenger on the same flight.[2] It is this group of business passengers which keeps many full-service airlines in existence. Low price carriers traditionally focused on the leisure travel market or more specifically, the 'visiting friends and relatives' (VFR) travellers, as was the case with Ryanair.[3] In doing so, they were tapping into a huge and virtually unlimited market. Leisure travellers constitute over two-thirds of most modern airline markets and their numbers are growing at a much faster rate than those in the business travel market. This imbalance has begun to shift, with research now showing that 40 per cent or more of LFA passengers are flying on business (Go 1999; McWhirter 2000). Mason (2000a) illustrates that self-employed business travellers or those working for small companies are now increasingly flying with LFAs. They tend to be more willing than those working for larger companies to trade in-flight service and frequent flyer points for lower fares. In fact, short haul business travellers are, en masse, becomingly increasingly price sensitive (Mason 2000b, p.1). Many large international corporations refuse to fly their employees business class for journeys of under three hours. Low fare carriers therefore have a vast existing and potential market that they can exploit.

The European airline industry did indeed experience its first significant competitive shake-up during the 1990s. As Morrell points out:

> Excluding those airlines based outside the EU, there was a net increase of six in the number of airlines serving intra-EU cross-border scheduled routes between 1992 – 1995 compared to a net loss of four carriers between 1989 – 1992 (1998, p.50).

In many cases these new entrants served low-density regional routes. As Bhide argues, 'most start-ups begin by pursuing niche markets that are too small to interest large competitors' (1992, p. 111). In other cases, charter airlines such as Air Liberté in France (now Air Lib) commenced scheduled flights in direct competition with established carriers. During the latter part of the 1990s, more than 100 new airlines commenced operations in Europe. During the same period, in excess of 70 went out of business or were absorbed by another airline. Of these airline start-ups, five can be classified as LFAs – easyJet, Go, Buzz, Virgin Express and Debonair.

Gudmundsson (1998) provides a useful typology of new-entrant airlines based on origin. These are first, start-up carriers (started post-deregulation); second, charter-based carriers (start-up or expansion to scheduled); third, intrastate (operating only within a state before deregulation); and fourth, regional-based carriers (moving from turboprop to scheduled jet operations). Although developed in the context of the US market, these categorisations may also be applied to the liberalised European market. Gudmundsson's research found that, in the US, the most unstable of these groups – in terms of net profits – were the start-up new entrants (1998, p.218).

The discernable post-deregulation competitive cycle is as follows. Stage 1: market deregulation provides the opportunity for new airlines to enter the market. Stage 2: these new entrants challenge established carriers on cost, price and often service. Stage 3: the larger established airlines restructure their cost base and sometime change strategic direction to meet the competitive challenge (defensive reaction). Stage 4: the larger carriers go on the attack, forcing many newer airlines out of business (legally or illegally) or acquiring them (offensive action). Stage 5: The industry roughly speaking consolidates into a bipolar structure – large established airlines and their subsidiaries and highly competitive smaller independent airlines.

The US scenario would indicate that Europe is likely to experience as ruthless a shakeout in terms of the survival rate of new entrant airlines.[4] This process has already begun – witness the 1999 liquidation of Debonair and the 2000/1 downsizing at Virgin Express.

What is a LFA?

Tom Haughey, Director of Marketing Development and Strategy at the Irish airport authority, Aer Rianta, provides a clear comparative distinction between Europe's LFAs and traditional scheduled carriers (Table 3.1).[5]

Table 3.1 European low fare versus full fare airlines

Low fare airline	Full fare airline
Simple brand – low fare	Complex brand – price + service
Online and direct booking	Mainly travel agents
Simple ticket price structure and ticketless check-in	Complex fare structures
Use of secondary, low-charging airports (some exceptions)	Focus on primary airports
High aircraft utilisation – quick gate turnaround time	Lower utilisation on short haul
Do not interline/point-to-point service	Interlining important part of service
Simple product – all additional services and facilities charged for, e.g. credit card bookings, late check-in	Complex integrated service product(s), e.g. ticket flexibility, business lounges, frequent flyer programme
Focus on ancillary revenue generation – advertising ('the plane as a billboard'), on board retailing	Focus on primary product
Mainly short-haul focus	Short and long-haul
Common fleet type acquired at very good rates	Mixed fleet

Whilst it is relatively easy to identify the core features of the LFA business model, many variations do exist. Nonetheless, it is widely accepted that the approach pioneered by Southwest Airlines in the US is the archetype LFA model. The Southwest (and Ryanair) low cost/low fare model is reliant on:

- short-haul routes
- no frills service (no meals, no in-flight entertainment, no advance seat selection, no frequent flyer points)
- minimal debt servicing costs
- standardised fleet (Boeing 737)
- use of cheaper, secondary airports
- cautious route network expansion
- ticketless reservation system *(not in the original Southwest model).*

easyJet management concur with most of these principles (although neglect to mention minimal debt servicing costs) and add a further essential practice – the direct sell, excluding the travel agent and selling directly to the customer – preferably via the Internet.[6]

As we will see in subsequent chapters, LFAs around the world have deviated from or developed on this basic model in many different ways.

Five LFAs can be identified in Europe: Ryanair, easyJet, Go, Virgin Express,[7] and Buzz. A sixth – Basiq Air – does appear to meet most of the criteria. However, operationally and strategically, it is virtually indistinguishable from charter and cargo airline Transavia – itself closely identifiable with KLM.[8] Of the five more obvious LFAs, three are or were associated with larger airlines. Three – easyJet, Go and Buzz – are based at a London airport and Ryanair also has a major base at London Stansted. The London market has also seen a prominent LFA go into receivership, with the 1999 collapse of Debonair.

A Salomon Smith Barney report[9] illustrates that only 3.4 per cent of intra-EU passengers use LFAs. This compares to a figure of 24 per pent in the US This would indicate that the potential for LFA growth in Europe – at the expense of the existing carriers – is considerable. Based on route analysis, the same report argues that on almost every route the LFAs have taken at least 5 percentage points in market share from the incumbents. This is in addition to the new market space that they have created – most of which they control.

Initially, little competition existed between LFAs, as they generally avoided operating on the same routes. This began to change in 2000/1, as the airlines expanded their route networks and some airport authorities endeavoured to attract more than one LFA. Witness for example the competition between Go and easyJet on the London to Nice and London to Scotland routes and the Ryanair-Go rivalry on Dublin to Scotland routes.

How do LFAs ensure considerable cost advantage over traditional airlines? Doganis (2001) argues that the LFAs begin with two initial cost advantages arising from the very nature of their operation: higher seating density and higher daily aircraft utilisation. By removing business class and reconfiguring their aircraft, LFAs can significantly increase the number of seats on their aircraft. The seat pitch of a LFA is usually 28 inches, compared to a conventional economy class pitch of 32 inches. This allows LFAs to fit more seats onto their aircraft, thus increasing the maximum capacity of each flight. For instance, easyJet has 148 seats on its Boeing 737-300 aircraft, compared with Bmi British Midland's 124 seats. Assuming similar operating costs and the same aircraft, easyJet's 24 extra seats per aircraft would result in its costs being 16 per cent lower than Bmi British Midland's (Doganis 2001, p.63).

On the issue of aircraft utilisation, LFAs ensure more flights a day per aircraft due to their rapid gate turnaround time. The average LFA takes about 25 minutes to disembark passengers, unload and load baggage, refuel and clean the aircraft, and embark new passengers. This can be as much as half the time it takes a traditional airline to carry out the same activities. The reasons behind this rapid turnaround time will be explored in more detail in Chapter 6. In brief, they derive from the use of uncongested secondary airports (whenever possible), the no frills service (requiring little catering and cleaning support), the non-assigned seating approach and the absence of freight (Doganis 2001, p.63). As a result, aircraft utilisation averages out at 11 hours per day for the LFA, compared with around 7 hours per day for a more conventional carrier (CAA 1998, p.143).

Overall, Doganis (2001) calculates that LFAs should be able to operate at seat costs that are only 40-50 per cent those of a mainline rival. If this is combined with a significant load factor differential and lower distribution costs, a LFA's cost per passenger can drop to about one-third those of a conventional airline's.

Research indicates that the absolute cost disadvantage of conventional airlines lies in their provision of a business class (CAA 1998, p.144). However, this element should be offset by higher yields. The real cost advantages of the LFAs are therefore smaller than the bare figures indicate. These cost advantages are sustainable and stem from the nature of the low fare product. Premised on a more basic no frills service, the LFA product cannot or will not be emulated by traditional full service carriers. Such an approach would damage a traditional airline's quality reputation, alienate passengers (particularly many business customers) and undermine its market position.

Positioning low fare carriers in the European airline industry structure

Given the plethora of airlines that exists in Europe, it is necessary from the outset to conceptualise where exactly low fare carriers are strategically situated. A study conducted by management consultants McKinsey & Co. has identified three different roles for airlines in the commercial air passenger industry: network manager, capacity provider, and service provider (Avmark Aviation Economist, April 1995). Low fare operators such as easyJet possess neither the scale nor the scope to be network managers, conceding this role to the likes of British Airways and Lufthansa. Service providers tend to concentrate on non-core functions such as the technical maintenance of a fleet. Many European airlines outsource such activities. For some this is a core activity, performed either by the airline itself or by a subsidiary, e.g. Lufthansa Technik. Since Ryanair, easyJet and others outsource most of these business activities, they cannot be classified as a service provider. The third role, that of capacity provider, comes closer to encapsulating the LFA. Such airlines include feeder/commuter carriers flying to a network manager's hubs on routes with less traffic. These companies tend to be the secondary carriers to and from airports dominated by network managers. Low fare airlines do not fit neatly into this category either – nor do other entrepreneurial, niche carriers such as Bmi British Midland. Although they may be classified in general as commuter carriers and have traditionally been secondary carriers, these airlines have broken free of this status on several routes. For instance, on the Dublin-London route, traditionally dominated by the network manager, Aer Lingus, Ryanair has achieved the position of largest carrier. Hence, we must move beyond the narrow McKinsey classifications if we are to understand the nature of the European airline industry and the place of LFAs in the industry's hierarchy. The structure in Figure 3.1 broadly concurs with that advanced by the Robinson-Humphrey Company (1997). They divide the European airline industry into major airlines; low fare, no frills airlines; regional feeder airlines; and charter airlines. We refine this structure to distinguish between major airlines and to differentiate between regional airlines in terms of scale and scope.

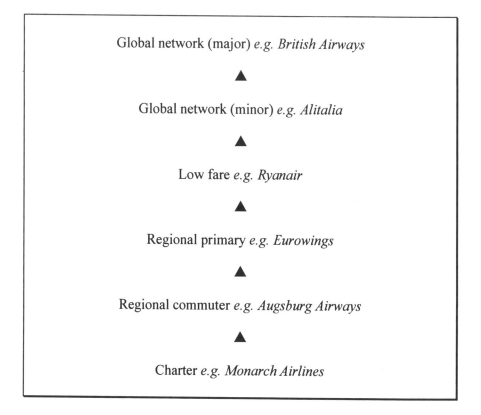

Figure 3. 1 The European airline industry structure

Such a classification allows us to clearly position low fare carriers within the airline industry. It also emphasises the fact that these companies are positioned between the mid-sized and the very small operators, thus competing with both bigger and smaller companies for market share on certain routes.

Converting charter airlines to low fare carriers

In the aftermath of European liberalisation, no regulatory distinction now exists between scheduled and charter airlines. Scheduled airlines can however be divided into those providing both domestic and international flights and those operating either one or the other. Most European scheduled carriers perform both kinds of service (Janić 1997, p.170). Charter airlines are distinguished by their pattern of operations, target markets and organisational structure. The key difference between the two is that a scheduled airline offers a consistent, repetitive service (e.g. flying from London to Dublin every weekday at 9am, year round), whereas a charter airline will alter its schedule according to demand, season and other variables. Put another way, a scheduled airline decides where to fly, whereas a charter airline is told where to fly. A scheduled airline determines its route network and sells tickets direct to the public or via travel agents and tour operators. A charter carrier sells its services to a tour operator (and is often owned by one) and it is the tour operator that determines where and when the carrier will fly. It is effectively a contracted-in process with little or no risk for the airline. More recently, some blurring is occurring as carriers such as Air 2000 have converted many of its flights from charter to scheduled service and sell 'seat only' tickets to the public. However, the fundamental differences remain in most instances.[10]

European deregulation had significant strategic implications for Europe's charter airlines. The Third Package of deregulation (1993) abolished the distinction between scheduled and charter carriers, permitting the latter to designate their flights as scheduled if they so wish (Graham 1997, pp.227-8). Charter airlines therefore now had the opportunity to develop scheduled services on their core leisure routes and/or on high-density inter-city routes. The alternative was to consolidate their core charter business through the development of long-haul services. As the history of charter airlines becoming scheduled carriers is fraught with failure, many charters chose not to compete on scheduled services. There were some notable exceptions such as Braathens (Oslo-London) and Maersk Air (Copenhagen-London). Morrell (1998) argues that although charter airlines may have appeared to be ideal low fare airline candidates, the cost and difficulty of converting their image and structure proved prohibitive.

Distinguishing between regional and low fare airlines in Europe[11]

It is increasingly difficult to define what constitutes a regional airline. The industry magazine *Airline Business* describes it as 'a carrier whose fleet is mainly composed of aircraft smaller than 100 seats, flying scheduled services on regional routes of up to 800km' (1997, p.29). The European Regions Airlines Association (ERA) broadly agrees with this definition. However, the seat configuration has now increased to 120, as Boeing 717 and Airbus 318 are both over 100 seats in capacity.[12] In acquiring these larger aircraft, many regional carriers are now moving into longer trunk routes, thus blurring the distinction between them and larger established airlines. These may be classified as primary or secondary regional airlines (depending on scale and scope), as opposed to the smaller regional commuter airlines.

By the mid-1990s, the 100 largest regional airlines in the world were carrying over 120 million people per annum, employed almost 90,000 people, and flew up to 3,000 jet and turboprop aircraft. Their combined revenue came to more than $9 billion, and their annual passenger growth rate was in excess of 11 per cent. The thirty-three regionals reporting profits in 1995 made a collective net profit of over $200 million and a net margin of 3.9 per cent (Airline Business, May 1996, p.24).

LFAs, whilst operating on a regional basis (short-haul flights within a specific geographical market), are not regional airlines as such. Four key factors distinguish regional from low fare carriers:

1. LFAs operate on high density or high traffic potential, city-to-city routes; regionals operate on some of these but also on short, low frequency routes.
2. Regional carriers are cost efficient but they are usually not as cost efficient as LFAs (non-standardised fleet and route structure being some of the causes). Also, they are often not price focused. Whilst their operational side can be very cost efficient (25 minute turnaround time), they may choose to add cost for customer service. This tends to be recouped through higher ticket prices.
3. LFAs tend to have a standardised fleet (usually Boeing 737 jets) but for regional airlines it can vary between sizes and between turbo prop and jet engine.
4. Unlike LFAs, regional carriers often provide premium class, full service with a better seat pitch.

European regional air transport was liberalised far in advance of the rest of the industry. As Morrell (1998) points out, the Inter-regional Directive, deriving from the European Commission's 1979 aviation memorandum (COM 79/311), introduced free access on inter-regional routes over 400 km operated by aircraft smaller than 70 seats. The directive had little impact on the structure or competitive dynamics of European aviation: only 14 new services were subsequently started between regional airports and many of these would probably have been permitted anyway under existing bilateral agreements (Wheatcroft and Lipman 1986). An example was the service started by Maersk between Southend in Essex and Billend – the nearest they could get at the time to a London-Copenhagen service (they later flew between London Gatwick and Copenhagen). It was not the bilateral agreement that prevented them from offering the inter-capital service but the

Danish government protecting SAS's market position. This was very common at the time – a flag carrier in a privileged position protected from private sector competition by its own government.[13] The limited existing and potential size of the markets on inter-regional routes further accounted for the relative lack of growth in this sector, even after it was opened up to competition.

A regional route can take three forms: (a) a route between two regions; (b) a route between a region and a major centre; (c) a route between major centres but using secondary airports. Depending on the size of the regional, it may offer services on one or all three of these route types. Three different categories of regional airline also exist. These are:

1. 'Regional commuter' – flying just between two regions and/or between a region and a major centre (19-80 seat aircraft).
2. 'Regional primary' – flying between major centres but using secondary or regional airports at one end or the other (70-120 seat aircraft).
3. A hybrid of the above.

European deregulation has been a great opportunity for ERA members. The ERA was in fact one of the actors pushing the European Commission towards liberalisation in the 1980s (see Chapter 2). Regionals can now fly anywhere within the European Economic Area (the 15 EU member states, plus Norway and Iceland). Deregulation has given 'lifeblood' to regional airlines.

Inter-modal competition is a worry for regional airlines. Rail competition in particular is a problem. Rail travel is heavily subsidised by regional, national and EU-level government. The same is not the case for air transport. In terms of potential regulatory barriers to competition, the prospect of environmental charges being levied on the air system alone is a real possibility and threat. It is not likely to be levied on trains.

How much of a competitive threat do LFAs pose to regional airlines? At their 2000 annual assembly in Switzerland, the ERA were 'relatively sanguine about any threat from the low cost sector' (Baker 2000a, p.77). Speaking at the ERA meeting, Andre Auer, former president of the European Civil Aviation Conference (ECAC) noted that regional airlines had 'lessons to learn' from the low fare airline experience but that the LFAs carried out a different job. As Andrew Clarke, Director of Air Transport Policy at the ERA notes, there is not much direct competition between these two air transport segments. Regionals compete more with trunk/large airlines as they often provide a feeder service into hub airports. LFAs serve 'thicker' routes with greater passenger capacity than typically served by a regional.[14]

On the issue of alliance networks, the feeder role of many regionals is a good marketing point. However, only 30 per cent of regional passengers are making connections, whereas 70 per cent are point-to-point. Whilst the feeder role should not be the be all and end all, it is an important role for business purposes. Feeder agreements with a big airline can be cost effective as it involves the pooling of marketing and advertising resources. This can ultimately deliver higher passenger numbers.

At the time of writing, the ERA has 65 scheduled service airline members in Europe. Of these, 15 are wholly owned by a major airline. 20 more are part owned by a larger airline. The remainder – some 50 per cent – have no ownership by a major airline. However, these last numbers are declining year by year as more and more large airlines buy into regionals. Morrell sees this activity as a defensive response by many flag carriers to the threat of new entrants unleashed by European deregulation (1998, p.49). It is also linked to the industry consolidation that has gripped the world aviation business, as companies such as British Airways endeavour to establish greater economies of scale and scope (Graham 1997). Part of the reason for the decline in the number of European regional independents also comes from within the regional airline industry. Ironically, this comes at a time of strong growth in traffic within the regional airline market. Traffic among ERA members grew by over 10 per cent in both 1999 and 2000 and about one third of members experienced growth in excess of 20 per cent. Some carriers far exceeded even this figure, with Italy's Air Dolomiti and Spain's Air Nostrum respectively posting a 36.9 and a 52.7 per cent increase in revenue passenger kilometres during the first half of 2000. The largest of Europe's regional airlines, Crossair, grew its traffic by 13.6 per cent during the same period. However, strong growth rates do not necessarily translate into increased profitability. High fuel costs, the unfavourable dollar exchange rate (having implications for leasing and maintenance costs), and additional operational expenses in congested European airspace have had a negative impact on the financial performance of Europe's regional airlines. Pressure to undergo fleet modernisation – particularly the expensive transition to all-jet fleets – adds to the difficulties of Europe's regionals to turn a profit. Only a little over half of the ERA's member airlines are showing an operating profit.[15] Such financial problems provide an impetus for regional airlines to deepen their relationships with major carriers – as well as leaving them vulnerable to takeover. For example, in Germany, Lufthansa's move in 2000 to acquire a 24.9 per cent stake in Eurowings served to improve Lufthansa's position in the regional sector while strengthening Eurowings plans for a complete regeneration of its fleet.

Load factor is a key means of distinguishing a regional carrier from a LFA. Unlike regionals, LFAs do not emphasise yield management: profitability for LFAs is dependent on high load factors because their profit margins are so low. What is the lowest average load factor that a low fare airline can sustain if it is to remain profitable? According to Conor McCarthy, director of aviation management consultancy company PlaneConsult and former Director of Operations at Ryanair, it all depends on the breakeven load factor (BELF) for a particular airline. The BELF is a combination of aircraft type, operating costs and yield. In Ryanair's case, the breakeven figure in 2001 was around 54 per cent. Ryanair has the lowest costs in Europe but also very low yield per seat. If Ryanair were to push up yields, they could lower the BELF even further. However, to do so risks jeopardising their price leadership position. If they were based in the US, with the same salaries and airport deals, they could have a lower BELF due to lower fuel costs and the absence of Eurocontrol. McCarthy estimates that 55-60 per cent BELF is a good achievement in the low fares arena.[16]

In most cases, LFAs cannot afford to have average load factors of less than 70 per cent if they are to remain profitable (the same is broadly true for the majors). Conversely, a regional carrier can sustain considerably lower load factors of 50 per cent and above but remain solvent, if not profitable. The average load factor for ERA members in 2000 was 56.4 per cent, up from 55.5 per cent the previous year.[17] As Table 3.2 illustrates, all but one of Europe's leading regional carriers have average load factors of under 70 per cent. As mentioned earlier, most regional airlines are very cost focused and many are highly operationally efficient. They do not usually transfer these cost savings to the customer as they are obliged to charge higher fares so as to offset the often low load factors on their flights. It is difficult to increase this load factor due to the low density nature of many regional routes.

Table 3.2 Europe's largest regional airlines (by passenger numbers)

European Rank	Airline	Country	Passengers (thousand)	Load factor (%)	World rank
1	Crossair	Switzerland	6,290	52.0	6
2	Lufthansa Cityline	Germany	5,660	59.5	9
3	KLM uk	UK	3,778	62.6	18
4	Delta Air Transport	Belgium	3,300	N/A	19
5	Eurowings	Germany	3,175	58.7	20

6	Air Nostrum	Spain	2,758	59.9	23
7	British Regional Airlines	UK	2,523	61.0	25
8	British European	UK	2,444	56.0	26
9	KLM cityhopper	Netherlands	2,167	68.3	27
10	Binter Canarias	Spain	2,116	77.1	28

Source: Adapted from the Airline Business Regionals Top 100 Rankings, May 2001.

Crossair – leading the regional market

The 1999 and 2000 *Airline Business* rankings of regional airlines, by passenger numbers, placed Crossair sixth in the world and first in Europe.[18] Based in Basle, Switzerland, Crossair is majority owned by the SAir Group (70.9 per cent).[19] Crossair has a wide range of alliances with other airlines. Its partners include other regionals such as Air Europe, Air Littoral and Tyrolean Airways, as well as flag carriers like Austrian Airlines, Swissair, TAP Air Portugal, Air France and British Airways. Its total fleet size is 84 aircraft.

Crossair is credited with having pioneered the regional airline concept in Europe and its founder, Moritz Suter, was one of the architects of the ERA. Since the ERA's foundation in 1980, it has grown from five members carrying under 60,000 passengers per annum to almost eighty members carrying 70 million passengers (O'Toole 2000b, p.39). The business proposition of Crossair emerged from its founder's work as a Swissair pilot in the 1970s. Through his work on Swissair's regional routes, he saw a market niche for a small-scale operator in markets too tiny for the flag carrier. Swissair management were eventually convinced of the potential of the feeder concept and Crossair commenced operations in July 1979 with a one hour scheduled service from Zurich to Nuremberg.

Crossair avoids competition with major carriers, preferring instead to take over routes that prove unprofitable for the majors, or to develop short hop new routes that bigger airlines could not operate profitably. Crossair is also a quality service provider, as witnessed by the fact that 80 per cent of its customers are business travellers (O'Toole 2000, p.40). Crossair's maintains its profitability through the aforementioned balance of relatively low operating costs and high yields. It is typical of the mainstream, successful European regionals and contrasts with LFAs by competing on quality rather than on price (hence its dependence on the business traveller rather than the VFR market for instance).

Air One – challenging on price

The Italian carrier, Air One, comes close to being classified as a low fare operator but is in fact more accurately described as a regional airline. As with companies including Braathens SAFE of Norway and the Spanish-focused Air Europa, Air One operates on a low cost, low price basis. However, it cannot be placed in the same category as Ryanair and its low fare contemporaries, as neither costs nor fares are proportionally as low and the regionals also tend to offer the same frills as full fare airlines.

Nonetheless, Air One is a low price competitor – relative to the full service airlines operating in Italy. It operates on a low cost basis and sets its fares relative to Alitalia, generally achieving prices of 30-35 per cent less than the national carrier (Feldman 1996, p.89). The company has sought cost reductions through more direct sales and outsourcing ground handling, aircraft maintenance, and other technical services. However, Air One deviates from low fare airline standard practices such as offering coach class seating only. Its cabins are dual class and it admits to targeting both business and leisure class passengers. The company also does not stick to the 'no frills' approach.

Air One commenced operations in November 1995, with its first route being Europe's fifth busiest – Milan Linate to Rome Fiumicino. Air One emerged from Aliadriatica, a light-aircraft training school started in 1983. In 1988, Aliadriatica was acquired by Toto Group, which added air taxi and regional routes as part of the Aliadriatica operations (Feldman 1996, p. 89). The Toto Group were interested in offering Milan-Rome scheduled services as early as 1990. However, the Italian authorities refused them permission to fly between Milan and Rome. Group Chairman, Carlo Toto argued that the rules were 'clearly designed so only Alitalia could win'.[20] EU liberalisation finally opened the way for the Toto Group. The third package of liberalisation, introduced in 1993, required countries to open up route competition. Despite three Alitalia lawsuits, Air One (the Toto Group's chosen name for its airline division) was finally granted permission to operate scheduled services between the main airports at Milan and Rome.

Another important development at this time was the hiring of Giovanni Sebastiani, a former Alitalia executive. Sebastiani both understood the operations and strategy of Alitalia and was experienced at dealing with Italian bureaucracy. His first achievement was to secure an increase in Air One's slot hourly allocation at Milan Linate from 22 to 32.

Within a year, Air One was offering 13 daily flights between Rome and Milan – later on reduced to seven. Its domestic network also includes Turin, Venice, Naples, Bari, Crotone, Pescara, Brindisi and Reggio Calabria.

In 1996, the airline's first full year of operations, it carried a total of 713,000 passengers. Traffic grew steadily during the subsequent years, reaching almost 1,400,000 in 1999.

Air One's fares are pegged at 22.6 per cent less than Alitalia's published tariff. When corporate discounts are factored into the equation, Air One's fares can be as much as 35 per cent less than Alitalia's. This is a long way off the fares offered by Ryanair or easyJet, relative to Aer Lingus or British Airways. Such an approach to fare pricing (pegging prices against those of a flag carrier) might indicate that Air One is a *lower* cost airline but not necessarily *low* cost as it does not fit the low fare model outlined elsewhere in this book.

As with low priced new entrants elsewhere in Europe, Air One did succeed in growing existing markets. For instance, in the first quarter of 1995, just prior to Air One's market entry, Rome-Milan had 795,879 passengers. A year later the total was 917,728. Of those, Alitalia flew 746,558, giving Air One 21 per cent (Feldman 1996, p.90).

Due to its short-haul network, Air One's main operating expense is handling, followed by maintenance, fuel and crew. Its operational performance has not improved since the company's formation and it has not shown a net profit since 1997 (Table 3.3).

Table 3.3 Air One: facts and figures

	1996	1997	1998	1999
Passengers	0.71 million	1.38 million	1.53 million	1.39 million
Load factor	n/a	58.5%	60.7%	n/a
Employees	226	417	600	n/a
Sales	$75.82 m	$137.34 m	$170.57 m	$165.0 m
Net profit	$0.00 m	$34.66 m	-$5.13 m	-$7.81 m
Net margin	0%	25.23%	-3%	-4.73%

Air One has encountered many problems. These include the generally pro-Alitalia nature of airport authorities and the endless bureaucracy of Italian government. Also, Air One experienced problems in introducing a standardised fleet of Boeing 737s, as it was the first airline in Italy to do so and therefore experienced problems in locating suitably trained mechanics and pilots. To date, it has accrued high development and operating costs and heavy losses and it is difficult to assess its long-term viability, particularly as an independent operator.

Comparing the hub-and-spoke system with the point-to-point model

A defining organisational difference exists between LFAs and traditional carriers. LFAs operate on a point-to-point basis whereas traditional carriers tend to utilise a hub-and-spoke system. The hub-and-spoke approach consists of an airline flying short-haul passengers from a number of their secondary airports into the hub, or base, airport. The passengers are then put onto one, usually larger, aircraft and flown to their final long-haul destination. For example, British Airways (BA) would use its regional subsidiaries to fly passengers from Belfast, Edinburgh and Glasgow to London Heathrow (or another hub, such as Manchester) and would fly them collectively from there to Amsterdam. The point-to-point system, by comparison, flies passengers directly from City A to City B, without using an intermediate airport. Using the same example as before, easyJet will fly passengers from Belfast, Edinburgh and Glasgow direct to Amsterdam but it will not fly people from all three destinations to London Luton with the aim of transferring them onto the flight from Luton to Amsterdam.

If a LFA passenger wishes to fly from City A to City B but must do so via the airline's hub, two separate flights have to be booked. For instance, a Ryanair customer wishing to fly from Dublin to Pisa must book a flight from Dublin to London Stansted and then another flight from Stansted to Pisa. No baggage transfer is provided, so the customer must collect his/her baggage at Stansted and recheck it for the flight to Pisa. If he/she misses the second flight due to delay or other problems, Ryanair is under no obligation to provide a refund or to offer another flight.

As Freiberg and Freiberg (2001) argue, the hub-and-spoke system is an efficient way to fill an airplane. However, it does not usually offer efficient aircraft utilisation. LFAs spurn the hub-and-spoke system on the basis that it increases costs. Baggage handlers, gate staff and other ground crew can be idle if an airplane spends more time on the ground waiting for passengers and their baggage to connect from feeder cities. In addition, the aircraft will accrue higher airport charges for spending longer at the gate (particularly at busier airports). With the point-to-point system, airlines calculate that using each aircraft for a maximum number of flights per day will generate more revenue and lower unit costs per flight. For instance, in the US, the leading LFA, Southwest Airlines, obtains 11.5 hours of daily flying time from its typical Boeing 737. This compares with an average of 8.6 hours per day for traditional carriers (Freiberg and Freiberg 2001, p.51). These figures are particularly striking when one considers that the average Southwest flight lasts little more than an hour.

In addition to the cost efficiencies gained, LFAs believe that the point-to-point model is more convenient for customers, most of whom would prefer to avoid the time and inconvenience of making flight connections.

Route network comparisons

Route network strategies have varied between Europe's LFAs, with companies like Ryanair seeking to maximise the number of city pairs between which it offers services, whereas airlines such as easyJet strive to increase density on a smaller number of city pairs (Figure 3.2). As of mid-2001, all of the LFAs – except for Buzz – also had more than one hub airport within their network. In a straightforward comparison of the number of city pairs within route networks, Europe's LFAs (including the quasi-LFA, Basiq Air) line up as follows:

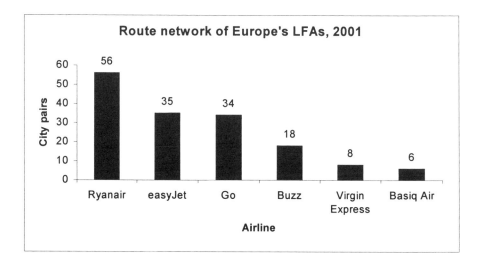

Figure 3.2 Route network of Europe's LFAs, 2001*
Source: data derived from the websites of each airline.
(*These figures are correct as of 20 September 2001)

This figure is indicative of individual LFA strategies in the 2000/1 period. Virgin Express's relatively low number of city pairs is due to its network contraction in the 1999/2001 period, in an effort to restructure, cut costs and refocus its market. Go has made steady gains on easyJet in terms of network expansion, as easyJet has preferred to concentrate on greater frequency rather than significantly expanded network. Ryanair has adopted the opposite approach, preferring to establish more city pairs without necessarily creating dense frequency. Basiq Air is included here as a point of comparison and due to its quasi-LFA status. Its city pairs are exclusively between the Netherlands, Spain and the south of France.

Challenges ahead and strategies for success

Despite the inevitability of a shakeout, reminiscent of early 1980s America, Europe's low fare carriers are here to stay. Ever-increasing industry liberalisation, together with customer demand, will guarantee a place in the market for cost efficient and reliable LFAs. Nonetheless, challenges abound for these price leaders. The first of these is competitor response from market incumbents. Unfair practice allegations have been levied for several years by LFAs against larger, established competitors. For instance, easyJet conflicted with KLM over an advertisement featuring a massive price cut to KLM's London-Amsterdam route and allegedly targeting easyJet by titling the advertisement 'Easy Choice'. Also, KLM appear to have launched Basiq Air in direct response to easyJet's decision to create a second hub at Amsterdam. Doganis (2001, p. 64) outlines several other challenges facing LFAs in the modern European market. First, competition is ensuing between LFAs as they expand their route networks. This has already commenced, e.g. the vigorous competition between Go and easyJet and between Go and Ryanair on a number of routes.

Second, there is a real risk of over capacity if growth rates overheat. Current projections (on average, 20 per cent per annum for the main LFAs) may be unrealistic. In the early years, Southwest cautiously targeted growth rates of only about 10 per cent per year and took 12 years to build a fleet of 50 aircraft (as did Ryanair). If Europe's LFAs are growing too rapidly they may endanger their own survival. This may occur due to pressure to reduce prices in order to fill excess capacity and a non-strategic approach to route development, resulting in the choice of marginal or highly competitive routes.

Third, controlling costs is a further challenge. As the LFA airlines mature, they may find it more difficult to negotiate low cost deals with airports and other service providers. This is already happening for Ryanair at Manchester and Dublin airports for instance. It has also happened for easyJet at Luton Airport, as witnessed by the 2000 dispute over the airport's attempts to quadruple its charges.

Building on the LFA model key principles outlined earlier, Doganis also offers a number of suggestions for LFA market survival (2001, p.65):

1. Keep it simple – need to maintain a 55-60 per cent cost advantage while offering a product that is well regarded by customers and seen as value for money
2. Stick to short haul routes
3. Operate a single aircraft type
4. Offer high density seating
5. Operate from secondary airports as much as possible
6. High frequency and punctual service
7. Sell 100 per cent by telephone or Internet and be ticketless
8. Minimal on-board catering, good quality but not free
9. Simple, one way, point-to-point fare structure
10. Avoid transfer traffic or hub feeding
11. Outsource functions wherever possible.

Another requirement for long-term survival involves becoming the number one or two carrier on most routes operated (measured by market share). This dominance, together with low fares, raises the entry barriers and gives the LFA a strong defensive position if new entrants emerge. It also provides the cash flow needed to service further growth.

Conclusions

The US experience indicates that the large number of low fare carriers that emerge in the wake of market deregulation will dwindle over time and that only a handful will ultimately survive. Many are driven out of business by insufficient access to landing slots or by predatory activity on the part of larger airlines. Others simply cut prices further than they can afford, effectively pricing themselves out of the market. This is likely to happen in Europe too. It is not yet clear which of the cheap carriers will triumph but Ryanair is the frontrunner for survival and growth. Chris Avery, aviation analyst at JP Morgan, adopts an optimistic interpretation of the European LFA industry.[21] Addressing criticisms that Europe's leading LFAs cannot continue to sustain above average growth, he notes that Southwest Airlines in the US have done so for three decades. He further argues that too much has been made of the differences between Ryanair, easyJet and Go and that they all in fact have sustainable business models.

As we will see in the following chapters, there is evidence to suggest that the original LFA model – as outlined in this chapter – is being most closely adhered to by Go and Ryanair.[22] All other LFAs are straying from the model in some way or another. easyJet and Buzz both fly into some expensive airports (e.g. easyJet operates from Glasgow Abbotsinch and London Gatwick; Buzz flies into Paris Charles de Gaulle). Buzz operates two different types of aircraft, the BAe 146 and the Boeing 737. Virgin Express offers two classes of service on its aircraft.[23]

In the following chapters we will consider how such deviations may have affected the operational efficiency of Europe's LFAs. We will reflect on whether Europe's LFAs should adhere rigidly to the Southwest/Ryanair model if they are to survive and thrive, or whether a certain amount of deviation is viable, so long as the extra costs incurred can be offset by resultant increased revenue.

Notes

1   For instance those conducted by the management consultancy firm, Arthur D. Little, and as argued by their consultant David Guillebaud in The Economist 'survey on travel and tourism', January 10, 1998.

2   The Economist 'survey on travel and tourism', January 10, 1998.

3   A growing proportion of Ryanair's customers are business travellers but these usually tend to be small businessmen who are close to the costs, often paying for travel out of their own pockets.

4   Gudmundsson states that in the decade immediately following US market liberalisation, 88 jet-operating airlines (scheduled, charter and cargo) were formed in the US, of which 83 failed (1998, p.217).

5   A version of this table was included in a presentation titled 'A new age for Europe: the impact of low cost airlines on European airport operations', given by Mr Haughey to a conference in Amsterdam on 27 February 2001.

6   Quoted in Airfinance Journal 'Super models', February 2000.

7   Interestingly, in an interview with this author, a senior Virgin Express manager, argued that Virgin Express is not and never was intended as a LFA. Rather, it was conceived more along the lines of British Midland, serving primarily business travellers at a good price and with good service. This position appears somewhat at odds with the original Virgin Express marketing, which emphasised the airline's no frills, low cost image.

8   Moreover, it appeared likely by early 2002 that parent company KLM would integrate the operations of Buzz, Basiq Air and Transavia, allowing only the Buzz brand to survive.

9   Airfinance Journal op cit.

10   This discussion derived from a correspondence between this author and a manager at the UK Civil Aviation Authority, 26 September 2001.

11   Much of the following analysis is based upon a discussion between this author and Mr Andrew Clarke, Director of Air Transport Policy, European Regions Airlines Association (ERA), 20 April 2001.

12   Although it should be noted that both of these aircraft types are generally bought by major and not regional airlines.

13 Taken from a correspondence between this author and a CAA official, September 2001.
14 Ibid.
15 Data derived from Aviation Week and Space Technology 'European regionals seek routes to profits', 9 October, 2000.
16 Based on a discussion between this author and Mr McCarthy, June 2001.
17 Ibid.
18 Although when ranked by revenue, Crossair is overtaken by Lufthansa CityLine, which was the second largest regional airline in the world in 2000 (Crossair being fourth).
19 Although a restructuring of the Swissair Group in October 2001 merged Swissair's short-haul operations with Crossair. Given the problems besetting Swissair at that time, many analysts commented that it appeared more like a reverse takeover, with Crossair management running the new parent organisation, Swiss Air Lines.
20 Carlo Toto quoted in Feldman (1996), 'Booting up competition', Air Transport World p. 89.
21 Quoted in Airline Business December 2000, p. 18.
22 Despite the fact that Ryanair continues to sell some of its tickets via travel agents – although this share is declining steadily and in November 2001, Ryanair announced their intention to move to 100 per cent direct sales.
23 Although the business class cabin was traditionally operated on behalf of Sabena and only Sabena sold seats in the business class section.

Chapter 4

Structure and Competition in the European Airline Industry

Introduction

EU air transport liberalisation has realised some noticeable achievements, particularly the emergence and growth of LFAs. However, Morrell (1998) points out that some of the expectations of liberalisation have not been met. In particular, flag carrier monopolies and duopolies persist across the EU. Most of Europe's air routes still have only one or two competitors. Not only that but as Uittenbogaart illustrates, at the height of the liberalisation process (1992-1996), the number of duopoly routes decreased from 40 per cent to 30 per cent, with a parallel rise in monopoly routes from 56 per cent to 64 per cent (1997, p. 217). However, the fact remains that leading LFAs such as Ryanair and easyJet are steadily eroding the figure and market deregulation has allowed them to do so. In 1992, 90 per cent of domestic European routes were run as a monopoly; by the end of 1997, this proportion had declined to 81 per cent. On cross-border EU routes, 96 per cent were operated on a monopoly basis in December 1992, falling to 93 per cent by December 1997 (CAA 1998, p. 190). These figures continued to fall and the proportion of monopoly routes within the European Economic Area[1] decreased from 76.2 per cent in July 1999 to 73.2 per cent in July 2000.[2] Concurrently, intra-EU traffic increased at an average annual rate of 4-5 per cent and commentators such as Barrett (1997) and Morrell (1998) agree that this is due to liberalisation and the resultant market competition – particularly from low price challengers. This view is supported by the EU's 2000 annual report on the European air travel industry, where it is argued that:

> It may be the case that low cost carriers are helping to keep the intra-European passenger forecast higher than would perhaps be expected for a mature market.

Competition did not develop in an even fashion across Europe though. It was particularly intense in the UK but much less so in other EU countries.

This chapter begins by charting the evolution and dynamics of the European airline industry during and immediately after the deregulation process discussed in Chapter 2. This leads into an assessment of the widely cited barriers – or limits – to airline competition in Europe. We will examine a number of these in detail, consider their impact on LFAs and comment on the extent to which there is a liberalisation deadlock in the EU. A key question is, 'why have almost all of Europe's LFAs emerged from the UK/Ireland?' This leads us to explore what factors – if any – prohibit the spread of competition (especially LFA competition) across mainland Europe.

Competition in the liberalised European airline industry

In his opening address to the 2000 annual meeting of the International Air Transport Association (IATA) held in Sydney, Australia's deputy prime minister and minister for transport, John Anderson, led the demands for a full liberalisation of the global air transport system and launched an attack on the present bilateral system, arguing that 'it promotes the well being of the flag carriers'.[3] This onslaught was not an isolated incident. Instead, it heralded a global sea change in the government – (large) airline relationship. Anderson's insistence that the airline industry no longer be treated as 'special' is indicative of an international shift towards greater air transport liberalisation. National flag carriers are specific targets of liberalisation advocates. Governments retain a majority stake in about 70 airlines around the world. Increasingly, these companies are being privatised – often in response to pressure from proponents of aviation liberalisation. In recent years this trend has been most noticeable in Europe, where national carriers such as Lufthansa, Air France and Iberia have been opened up to private capital.[4]

The global shift towards a more liberal air transport regime is more than rhetoric. As discussed in Chapter 2, the free market Transatlantic Common Aviation Area (TCAA) concept has received strong support from both the European Commission and the Association of European Airlines. IATA has also produced a policy document that lists five principles that should be adhered to during the liberalisation of air transport. Interestingly, the US – normally a leading proponent of global economic liberalisation – is reluctant to embrace the European TCAA proposal. In suggesting the lifting of limits on cabotage and ownership rules, the TCAA is viewed sceptically by many US trade unions, airline managers and policymakers (Walker 2000, p. 29).

The previous chapters have delved into various aspects of the nature and extent of change experienced in the European airline industry since the early 1990s. The competitive dynamics unleashed by market liberalisation, together with the spread of global industry alliance and consolidation have transformed the industry landscape. Larger, established airlines – above all former or existing flag carriers – have been particularly affected. Many have been forced to restructure, often with the help of state aid. Most have chosen to enter into strategic alliances, often with a number of international partners. The earlier mentioned Lufthansa/United Airlines led Star Alliance and the British Airways/American Airlines dominated Oneworld Alliance are two examples of the strategic groups that have emerged in the global airline industry.

Competitive pressure is also bringing down fares and allowing passengers greater choice. European Commission (1999) research indicates that when competition is introduced on a particular route, consumers enjoy, on average, fare reductions of between 10 and 14 per cent – depending on the type of fare. These reductions are usually considerably higher when a low fare airline enters a route. The aforementioned 1999 European Commission report contained interesting data on the impact of market liberalisation on Europe's airline industry. For instance, between 1992 and 1998, the total number of scheduled carriers within the EU grew from 132 to 164. Furthermore, data on entry and exit of carriers in the market place (Figure 4.1) pinpoints the dynamic and competitive nature of air transport.

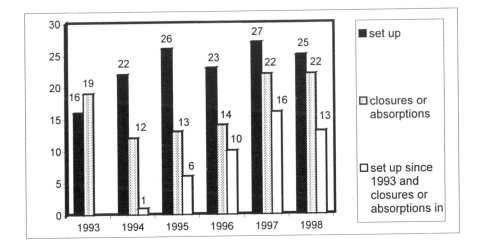

Figure 4.1 Entry and exit of carriers in the EU
Source: Reed OAG and the European Commission, 1999.

Of particular note here is the evidence that a 'shake-out' began even before the 1997 completion of the liberalisation process. Of the 139 airlines established in the wake of the third and final EU liberalisation package (1993-8), 102 declared bankruptcy or were taken over during the 1995-9 period. This attrition rate of almost 70 per cent is well above average for European start-ups. It is especially unusual in an industry that had previously experienced relatively low rates of new entrant activity and industry consolidation. Although not substantively dissimilar to the EU experience, post-deregulation consolidation in the US took considerably longer to manifest itself. Hanlon (1999) points out that airline consolidation was not clearly manifest until seven years after liberalisation. However, the eventual outcome was similar: hardly any of the original new entrants survived as independent operators (Hanlon 1999, p. 43). This may indicate that European airline consolidation is not yet complete. At the end of the 1990s, the total number of scheduled passenger airlines in the EU (plus Norway and Iceland) stood at 137 (AEA 2000, p. 6). This large number appears unsustainable.

European Commission (1999) figures also show that the impact of liberalisation can further be seen in the growth in the number of crossborder, intra-EU routes from 1992. The total number increased by 31 per cent during the 1992 to 1997 period. This is significant and illustrative of the impact that deregulation has had on the structure and market dynamics of the European aviation sector.

Europe's traditional carriers: facts and figures

As elsewhere in the world, Europe's largest airlines performed sluggishly during the 1990s and into the new millennium. Global companies such as BA, Air France, Swissair and Lufthansa underwent restructuring, rebranding and refocusing in an effort to revive their respective profits and share value. The larger carriers took leading roles in global alliance networks. The remaining flag carriers (such as Alitalia and Iberia) scrambled to find suitable partners and, in many cases, to prepare themselves for privatisation. Added to these challenges, industry deregulation brought with it a raft of new competitors. Many of these start-ups competed on price and often targeting the soft underbelly of the market incumbents: overpriced, high yield and high capacity intra-European routes.

Tables 4.1 and 4.2 illustrate the operating performance, capacity and yield of Europe's once dominant airlines during the latter part of the 1990s.

Table 4.1 AEA airlines traffic capacity and yield (international routes per calendar year)

	1997	1998	1999	% change 99/98
Passengers (000)	164,246	174,960	184,933	5.7
Passenger kilometres (mill)	452,620	485,354	516,046	6.3
Seat kilometres (mill)	625,566	674,027	723,216	7.3
Passenger load factor %	72.4	72.0	71.4	-0.6 pt
Passenger yield (current US cent/RPK)	10.2	9.9	9.1	-8.1
Average number of seats per aircraft	207.5	212.2	214.8	1.2
Average stage distance (kms)	1,505	1,549	1,565	1.0

Source: The Association of European Airlines Yearbook 2000.

Table 4.2 AEA airlines operating results (international routes per financial year)

	1997	1998	1999	% change 99/98
Overall load factor %	68.9	68.6	67.9	-0.7pt
Break-even load factor	65.2	64.0	67.2	3.2pt
Yield (US cent/RTK)	76.9	73.7	68.5	-7.0
Unit cost (US cent/ATK)	49.4	47.2	46.4	-2.4
Operating ratio before interest	106.8	107.2	103.5	-3.7pt
Operating ratio after interest	104.5	104.4	103.5	-0.9pt
Profit/Loss after interest (current US$ million)	2,333	2,276	619	

Source: The Association of European Airlines Yearbook 2000.

It should be noted that this data is based only on the traffic and operating results of Association of European Airlines (AEA) members. This includes all of Europe's previous and existing national flag carriers (EU and some other states such as Iceland and the Czech Republic), as well as airlines like Bmi British Midland and Adria Airways. Total membership as of June 2001 was 27 airlines. Membership excludes all of the LFAs and charters, as well as most regional carriers. In 1999 and 2000 the AEA airlines managed to break even but not much more. European load factors were depressed during this period by the very low level of traffic growth experienced by AEA members. This contrasts vividly with the LFA sector, where traffic rates were growing at rates of up to 35 per cent per annum for companies such as Ryanair.

The limits of liberalisation

As mentioned in Chapter 3, of the five LFAs operating in Europe, three are UK-based (easyJet, Go and Buzz) and one has a significant UK hub at London Stansted Airport (Ryanair). The fifth, Virgin Express, is based in Belgium but does have a service to and from London Heathrow. The question that arises is therefore, why is it that most LFAs in Europe were founded and operate within and from the UK and Ireland? Reasons vary. They include the historical and cultural specificities of the region, the large number of first and second generation Irish citizens living and working in the UK, and the more open and competitive business environment which exists there. As *The Economist* pointed out for instance, deregulation in Europe is still mostly limited to flights from the British Isles and the most promising contenders among the cheap airlines are all based in either Britain or Ireland ('survey of travel and tourism', 10 January, 1998). An extensive number of reasons emerge to explain why the UK and Ireland constitute the epicentre of the European LFA industry. The next section will list and provide industry perspectives on these variables.

Barriers to LFA competition across Europe

Low fare carriers identify[5] a range of factors that explain why the LFA business is concentrated in the UK and Ireland and has been slow to develop across mainland Europe. First, 'the island factor', i.e. the geography of the UK and Ireland means that international travel by car is not as easy as it is elsewhere in Europe. Such journeys also cost more, as other modes of transport – ferryboat or channel tunnel train – must be factored into the overall cost.

Second, linked to this, is the 'intermodal competition' variable, i.e. competition between airlines, ferryboats, trains and cars. This tends not to be as vigorous in the UK and Ireland as it is on mainland Europe. When people choose to fly within or from the UK it is normally because other modes of transport are not viable. For many other European countries, a high speed train may be a perfectly acceptable alternative to an airplane, particularly on journeys of up to 500kms. It can be argued that shorter average travel distances and inter-modal competition (especially from high speed trains) will mean that air route density in Europe will never reach US levels (Berechman and DeWit 1996; Burghouwt and Hakfoort 2000). Senior management at leading European LFAs such as Ryanair argue that airlines cannot compete with other modes of transport for journeys of less than 250 miles. Nevertheless, Feldman (1998) argues that the concern that high-speed rail might replace some air traffic is not well founded. It is true that when the TGV was introduced on the busy Paris to Lyon 400-kilometre route, flights between the two cities dropped by 35 per cent and traffic dropped an estimated 60 to 70 per cent. But there are few other air routes in Europe that could actually be replaced by rail (see Appendix 1 for some examples). Almost three-quarters of all passenger seats offered within Europe are on flights covering distances greater than 400 kms. Nearly 24 per cent of the rest are on routes that offer fewer than 800 daily passenger seats (the estimated minimum to justify high-speed rail), or over water, or on routes where there is existing rail competition (high-speed or upgraded fast services). This leaves only two to three per cent of Europe's air traffic potentially vulnerable to competition from high-speed rail. Henry Essenberg, former chief executive of Air UK (now called KLMuk), commented that a lack of intermodal competition did play a role in the emergence of the UK as the main site for LFA start-ups in Europe. This is because 'the UK's railways offer less of a competitive challenge to airlines than France's high speed services' for instance.[6] The European Regions Airline Association (ERA)[7] urge caution, commenting that inter-modal competition is a variable but it can be over-emphasised. There are plenty of routes on mainland Europe where inter-modal competition is not viable (e.g. in the Baltic area or the Alps). Also, Europe's cross-border high speed rail service is still quite limited. Apart from the Thalys and Eurostar services, there are as yet few other transborder intercity train services in Europe.

Third, the UK is the largest leisure air travel market in Europe, therefore the market potential for LFAs is considerable. The British love of sun holidays has created a huge and concentrated market demand in the UK for budget flights. The travel retail sector is not as developed in most markets outside of the UK and Ireland, particularly group travel.

Fourth, as senior executives at the Irish airport authority, Aer Rianta,[8] argue, the 'visiting friends and relations' (VFR) market is very important in explaining why LFAs are so strong in the UK and Ireland. Ireland-UK is a 'quasi-domestic' market, given their heavily integrated economies and societies. It is also a very price sensitive market as traditionally many Irish expatriates in Britain were working class. This created what Porter (1996) described as a 'needs based strategic market position', wherein LFAs were able to successfully create new market space. The size and generally increased affluence of the Irish expatriate community in the UK are key factors in the growth of Ryanair. The Ireland-UK market constitutes a large part of the total European market, in sheer passenger numbers alone. The number of people flying between Dublin and London increased from 1.7 million in 1991 to more than 3 million by 2000, making it the busiest cross-border city pair route in Europe. Italy is potentially the most dynamic LFA market in Europe due to its size and geographical structure. Also, the VFR market in Italy is significant. Aer Rianta believe that without the VFR segment, there is little market potential for LFAs in Europe. Officials at the Irish Department of Transport and Energy also emphasise the importance of what they call the 'ethnic market' to LFA development.[9] In addition to Ireland-UK, they also cite UK-Italy and Germany-Turkey as lucrative or potentially lucrative markets for LFAs. UK-Italy is already a major part of Ryanair and Go's respective route networks. The Germany-Turkey market has yet to be exploited. Turkey's non-membership of the EU may make it a more problematic destination for LFAs – at least in the short to medium term.

Fifth, technology plays a part in this phenomenon. Credit card use, Internet access and online purchasing are all well developed and widely disseminated in the UK. This is not the case in any other large European market. Taken together, these three trends facilitate the direct Internet sales process favoured by LFAs.

Sixth, significant 'invisible barriers' to competition persist at many mainland European airports. Slot restraints exist but are not really the key issue as they are usually found at expensive, major airports that LFAs usually do not fly to anyway. 'Latent discrimination' does affect LFAs at many other airports but is difficult to prove categorically. Buzz management cite as one example efforts by the authorities at Charles de Gaulle airport in Paris to force them to operate from a charter terminal that has fewer facilities than other terminals. Many other instances of latent discrimination exist. For example, it is relatively common for Buzz aircraft to arrive at their gate only to find it still occupied or to arrive at an airport and be forced to wait for buses to ferry their passengers to the arrivals hall. Such delays are a serious disruption for LFAs, reliant on a rapid gate turnaround time in order to maximise aircraft utility and minimise costs. This discriminatory behaviour exists primarily due to close and long standing relationships between airport authorities and national flag carriers. Europe's national airlines remain entrenched at many airports. This can result in airport authorities at worst, clearly and deliberately hampering the operations of rival airlines and at best, providing an inferior level of service to other airlines than provided to the flag carrier. Virgin Express managers further argue that national airlines use slot constraints and airport congestion to their advantage as their 'grandfather rights' ensure that they maintain a dominant position within key airports. Ryanair executives believe that airport authorities can constitute a barrier to the emergence and growth of LFAs but it depends on which airport authority one has in mind. Some ticket taxes are in reality per-passenger charges levied on airlines by individual airports rather than by national authorities. This is because private companies or local region or city governments run the vast majority of European airports. Therefore an airport can have a major impact on an airline's overall cost per passenger. This cost ratio is amplified for LFAs, where, for instance, a flat st£5 charge constitutes a much larger proportion of the total ticket price than for a full fare carrier. Ryanair believes that cultural differences can play a role and that French and Italian airport authorities are generally more difficult to deal with than German, Scandinavian or Austrian airports for instance. Having said that, noticeable exceptions exist. For example, Ryanair management cite Pisa and Brescia as two Italian airports that are run by commercially minded, entrepreneurial people who are open to new ideas and to airline suggestions. In general, Europe's leading LFA, Ryanair, perceives no embedded structural reasons preventing a LFA from setting up operations elsewhere in Europe.

Seventh, LFA executives acknowledge a correlation between risk capital and culture and the emergence of LFAs. The UK is the most vibrant venture capital market in Europe and arguably has the most entrepreneurial culture. This relatively easy access to risk equity and propensity to gamble makes the UK an obvious location for the launch of a LFA. Access to venture capital may be a problem in other European countries, as sources of venture equity are not as plentiful in many mainland European countries as they are in the UK and Ireland (Lawton 2001). Many start-up airlines fail due to a lack of sufficient finance to stay the course. Morrell argues that some new entrants with sounds business plans have failed to get started due to their inability to raise the necessary finances (1998, p.57).

Eighth, LFA sources argue that the inflexibility of the workforce in certain countries is also a problem. For example, employing French pilots is not appealing due to their high degree of unionisation and well-established track record of frequent recourse to strike action. Countries such as Belgium (where Virgin Express is based) have very restrictive social laws and powerful trade unions. These tend to deter the entry or emergence of LFAs. By contrast, The UK has the most liberal labour/social regime in the EU. Stelios Haji-Iaannou, founder of easyJet, cites labour law flexibility as an important factor in his choice of the UK as the headquarters for his airline.[10] LFA executives argue that unions have really hampered the setting up of LFAs by majors such as Air France, Iberia and Lufthansa. Also, social structure is important, measured in terms of pension contributions, government levies, PSRI contributions and so forth. If you compare and contrast these costs between European countries you will find that it is an important determinant of LFA choices of location for start-up and operation.

Ninth, there is evidence to support the notion that the UK had a first mover advantage. In the late 1980s an airline such as Air Europe was desperate for low fares out of London Gatwick and, unlike other European governments, the British government was willing to let its flag carrier be undercut on prices. Pressure from the industry, combined with the liberal economic ethos of the Thatcher government, combined to ensure that vigorous air transport price competition emerged in the UK ahead of other European states. It is only surprising that it took until the mid-1990s before LFAs were established in Britain.

Tenth, it should also be remembered that the UK has always been strong in aviation. This means that airlines based in the UK have both a ready supply of trained labour and management as well as a wide range of suppliers to choose from. These factors cannot be overlooked in any assessment of why most LFAs started in and operate form the UK. Stelios Haji-Iaannou of easyJet argues that one of the UK's advantages as a base and start-up location for a LFA is that it has more services such as aircraft maintenance than other European countries.[11]

Ryanair's Head of Regulatory Affairs argues that abusive behaviour from other carriers is also a restriction. For instance, Lufthansa began serving the Hamburg–Frankfurt–Stansted route with predatory pricing as soon as Ryanair entered the market. Ryanair launched a complaint with the EU. The German regulatory authority subsequently permitted Lufthansa to acquire Eurowings, albeit with some conditions. Go have registered similar complaints against Lufthansa on the Stansted-Munich route, as have easyJet vis-à-vis KLM on London to Amsterdam.

Morrell (1998) argues that four categories of barriers to entry in intra-EU markets exist. He describes the first as 'administrative' obstacles or the reluctance in certain EU countries to implement all elements of the deregulation packages. Morrell cites examples such as the French government's initial resistance to open Paris Orly Airport to competition and the Greek government's delays in processing applications for new operating licences. State aid (see Chapter 2) is also part of this problem. Morrell's second barrier is 'infrastructure capacity constraints', particularly slot allocation and to some extent air traffic control bottlenecks. Sources at Ryanair argue that this is overstated. They claim that for them, only London Stansted is affected by slot constraints and steps are being taken to address the problem there. A third obstacle is 'monopolies in input markets', which significantly increase the cost of new entrant operations. By this Morrell means issues such as baggage handling monopolies at most European airports. This obstacle has been tackled by the European Commission and is being phased out. Morrell's fourth and final category is 'economies of scale', examples of which include distribution channels, which tend to be dominated by large established airlines.

There are two key areas in which government regulatory bodies and publicly owned airport authorities still appear to undermine the emergence and growth of LFAs across mainland Europe. These are first, airport charges and second, slot allocation.

Structural barriers to the emergence of LFAs: airport charges

Airport charges are generally cited as a significant structural barrier to the emergence and growth of LFAs in Europe. Ryanair cite landing charges as a major factor in their selection of hub airports.[12] Ryanair, is consequently a vocal advocate of lower airport charges at select European airports. In the case of Dublin Airport, the accusation is refuted by both the Irish Government[13] and the Irish airport authority, Aer Rianta.[14] However, European Commission (1999) figures indicate that Ryanair's argument has some validity. The EU study compares fares on major European routes, namely average fares from 20 capital and main hub cities (CEC 1999). Fares per kilometre depended on the distance flown. However, even taking into consideration distance, there are large disparities in airport charges across the EU. In particular, fares are higher from airports such as Vienna, Frankfurt, Paris CDG, Brussels, Copenhagen and Stockholm. In the case of Dublin, the average business fare is amongst the highest in Europe and the average economy fare is higher than at other large Ryanair airports such as London Gatwick. There may be several factors explaining this situation, such as local labour cost levels, the degree of competition (or lack thereof), congestion and local market conditions (e.g. the cost of parts and supplies). Ryanair's Head of Regulatory Affairs argues that licensing is not a problem around Europe but airport charges are, particularly ground handling fees. He comments that although there is liberalisation at a European market level, it does not exist at a national airport level. Operating into secondary airports alleviates problems of costs and restrictions.

Slot allocation, ground handling and airline competition

In 1993 the European Commission introduced a regulation governing the allocation of airport slots[15] in Europe (Council Regulation (EC) No. 95/93 of 18 January 1993). This was prompted by the significant and consistent growth in air traffic across the EU, combined with the delays and difficulties experienced in increasing airport capacity.[16] Fostering greater competition was an explicit objective of this regulation. Two key aims were '…to facilitate competition and to encourage entrance into the [EU air transport] market' and to ensure that slots at congested airports are allocated on the basis of 'neutral, transparent and non-discriminatory rules' (CEC 1993). As such, this regulation can be seen as a further legislative tool aimed at facilitating the emergence of LFAs from the mid-1990s on. By the late 1990s, the results appeared mixed. In 1998, then European Transport Commissioner Neil Kinnock argued that infrastructure constraints were proving to be a serious impediment to new entrants and, in particular, the issue of slot allocation was increasingly becoming a matter for concern.[17] Commissioner Kinnock targeted the protection of 'incumbent carriers which currently benefit from unrestricted grandfather rights' as a notable product of the existing slot allocation system. This in turn 'limits the positive impact of the liberalisation process' (1998, p.4). Subsequent efforts by the European Commission to ensure compliance with the 1996 directive may have proven effective. A study commissioned by the European Commission and conducted by PricewaterhouseCoopers consultants in 2000, found that European airlines were generally satisfied with the approaches being adopted in most EU Member States in relation to capacity assessments. Problems of infrastructure enhancement were identified at two airports though, Madrid-Barajas and Paris-Charles de Gaulle (PwC 2000, p. 23). An important finding of the study was that apart from the specific capacity constraint issues just mentioned, the airlines surveyed reported no concerns about inappropriate constraints at any airport (PwC 2000, p. 26). This would indicate that national airport authorities across the EU do not undermine or restrict the emergence and/or growth of LFAs through restrictive slot allocation practices. While problems persist over grandfather rights at certain airports ensuring the dominance of one or two airlines (e.g. BA's dominance at London Heathrow), airport authorities are actively seeking creative solutions to these problems. Besides, LFAs generally choose not to fly into such airports anyway, as they tend to be expensive and congested. On the issue of slot allocation there is therefore no evidence that the business environment is more hostile on mainland Europe than in the UK.

A further useful piece of EU legislation for LFAs was the 1996 Council Directive on access to the ground handling market at EU airports. Ground handling services at many EU airports has traditionally been run by monopolies, often by or on behalf of a national airline.[18] Other airlines using the airport have no control over the quality or price of the service. This directive was explicitly aimed at the 'opening-up of access to the ground handling market [so as to] help reduce the operating costs of airline companies and improve the quality of service provided to airport users' (CEC 1996, p.36). Moreover, as from 1 January 2001, at least one of the authorised suppliers may not be directly or indirectly controlled by the managing body of the airport or any airline that accounts for more than 25 per cent of the airport's total passenger or freight traffic (CEC 1996, article 6). This article prevents airport authorities from maintaining or establishing a monopoly position in ground handling and charging airlines premium prices for the service.

European growth potential

easyJet believe that there is substantial intra-European growth potential. Annual growth in air travel is projected by IATA to be 5.1 per cent annually during the early 2000s.[19] This would signify an increase in total EU passenger numbers from 176 million in 1999 to 215 million in 2003.[20] LFAs only account for 5 per cent of intra-European travel but this is likely to grow to as much as 15 per cent by 2010. Moreover, the LFA market is heavily concentrated on London right now. easyJet believe that there are more than 300 potential regional and secondary airports that they might offer services to across the EU.[21] easyJet advance a number of difficulties in realising this potential pan-European growth. These include first, a need to 'educate the public' on the benefits of LFAs and air travel more generally. There is a lower propensity to travel across mainland Europe than there is in the UK. Moreover, there is closer proximity of concentrated populations. Reliable and price competitive alternative modes of transport also exist, particularly high speed rail. In addition, the level of internet and credit card use is relatively low in many mainland European countries, compared to the UK. Second, dominant flag carriers have anti-competitive behaviour tendencies. easyJet have experienced problems with KLM in their UK-Netherlands operations and with Swissair on their Geneva-based services for instance. Third, language and cultural issues continue to pose obstacles. Fourth, significant regulation and bureaucratic barriers remain at many airports. Fifth, there are embedded constraints to growth due to Europe's congested infrastructure.

Final comment

Returning to our initial argument, the findings indicate that many widely held beliefs about LFA competition in Europe are in fact false. First, airport charges can be a deterrent for LFAs but only if they fly into larger airports. However, for the most part, LFAs fly into smaller airports, due to their cost and time-focused strategy. They can therefore usually avoid the barrier posed by high airport charges. Second, airport slot allocation and baggage handling have traditionally been a barrier to entry for many smaller airlines. Recent EU legislation has tackled these problems though and they are likely to become less of a problem during the coming years. Third, intermodal competition can be a factor preventing the spread of LFAs but only on short, intercity routes (less than 250 km). High speed rail services still do not exist between most of Europe's major population and commercial centres. The services that do exist tend to be relatively expensive and take considerably longer than air travel (see Appendix 1 for some examples). Fourth, access to venture capital is a problem for many business start-ups in Europe but it is not a problem confined to aviation. However, the situation is gradually improving and is likely to prove less of an obstacle in the future. It may be a factor contributing to the development of LFAs in the UK, as the UK venture capital market has long been the largest and most vibrant in Europe. Fifth, no regulatory barriers or deliberate state-imposed structural obstacles exist to LFA competition. However, high social costs and inflexible labour markets can prove a major disincentive to LFA activity.

Few competitive barriers actually exist elsewhere in Europe and positive factor conditions are not exclusively found in the UK. However, the UK did embrace airline deregulation before most other EU member states and may have some first-mover advantage in attracting LFAs. Also, labour market flexibility, relatively low social costs and ready access to venture capital combine to make the UK a more attractive base for Europe's LFAs.

The lesson to date is that LFAs develop and succeed primarily in those countries/regions where social costs are relatively low, there is a strong pro-business culture and airports are commercially oriented (if not privately owned). These are not variables that any one country has comparative advantage in – they can exist in any EU member state. In all aspects of regulation and most aspects of the business environment, a level playing field exists across the EU post-deregulation and – with the exception of a handful of airports – no barriers exist to the market entry of LFAs. There is therefore no reason why LFAs cannot emerge and grow in all EU member states during the coming years. The liberalisation deadlock is in fact a myth, as the European market and its airline route network are open to competition. Rather, the onus rests with entrepreneurs and existing LFAs to enter and develop those routes where monopolies and duopolies persist.

Notes

1   The European Economic Area comprises the 15 member states of the EU plus Iceland, Norway and Lichtenstein.
2   Data derived from the EU's 2000 annual report on economic and fares data in the European air travel industry, p. 4.
3   Report by Karen Walker, 'Worlds apart', Airline Business, July 2000, p. 28.
4   The Economist, 'The Sky's the Limit: a survey of air travel', 10 March, 2001, p. 6.
5   This discussion is based on a series of interview conducted with senior executives at Buzz, easyJet, Ryanair and Virgin Express, March to August 2001.
6   Cited in Michael Skapinker (1997) 'Why the air is thick with budget fares', The Financial Times, 3 September, p. 10
7   Interview conducted with Mr Andrew Clarke, Director of Air Transport Policy, European Regions Airlines Association (ERA), 20 April 2001.
8   Interviews conducted by this author in Dublin in March 2001.
9   Interview conducted with senior civil servants responsible for aviation and airport policy, Department of Public Enterprise, Dublin, 9 March 2001.
10   Cited in Michael Skapinker (1997) 'Why the air is thick with budget fares', The Financial Times, 3 September, p. 10.
11   Ibid.
12   Interview conducted with senior Ryanair management, Dublin Airport, 8 March 2001.
13   Letter sent by Mr Matt Benville, Principal Officer, Airports Division, Department of Public Enterprise, Dublin, to Mr Kieran Sheedy, Department of Tourism, Sport and Recreation, 16 January 2001. The letter was in part a response to Mr Sheedy's specific query about Ryanair's allegations in respect of changes in air services.
14   Interview conducted with M. John Burke, CEO of Aer Rianta and Mr Tom Haughey, Director of Marketing and Strategy, Aer Rianta, Dublin, 8 March 2001.
15   An airport slot is defined as 'the ability to plan and operate at an airport within a specified time period...with the expectation that all necessary resources will be available to accommodate that operation' (PwC 2000, pp. 28-9). These resources usually include most importantly runway, stand and terminal capacities.
16   Much of the discussion in this section is based upon or directly derived from a PricewaterhouseCoopers report for the European Commission on common rules for the allocation of slots at EU airports, May 2000.
17   Neil Kinnock, opening remarks for 'Meeting the global challenge: the outlook for civil aviation in the EU' (organised by Forum Europe), Brussels, 27 January 1998, p. 4.

18 This assessment is derived from the UK Department of Transport's 'EC liberalisation information pack', Spring 1997, p. 3.
19 These projections were released before the industry crisis of late 2001.
20 These projections were made prior to events of 11 September 2001. However, traffic figures released by Ryanair, easyJet and Go in the aftermath of the US attacks, suggested that their passenger numbers were continuing to grow.
21 Ibid.

Chapter 5

Getting the Balance Right: Price-Based Competition and the Cost-Service Trade-Off

Introduction

Achieving operational cost reductions through lower service reliability standards and customer satisfaction can undermine an airline's long-term competitiveness. Airline success essentially rests upon providing a safe and reliable product. Standards of service reliability and customer satisfaction in this case can be interpreted as being on time, not losing baggage, providing comfortable seating, having a rapid check-in, low rates of flight cancellation, and having an informed and friendly customer service.[1] Studies[2] illustrate that corporate loyalty is largely dependent on high levels of customer satisfaction. Efficient and readily available customer services will ensure both repeat business and personal recommendations to potential customers.

We argue in this chapter that the price to service equation does not need to be a zero-sum game. You can have a win-win situation, with low prices and high quality service. The US low fare leader, Southwest Airlines, have proven this argument to be sustainable and illustrate that low prices and good service can exist coterminously within the organisational structure of a LFA. The record has been more mixed for Europe's leading LFA, Ryanair. The airline has occasionally been accused by the media and consumer groups of neglecting customer service (defined in a variety of ways) in their quest to lower costs. Other European LFAs, most notably Go and Buzz, have sought to differentiate themselves from Ryanair by placing greater emphasis on customer service. The key issues addressed in this chapter are therefore first, how to best define and measure customer service for airlines; and second, to consider whether customer satisfaction and service quality are interchangeable or distinct concepts.

Defining and measuring airline service quality: the AQR model

Definitions of service quality abound but a broadly accepted explanation might be that it is derived from four core elements: listening to customers, surprising customers, recovering from service problems and practising fair play. All of these involve understanding customer expectations and perceptions and then meeting or exceeding them (Berry, Parasuraman and Zeithaml 1994; Rhoades and Waguespack 2000a). A number of models have been developed to apply this definition to the airline business and break it down into measurable variables. Of these, perhaps the most prominent – at least in the US – is the Airline Quality Rating (AQR) scheme devised by Bowen and Headley and first implemented in 1991.[3] The AQR was first launched as an objective method of comparing airline quality on combined multiple performance criteria. The annual rating reflects detailed scores for the calendar year, based on 15 elements that focus on airline performance areas important to air travel consumers. Using the AQR system of weighted averages and monthly performance data in the areas of on-time arrivals (OT), involuntary denied boardings (DB), mishandled baggage (MB), and a combination of 12 customer complaint categories (CC), major airline comparative performance is reported. The formula for calculating the AQR score is:

$$AQR = \frac{(+8.63 \times OT) + (-8.03 \times DB) + (-7.92 \times MB) + (-7.17 \times CC)}{(8.63 + 8.03 + 7.92 + 7.17)}$$

The customer complaint categories are flight problems, oversales, reservations/ticketing/boarding, fares, refunds, baggage, customer service, disability, advertising, tours, animals and other. Data for all criteria is drawn from the U.S. Department of Transportation's monthly *Air Travel Consumer Report* (http://dot.gov/airconsumer/). Applying this formula to the major US airlines, Bowen and Headley have developed a widely regarded quality rating, much feared by the airline companies (Table 5.1).

Table 5.1 Airline Quality Rating Average AQR Scores*

	2000 AQR		1999 AQR		1998 AQR	
	Score	Rank	Score	Rank	Score	Rank
Alaska	-1.54	2	-1.85	5	-2.08	8
America West	-3.43	10	-2.12	8	-1. 54	6
American	-2.08	6	-1.99	7	-1.26	3
Continental	-2.11	7	-1.58	2	-1.07	2
Delta	-1.47	1	-1.69	3	-1.37	4
Northwest	-1.83	5	-1.72	4	-2.08	9
Southwest	-1.64	3	-1.28	1	-1.41	5
Trans World	-2.71	8	-2.13	9	-2.08	7
United	-3.01	9	-2.39	10	-2.16	10
U. S. Airways	-1.74	4	-1.91	6	-0.86	1
Industry	**-2.05**		**-1.85**		**-1.61**	

* Average AQR scores are based on monthly AQR score calculations using the AQR weighted average method. The calendar year is used and monthly AQR scores are totalled and divided by 12 to arrive at the average AQR score for the year.

Airline Quality Rating Criteria overview

The individual criteria used to calculate the AQR scores are summed up in four basic areas that reflect customer-oriented areas of airline performance. Definitions of the four areas used in the AQR 2001 (2000 data) are outlined below.

OT   On-Time Performance (+8.63)
Regularly published data regarding on-time arrival performance is obtained from the US Department of Transportation's (DoT) *Air Travel Consumer Report*. According to the DoT, a flight is counted 'on time' if it is operated within 15 minutes of the scheduled time shown in the carriers' Computerized Reservations Systems. Delays caused by mechanical problems are counted as of 1 January 1995. Cancelled and diverted operations are counted as late. The AQR calculations use the percentage of flights arriving on time for each airline for each month.

DB   Involuntary Denied Boardings (-8.03)
This criterion includes involuntary denied boardings. Data regarding denied boardings could be obtained from the DoT's *Air Travel Consumer Report*.

Data includes the number of passengers who hold confirmed reservations and are involuntarily denied boarding on a flight that is oversold. These figures include only passengers whose oversold flight departs without them onboard. The AQR uses the ratio of involuntary denied boardings per 10,000 passengers boarded by month.

MB   Mishandled Baggage Reports (-7.92)
Regularly published data regarding consumer reports to the carriers of mishandled baggage can again be obtained from the DoT's *Air Travel Consumer Report*. According to the DoT, a mishandled bag includes claims for lost, damaged, delayed, or pilfered baggage. Data is reported by carriers as to the rate of mishandled baggage reports per 1,000 passengers and for the industry. The AQR ratio is based on the total number of reports each major carrier received from passengers concerning lost, damaged, delayed, or pilfered baggage per 1,000 passengers served.

CC   Consumer Complaints (-7.17)
The criteria of consumer complaints are made up of 12 specific complaint categories monitored by the DoT and reported monthly in the *Air Travel Consumer Report*. Consumers can file complaints with the DoT in writing, by telephone, via e-mail, or in person. The AQR uses complaints about the various categories as part of the larger customer complaint criteria and calculates the consumer complaint ratio on the number of complaints received per 100,000 passengers flown.

The AQR industry average score shows an industry that is declining in quality relative to customer performance criteria. Alaska Airlines, Delta Air Lines, and US Airways were the only airlines to show improvement in their overall AQR scores for 2000 (Figure 5.1). American Airlines was most constant from 1999 to 2000, with only a slight decrease in their AQR score. America West Airlines registered the largest decline in AQR score. Continental, Northwest, Southwest, Trans World, and United all declined as well, but at more moderate levels. In all, seven of the ten airlines rated posted lower AQR scores in 2000 than in 1999.

For the low fare leader, Southwest Airlines, its performance in 2000 took it from the top position in 1999 to the third rated carrier in 2000. Southwest recorded the second largest decrease (4.8 per cent) in on-time arrival percentage of the ten airlines. However this may be seen as an anomaly because according to the US Air Travel Consumer Report database,[4] for the period September 1987 to June 2001, Southwest recorded the best on time arrival[5] rate of all the major US carriers. At all reported airports, Southwest achieved an overall average of 82.3 per cent on time arrival rate. This compares with 75.3 per cent at United and 77.4 per cent at Delta for example. It is also well above the average of 78.2 per cent for the 12 largest airlines in the US cancelled and diverted flights are counted as late in these reports. Extracting the records on flight cancellations, we can see that again Southwest fares well. For instance, the 2000 Air Travel Consumer Report illustrated that at all reported airports Southwest had only one per cent of operations cancelled; compared with 5.7 per cent at American Eagle and four per cent at United by comparison. Southwest was again the best placed major carrier in this category.

Involuntary denied boarding rates, mishandled baggage rates, and customer complaint rates were all worse for Southwest in 2000. For instance, the Air Travel Consumer Report shows that in June 2001, Southwest was the third worst offender of the eleven majors in terms of mishandled baggage reports filed by passengers (5.21 per 1,000 passengers, compared with 2.83 at Alaska Airlines or 4.3 at US Airways). Furthermore, Southwest does not do well on the 'denied boarding' service measure. This means that the airline oversells on a flight and is forced to deny boarding to passengers who have confirmed reservations. In the period January-March 2001, Southwest denied boarding to an average of 1.57 passengers per 10,000, making it the third worst offender of the US majors. This position saw Southwest slip from fourth worst the previous year.[6]

Nonetheless, at a time when industry customer complaint rates (2.98 per 100,000 passengers in 2000) are climbing, Southwest has, by far, the lowest rate of any of the ten major carriers (0.47 per 100,000 passengers). For example, during the first six months of 2001, this percentage was 0.44, compared with a high of 4.05 at America West or 3.56 at United. Similarly, for the first six months of 2000, Southwest's rate was 0.55 per cent, compared with 8.34 at America West or 4.39 at United.

As Rhoades and Waguespack point out, unlike other quality rankings, the AQR uses published, publicly available data to construct a multi-factor weighted average of airline quality for the major US carriers (2000b, p. 88). As already indicated, a lot of the data is collected from the Air Travel Consumer Report published quarterly by the US DoT. As might be expected, criticisms have been levied by airlines at the AQR. The carriers are especially critical of the weighted scheme. For instance, carriers objected to the AQR's initial assignment of a negative weight to load factor (Rhoades and Waguespack 2000b, p. 88). Bowen and Headley took on board this criticism and the load factor measure was not included in the AQR from 1998 onwards. Airlines also complain about the nature of the complaints registered by the AQR. They argue that the issues assessed are all to do with basic service (on-time departure, flight problems, etc.) and fail to measure passenger amenities such as ease of check-in, schedule availability, and so forth. This leaves the AQR open to accusations that it is imbalanced and does not in fact accurately reflect the priorities of customers. Nonetheless, despite its limitations, the AQR formula remains a simple and informative method of evaluating airline service performance.

The AQR model – or a similar quality measure – cannot be applied to the European airline industry. The reason is straightforward: it is a simple method, if the data is available.[7] Unlike the US, no common statistical database or impartial studies exist in Europe (the EU) for comparing common airline performance elements. There is no organised way to check for quality across the various air transport suppliers in Europe. The model remains relevant though and is a useful reference point for any assessment of airline service quality in Europe.

Passenger priorities and contrasting approaches to customer service

The long term success of the Ryanair-Southwest cost reduction model is tempered by one important variable – attitudes to customer services. Ashton-Davies argues that to be effective, short-term cost reduction must be driven by a focus on customer service if it is to be converted into long-term competitive advantage (1996, p.12). Customer satisfaction is the essence of sustainable competitive advantage in many service sectors, particularly air transport. In numerous travel industry studies, leading US marketing consultancy, J.D. Power and Associates, found that there is a significant correlation between loyalty and overall customer satisfaction:

> As satisfaction declines, so does the likelihood of the traveller to use an airline again and to recommend the carrier to others (J.D. Power III, 1997).

A visible divergence emerges between the two airlines on this issue. Southwest prides itself on having a very good, award-winning customer service, with a well-trained and attentive ground crew. Taking their respective mission statements as a point of departure, we can see that Southwest places customer satisfaction high on their list of priorities. Southwest states that it is 'dedicated to the highest quality of customer service, delivered with a sense of warmth, friendliness, individual pride and company spirit' (Southwest Airlines mission statement, 1998). Ryanair, by comparison, consistently define customer satisfaction almost exclusively in terms of price. Safety and reliability (on-time performance and minimal lost baggage) are also important.[8] It is assumed that low price and value for money, together with a safe and relatively efficient service will ensure client approval. This is not necessarily always the case. Surveys conducted by market research companies[9] have identified ten factors which together drive overall airline customer satisfaction. Of these, efficiency (translated as 'on time performance') was indeed ranked highest, seen as the most important factor by just over one in five respondents. However, factors such as rapid airport check-in, seating comfort, food service, and post-flight customer services were all considered important variables. Other factors considered important in customer satisfaction surveys include frequent flyer programmes, which – unlike Southwest and most other US LFAs – Ryanair does not operate. The 1999 IATA Corporate Travel Survey indicated that business travellers in particular continue to like quality in-flight service, onboard comforts and perks such as frequent flyer programmes. A wider survey of passengers found that for all cabin classes the factors influencing choice of airline for short-haul flights are as follows:

- Schedules (51 per cent)
- Frequent flyer programme (26 per cent)
- Low fares (25 per cent)
- Company travel policy (16 per cent)
- Punctuality (15 per cent).

Granted, these factors are ranked according to an average from all classes, including first and business. It might be argued that LFA customers have different priorities. In fact, when we break down the IATA survey and examine the priorities for economy class passengers only, schedules (48 per cent) and low fares (33 per cent) are the two most important factors when choosing an airline for a short flight.[10] This is acknowledged by leading LFAs on both sides of the Atlantic. The problem arises when customer priorities and customer satisfaction are not identical. Although a passenger may prioritise schedule and price, that is not necessarily the sum total of factors needed to satisfy him/her on a flight. For instance, if a flight is diverted and the airline fails to provide ground transportation to take passengers back to the intended airport destination, a very frequent schedule and extremely low ticket price are not likely to ensure that the passengers are satisfied customers. Individual LFAs adopt different approaches to addressing – or ignoring – this 'service gap' between customer priorities and customer satisfaction.

A 1998 Ryanair equity research report by Goodbody Stockbrokers argued that while it is difficult to compare cultures of companies on different sides of the Atlantic, Southwest clearly has a reputation for customer (and employee) satisfaction.[11] A significant difference between Ryanair and Southwest is that Southwest has its own staff at every airport it serves, whereas Ryanair outsource its ground crew operations to another company, Servisair, at every airport it serves[12] (except for its Dublin Airport base). Southwest therefore ensures that its customers are always dealing directly with the airline for customer inquiries, tickets, passenger handling and baggage. This ensures that Southwest management can directly monitor customer services and that Southwest can ensure that its corporate culture is conveyed directly to its passengers.

The level of customer service offered by an airline can legitimately vary, depending on ticket class or on the nature of the airline company. There is no expectation, on the part of either industry watchdogs or customers, that a LFA should provide the same level of customer service as a large full price carrier. However, as the British consumer lobby group, the Air Transport Users Council (AUC) argue:

> We entirely accept that low fares can only be achieved if costs are contained but there is a minimum acceptable level of service that air travellers have a right to expect from any airline (1998, p.3).

Reliability (defined here as on time performance and adequate safety standards) and courteous service constitute such a minimum service level.

Southwest has always managed to strike the balance between cost savings and customer service. It is regularly ranked highly in such customer satisfaction surveys. Although the low fare leader, the company attains annual customer satisfaction awards such as the 'Triple Crown' for best baggage handling, fewest customer complaints, and best on-time performance of all major airlines. As seen in surveys such as the AQR, it has achieved the best consumer satisfaction record of any continental US carrier several years in succession. Chairman Herb Kelleher argues:

> Anybody can do it...All they have to have is the lowest fares, the highest frequency, and the best customer service from the most fun-loving, warm, welcoming, spirited, hospitable employees in the airline business (Freiberg and Freiberg 2001, p. 270).

Southwest put their employees first, not customers. They do so in the belief that happy employees will provide better service and therefore create happy customers. This calculation appears to work, as proven by the customer satisfaction ratings consistently achieved by Southwest.

Ryanair, in contrast, has won numerous awards but notably, has not received any for customer service. In August 2001, Ryanair was voted the 'Best Airline Company in Europe' by the US magazine, Global Finance. It was selected 'because of its outstanding performance in revenue and profitability, market capitalisation and aggressiveness in market building'.[13]

No mention was made of customer service or satisfaction. In 1999, 2000 and 2001, Ryanair received the 'Best Managed National Carrier' in the world award from Aviation Week & Space Technology magazine. It has also been deemed the 'Best Value for Money Airline' on numerous occasions and was deemed 'Irish Company of the Year' by Business & Finance magazine in 2000. Ryanair management agree that Southwest has consistently delivered an excellent product and excellent customer satisfaction and concede that is where Ryanair wants to be for the future.[14] This may be difficult to achieve whilst the company continues practices such as outsourcing its airport customer services. It is not impossible though. A no frills service with maximum cabin space utilisation can be offset by low cost brand reinforcement techniques such as friendly and obliging staff – both in the air and on the ground. Other LFAs in Europe, most notably easyJet and more recently, Go, appear to have successfully established such an image. In this respect, Ryanair can learn lessons from other low fare carriers.

Are service quality and customer satisfaction synonymous?

At the crux of this discussion is the relationship between customer satisfaction and service quality. Do high levels of service quality necessarily equate to high levels of customer satisfaction? Can you have a satisfied customer without providing adequate quality of service? There are two points to be made here. First, service quality can be a very subjective concept. Objective measures of service are very difficult to find. This is due in large part to the fact that humans are by nature subjective and they are not perfect measurement subjects. As a consequence, it may make more sense to argue that 'value' is a better, less value-laden term of reference or measurement than either 'satisfaction' or 'quality'. Second, the term 'service' can mean different things to different people and in different business contexts. In the case of commercial aviation, service can be dichotomised (Figure 5.1).

Core Service Standards
• Safety
• Reliability
• Customer support
• Problem responsiveness

Ancillary Service Standards
• Complimentary food and beverages
• Free newspapers
• Frequent flyer programme

Figure 5.1 The dual tracking of airline service standards

In applying this discussion to the LFA sector, companies such as Ryanair clearly believe than the only purposeful and cost justifiable service standards in their business are the kinds of issues termed 'core' service standards in Figure 5.1. Ancillary services should either be discontinued or incur extra charges for the customer. Moreover, Ryanair's CEO Michael O'Leary consistently argues that low price and value for money are the only measures of customer satisfaction that matter to his company. By contrast, other LFAs such as Buzz believe that low price and a 'veneer of quality' ensures satisfied customers and secures repeat custom and long term advantage. In both cases core service standards such as aircraft safety and baggage delivery (reliability) are considered fundamental to market success. Based on the evidence of passenger numbers, revenue and profit margins to date, the Ryanair approach appears to be most commercially effective. It remains to be seen how this might develop once the sector reaches market maturity.

An ad hoc comparative survey of LFA service and value was conducted in May 2000 by four British journalists.[15] The journalists each chose a route with one of Europe's four main LFAs and evaluated the return flight-based on their overall experience – using the following criteria: booking/price/ticketing, check-in, boarding, take off, cabin décor, catering, flight attendant service and arrival. Whilst the analyses are subjective and the findings based on too narrow a sample, the survey does provide an interesting glimpse of the passenger experience on each airline. The comparative scores are aligned in Table 5.2.

Table 5.2   Ranking Europe's LFAs by service and value

Airline	Service	Value
Ryanair	6	8
Go	7	6
Buzz	7	7
easyJet	8	7

Although highly subjective, these findings are revealing, particularly because they indicate that first, Europe's LFAs all maintain good standards of service and value and second, because there appears to be little between the four main LFAs in either service standards or value for money.

Another, more extensive service/value survey conducted in 2000 sustained the view that Europe's LFAs are relatively popular with customers.[16] This survey considered the following variables when formulating their findings: cabin air quality, cabin crew, catering, check-in staff, cleanliness of aircraft interior, entertainment, leg room, seat allocation, seat comfort, toilets and value for money. The ultimate key question was, 'would you recommend this airline to a friend?' The sample size varied from airline to airline. This survey is worth noting because it places the European LFAs on a benchmark scale with leading global airlines such as Singapore Airlines and Air New Zealand. Three out of five of Europe's LFAs were placed in the global top ten, well ahead of all charter services and many traditional rivals (Table 5.3). Ryanair and Virgin Express fared less well, being placed 29th and 37th respectively. This was a drop for Ryanair on the previous year. Charter airlines fared particularly badly on this survey, with most air passengers surveyed expressing a preference not to travel on a charter.

Table 5.3   Would you recommend this airline to a friend? The global top ten

Rank	Airline
1	Air New Zealand
2	Singapore Airlines
3	Palmair
4	Emirates
5	SAS
6	easyJet
7	Thai Airways

8	Buzz
9	Virgin Atlantic
10	Go

On specific regional routes, the LFAs also outscored their mainstream, regional and charter rivals. For instance, on routes between the UK and Spain/Balearics, easyJet and Go were more popular than all other carriers, including the likes of BA, British Midland, Iberia, Spanair, Air Europa, Monarch and Britannia. Similarly, on UK-France routes, easyJet, Buzz and Ryanair were voted service/price leaders, well ahead of airlines such as BA, British Midland and Air France.

On-time performance as a measure of customer satisfaction

In addition to safety, other core operational factors are not adversely affected by the drive for constant cost cutting. In particular, as Table 5.4 attests, Ryanair's punctuality record rate appears generally better than its competitors.

Table 5.4 Dublin-London punctuality statistics, 2000

CAA on time statistics, Dublin-London (January-December 2000)			
1	Ryanair	Luton	83%
2	Ryanair	Gatwick	74%
3	Ryanair	Stansted	70%
4	BA CityFlyer	Gatwick	77%
5	British Midland	Heathrow	66%
6	Aer Lingus	City	68%
7	Aer Lingus	Gatwick	69%
8	Aer Lingus	Heathrow	61%

Overall Dublin-London punctuality 2000

1.	BA CityFlyer Express	77%
2.	Ryanair	74%
3.	British Midland	66%
4.	Aer Lingus	64%

This denotes a slippage in punctuality for Ryanair though, as it was the most punctual in 1999:

Overall Dublin-London punctuality 1999

1.	Ryanair	77%
2.	Aer Lingus	74%
3.	British Midland	68%
4.	British Airways	64%

However, it is an improvement in percentage terms over the 72 per cent punctuality rate for 1998 (and second position behind Aer Lingus).

The London-Dublin route is the busiest cross border city-pair in Europe,[17] with a weekly seating capacity (both directions) of 114,563 in 2000 and five scheduled carriers competing for business. On-time departure is a significant measure of customer satisfaction on such a competitive and congested route.[18] The figures above indicate that despite bad media publicity concerning punctuality and general performance, Ryanair in fact performs better than its rivals in these terms. As with Southwest, almost 80 per cent of all Ryanair flights depart within fifteen minutes of the scheduled departure time. This may have something to do with the airports from which they fly, which are generally less congested ones such as Glasgow Prestwick or Paris Beauvais. It should also be noted that these statistics do not account for cancellation rates. Management at Irish airport authority, Aer Rianta, have stated[19] that Ryanair operates a 'may fly' policy, whereby its daily flight schedule is only confirmed the evening before. The airline has told Aer Rianta officials that its flight timetable is an 'indication' of operations rather than a fixed schedule. Its published schedule may then differ significantly from its operational schedule on any given day and flights can be cancelled on short notice. Reasons for this vary but the company has been accused[20] of seeking to maximise the passenger load factor per flight – and minimise per unit operating costs – through deliberately amalgamating flights that individually fail to reach a satisfactory load margin. Ryanair's Head of Regulatory Affairs agrees that 'doubling-up' – although rare – does happen when Ryanair has flights that are close together, e.g. on high frequency routes such as Stansted-Dublin.[21] Industry experts[22] agree that some doubling-up does occur at Ryanair but it is not too prevalent. It can be attributed to the fact that 'high frequency routes take the pain when there is a bad day'. The practice does nonetheless concur with CEO O'Leary's emphasis on optimising the load factor. Ryanair's lower fares and subsequent low profit margins means that the airline needs a load factor per flight in excess of 55 per cent in order to make a profit.

'Doubling up' of flights is not uncommon amongst airlines but when practiced on a regular basis, not acknowledged by airline management, and usually not compensated for, such practices serve to seriously undermine an airline's standards of service reliability and weaken consumer confidence in the airline. In particular, these tactics alienate business passengers and those making connecting flights.[23]

In an analysis of 1,000 written complaints received from 1 April 1997 to 31 March 1998, the UK Air Transport Users Council found that on time departure was uppermost in the minds of passengers, with the largest portion (20 per cent) of complaints relating to departure delays or cancellations. Time is an increasingly important factor for airline passengers and poor performance in this sphere may prove a significant determinant for customers when choosing future flights. For LFAs, it is a crucial test of their ability to meet customer expectations, often under stricter conditions – fewer aircraft and shorter turnaround margins – than larger competitors

Airport location

Another important variable in determining customer satisfaction (and securing/maintaining business passengers) is airport location. The use of secondary airports is an important element of a LFA's low cost model. It ensures lower airport landing and handling charges but it also allows the airlines to realise rapid turnaround times of 25-30 minutes and therefore increase the average daily utilisation of their aircraft. Many passengers – including those travelling for business – are willing to endure the generally inconvenient location of LFA airports in order to secure a significantly lower fare than other scheduled carriers. However, there is a danger that many chosen airports are simply too far from the intended metropolitan hubs to be attractive to many passengers. In Europe, this is particularly the case for Ryanair, which tends to use regional rather than secondary airports for many of the city pairs it serves (Table 5.5).

Table 5.5 A selection of Ryanair airport locations

Route	Closest major city	Distance from major city
Stansted-Carcassone	Toulouse	43 miles
Stansted-St Etienne	Lyon	35 miles
Stansted-Kristianstad	Malmo	47 miles
Stansted-Skavasta	Stockholm	55 miles
Stansted-Torp	Oslo	65 miles
Dublin-Charleroi	Brussels	37 miles
Dublin-Beauvais	Paris	35 miles

Source: Ryanair: preparing for fleet expansion, report produced by Goodbody Stockbrokers, Dublin, August 1998 and Ryanair website.

Secondary airport destinations are a common theme in the strategies of Ryanair and its US role model, Southwest Airlines. However, there appears to be some difference between what the companies consider a secondary airport. Rival LFAs[24] do not believe that the Ryanair model is the same as the Southwest model as they fly into very different airports. In the case of Southwest, this appears to be a tertiary airport, whereas for Ryanair it usually comprises a regional airport. Southwest's airports are in fact often closer to the metropolitan hub than their larger rival airports. For example, Southwest flies into Midway Airport, 7 miles from downtown Chicago, compared with a distance of 25 miles for Chicago O'Hare. Similarly, Dallas Lovefield (Southwest's first airport) is 6 miles from downtown Dallas, compared with a distance of 30 miles for Dallas Forthworth International Airport. By comparison, as Table 5.5 illustrates, Ryanair serves Oslo by flying into Torp Airport, which is 65 miles away; and serves Stockholm via Skavasta, 55 miles from the Swedish capital.

This difference in approach to the notion of a city's secondary airport is significant and may pose a problem for Ryanair in retaining the loyalty of business passengers in particular. Increased competition from other LFAs such as Go and easyJet, serving more convenient airports, may erode Ryanair's share of the cost conscious business market and the frequent traveller segment of the leisure/VFR market. Also, serving far flung regional airports may make other modes of transport more of an option. For example, a passenger may prefer to take the Eurostar high speed train from London to Paris rather than fly to and from distant airports such as Beauvais.

Concluding remarks

The success of any airline company hinges upon providing a safe and reliable product. For LFAs, low operating costs and cheap ticket prices are also key requirements for market success. Of these variables, the most contentious is what precisely constitutes a 'reliable product'. The essential features of a reliable airline product are being on time (departing and arriving), having low rates of flight cancellations, ensuring baggage is not lost or damaged and having informed and helpful customer service personnel who are there to assist passengers, particularly when problems occur.

Achieving operational cost reductions through diminished service standards can weaken an airline's brand image and loyalty and undermine its long-term market competitiveness. Cost reduction is therefore a necessary modus operandi for LFAs but should not be achieved at the expense of an unreliable service product. As the example of Southwest Airlines clearly illustrates, the price/service trade-off does not need to be a zero-sum game. A win-win situation can evolve, with low costs and prices and a reliable and well-regarded service product.

Notes

1   These features of airline service reliability were outlined by Prof. David Kennedy of University College Dublin at the Air Transport Research Group Symposium, UCD, Dublin, July 1998.
2   Travel industry studies conducted by US marketing information firm, J.D. Power and Associates.
3   Brent Bowen is a professor in the University of Nebraska at Omaha and Dean Headley is a professor at Wichita State University. The ensuing discussion of the AQR is derived from a paper given by these authors at the Aviation Management Education and Research Conference, The Molson Business School, Montreal, 16-17 July 2001. The material is reproduced and applied with the kind permission of Dean Headley and Brent Bowen.
4   The report is produced annually by the Office of Aviation Enforcement and Proceedings of the US Department of Transportation.
5   According to the US Department of Transportation, a flight is counted as on time if it departs or arrives within 15 minutes of the scheduled time.
6   Data derived form the June 2001 Air Travel Consumer Report.

7   This fact was pointed out in a conversation between this author and Prof. Dean Headley, co-author of the AQR, 29 September 2001.

8   Interview with Mr Sean Coyle, Ryanair's Commercial Director, Dublin Airport, 8 March 2001.

9   For example, J.D. Power and Associates, in association with Frequent Flyer magazine, conduct an annual survey on customer satisfaction in the US airline industry.

10   The IATA survey is discussed in Redmile (2000) 'Passenger priorities', p. 70.

11   Goodbody Stockbrokers, equity research report on Ryanair, August 1998, p. 23.

12   Problems emerged in the Ryanair'Servisair relationship in early 2002, resulting in Ryanair terminating the contract at London Stansted and securing an alternative contractor.

13   Data derived from a news update dated 2 August 2001, on the www.Ryanair.com website.

14   Interview with senior Ryanair management, Dublin, November 1997.

15   Special report on low cost airlines in the Escape supplement of The Observer newspaper, 21 May 2000, pp. 5-11.

16   'Which airline?' survey conducted by Holiday - Which? Magazine, Spring 2001. The survey questionnaire was sent to 60,000 of the magazine's readers and the response rate was 31,410.

17   According to the EU's 2000 annual report on economic and fare data for the European air travel industry.

18   On-time arrival is considered more important in US measures of service quality but European studies tend to focus on departure times.

19   This argument was substantiated by a senior Aer Rianta source in a discussion with this author, August 1998.

20   Such accusations have emanated from sources in Aer Rianta as well as in newspapers articles by Gerry Byrne in the Irish Sunday Independent, 14 June 1998 and by Joanna Walters in The Observer, 16 August 1998.

21   Interview with Mr Jim Callaghan, Ryanair's head of regulatory affairs, Dublin Airport, 8 March 2001.

22   Discussion with Conor McCarthy, Director of PlaneConsult, Dublin, 9 March 2001.

23   This fact was highlighted by journalist Gerry Byrne in the above mentioned newspaper article and in discussions which Mr Byrne has had with this author.

24   Interview with a Buzz manager, Stansted Airport, 21 May 2001.

Chapter 6

Leader of the Pack:
The Ryanair Model[1]

Introduction

Ryanair was established in 1985 but it was not until its 1991 restructuring that it took on the role of Europe's first LFA. In 1990, Ryanair was serving 26 city-pairs and carrying 700,000 passengers but was in financial difficulties. A decade later the airline was serving 47 city-pairs, carrying 5.6 million passengers annually and operating at annual net profits of €72.5 million[2] (up by 24 per cent since the previous year). By 2001, Ryanair had become the ninth largest airline in Europe, measured in terms of passengers carried (7.4 million to financial year ended 21 March 2001). Growth projections indicated that by 2004, Ryanair could overtake long established rivals and become the fifth largest airline in Europe. This tremendous growth is attributable to the nature and efficiency of Ryanair's low cost operational model and senior management's dogged determination to adhere rigidly to the low fare business model.

This chapter examines the application of conceptual strategy models to Ryanair and, more broadly, to the European LFA sector. We look at the long-term viability of needs-based positioning, premised on price leadership and the strategic pitfalls of cost reduction efforts. We discuss the limits of a price-based corporate strategy when the needs and expectations of customers evolve. Although the strategic positioning framework is applied explicitly to Ryanair in this chapter, its model and findings apply equally well to the other LFAs discussed in subsequent chapters. The chapter also examines the cost reduction techniques of Ryanair and advances an operational model for other small and medium-sized carriers in Europe. This involves a critical assessment of Ryanair's cost reduction methods and their success in terms of achieving a consistent decline in unit cost. The main argument advanced is that through refining and adapting for the European context the set of techniques of US-based Southwest Airlines, Ryanair pursues an authentic and successful cost reduction strategy. This enables the company to redefine European airline cost structures and floors and consistently provide the lowest prices and best value to its customers. Through emulating Ryanair's best practices, European low fare and regional airlines can strengthen their market position and remain a viable competitive challenge to the larger, more established airlines.

Building a LFA strategy

In choosing a competitive strategy, a key consideration for company strategists is how to configure the value equation so as to best meet customer needs and demands. For many companies this means striving to achieve the lowest possible prices for their products or services. Low prices cannot be sustained unless a company maximises its operational efficiency. This means that the company has to perform similar activities better than rivals. One way of doing so is to pursue a rigorous and relentless policy of cost cutting. Many low price companies believe that there is always room for improvement when it comes to achieving low operating costs. Some of the most vigorous competitive rivalry occurs in the low price segment of the market. Across a wide range of industries, throughout the global economy, traditional market leaders are under attack from low price competitors. These low price firms are steadily eroding the profit margins and market share of their more established rivals. This, often cut-throat, competition is particularly evident in the airline industry. Beginning in North America and spreading more recently to Western Europe, the airline passenger market has witnessed a growing intensity in price-based competition. This intensified competition has been facilitated by policy deregulation initiatives. The nature of competition in European air transport has been transformed by national and European liberalisation initiatives. The corporate beneficiaries of this change are the new breed of independent LFAs. As we saw in earlier chapters, these small companies used the freedoms offered by the European Single Market to shake up the industry's competitive dynamics and cost structures and offer the customer an alternative form of service, premised on low prices and basic service.

All airlines ultimately seek to lower costs and maximise economies of scale. Economies of scale require significant investments in airplanes and support facilities. This means high fixed costs and consequently, capacity utilisation is critical.[3] Although it has its pitfalls, cutting prices is one tried and trusted way of filling seats and maximising capacity. Ryanair is the most cost efficient scheduled airline carrier operating in Europe. Its success rests on a combination of low costs and low fares, together with an extensive route network to rival larger, more established carriers. Its maverick status – non-membership of assorted airline associations, non-participation in alliances – arguably leaves the company open to attack from larger competitors. However, given the firm's ever expanding route network, its low breakeven load factor[4] and its increasing revenue, Ryanair may be viewed as a model for both small and large European low fare and regional carriers.

Ryanair: the emergence of a low price challenger

The largest and most successful of Europe's LFAs is the Irish operator, Ryanair. It is also the longest established, having first commenced scheduled services in June 1985, operating a fifteen seater aircraft between Ireland and England. The company's restucturing saw the emergence of Europe's first LFA. The subsequent CEO, Michael O'Leary, effectively invented the European low fare airline business in 1991, when he helped re-establish Ryanair as a Southwest clone, adapted for a European market.

The market entry of this independent, privately owned airline, symbolised the first real threat to the near monopoly which the state-owned carrier Aer Lingus had on routes within Ireland and between Ireland and the UK. Ryanair's strategy was simple: offer a no-frills, low fare service to all. In essence, the Ryanair recipe for success is captured in a simple equation:

$$\text{Lower fares} = \text{more passengers} = \text{lower costs} = \text{lower fares}$$

This formula proved hugely attractive to an increasingly cost conscious travelling public. No attempt was made to distinguish between different passenger groups – business people, students seeking summer work, emigrants visiting their families – all constituted Ryanair's target market and all shared the same non-assigned seating arrangement. This 'egalitarian' scenario was in stark contrast to the more opulent, segregated and expensive service offered by Ryanair's main rival, Aer Lingus. The state carrier had grown rather lax and was genuinely shaken due to the competitive threat posed by the new entrant. However, Ryanair was never the threat that Aer Lingus perceived it to be. Rather than simply eating into Aer Lingus's existing customer base, Ryanair's arrival helped precipitate a growth in the total air travel market, particularly between Ireland and the UK. A Morgan Stanley report illustrates that typically passenger traffic on a route grows at an enormous rate after Ryanair's entry, often doubling or even trebling the existing traffic within a few years (1997, p.15). Ryanair has certainly been a causal factor in the growth of traffic on major routes such as Dublin-London. In the decade prior to Ryanair's launch, passenger numbers on this route grew at a minuscule rate, going from 800,000 to around 1 million people per annum. Since 1985, this figure has soared, reaching the 4 million mark by the late 1990s. Similar growth rates are evident on other routes such as Dublin-Manchester and Dublin-Glasgow. This growth occurred primarily in what has been described earlier as the visiting friends and relatives (VFR) traffic. Lower prices will act as the prime catalyst for growth in this market segment – a fact substantiated in surveys of Ryanair passengers.[5] Although Aer Lingus's market share may have dwindled on certain routes, its volume remained stable or even grew. The aforementioned growth on the Dublin-London route for instance benefited all carriers. The consumer benefited enormously from the increased competition, seeing air fares being virtually halved as cartels such as that controlling the Dublin-London route were broken.

Another example of Ryanair's ability to stimulate air traffic can be found in their entry into the London-Venice market in 1997, at which point passenger traffic on the route began to increase at a rapid pace. The VFR market was again the basis for market growth, with a large Italian expatriate community living in the greater London area. As Figure 6.1 illustrates, passenger growth on this route was slow during the early to mid-1990s, increasing by a mere 100,000 passengers during the entire 1993-1997 period. In the three years immediately following Ryanair's market entry passenger numbers grew by at least 100,000 passengers per annum.

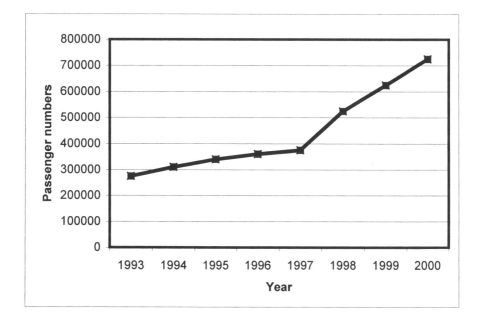

Figure 6.1 'The Ryanair effect': London – Venice
Source: UK Civil Aviation Authority statistics and a Power Point presentation produced by Mr
    Jim Callaghan, Ryanair's Head of Regulatory Affairs.

The long term viability of low price strategy

The low cost competitive context

During the 1990s, Ryanair established itself as the leading independent
European LFA, consistently expanding its route network and increasing its
profit margins. It believes that it is out on its own and is a company that
breaks barriers. Its core ideology is encapsulated in its mission statement:

> Ryanair will become Europe's most profitable, lowest cost scheduled airline by
> providing its low fares/no frills service in all markets in which it operates to the
> benefit of our passengers, people and shareholders (Corporate mission statement
> 1997).

If we deconstruct this corporate vision along the lines offered by Collins
and Porras (1996), we can identify Ryanair's core values and core purpose.

These provide the overall framework within which the company's strategy is formulated. Ryanair's core values – its constant and enduring guiding principles – are low price, value for money, and efficient service. These values should not alter, regardless of market or environmental changes (Collins and Porras 1996, p.67). The company's core purpose, by distinction, is its very reason for being. For Ryanair, this is to provide cheap, safe, and reliable air travel for all.

Strategic fit and cost minimisation

Ryanair's competitive advantage derives in large part from the way its activities fit and reinforce one another. It locks out imitators by creating a chain that is as strong as its strongest link (Porter 1996). Like the leading US low fares carrier, Southwest Airlines (see Chapter 8), Ryanair's activities complement one another in ways that create real economic value. One activity's cost is lowered because of the way other activities are performed. Similarly, one activity's value to customers can be enhanced by a company's other activities. That is the way strategic fit creates competitive advantage and superior profitability. The fit among activities substantially reduces cost or increases differentiation (Porter 1996, p.73).

In the early 1990s, following a period of heavy losses and low growth, Ryanair looked across the Atlantic for successful strategy models. The obvious example was the long established and highly successful low fare carrier, Southwest Airlines. Ryanair's emulation of Southwest's winning strategy is sustained in reports such as that conducted by US equities research firm, the Robinson-Humphrey Company (1997), who concluded that Ryanair is 'the Southwest Airlines of Europe'. Despite the apparent customer service shortcomings illustrated in Chapter 5, Ryanair's emergent strategy resembled Southwest Airlines in a number of ways. These similarities included:

- Establishing a corporate ethos of ongoing and rigorous cost reduction
- Translating these savings into lower prices than competitors and thus establishing a price leadership market position
- Growing existing markets through stimulating demand with low prices
- Being innovative, e.g. developing markets neglected by established competitors such as secondary routes or 'visiting friends and relatives' customer segments.

Commentators such as Guild (1995) point to a number of infrastructure problems that make it difficult to apply the Southwest model to the European air transport market. These include inflexible labour markets and the high costs of European air traffic control and landing and ground handling fees. Ryanair has largely overcome such competitive impediments through negotiating deals on fees with airport authorities for instance, particularly those seeking to increase their rate of air traffic. According to Southwest founder and CEO, Herb Kelleher, 'Ryanair is the best imitation of Southwest Airlines that I have seen'.[6]

The sustainability of Ryanair's cost-based strategy

Ryanair's cost structure requires some analysis so as to establish the authenticity and sustainability of the carrier's cost reduction tactics. Are lower operating costs achieved through a genuine strategy of lowering the cost of fuel and ticketing or in-flight services and increasing productivity levels, or through an artificial form of cost reduction based on, for example, salary freezes or introducing more part-time positions? How sustainable is the Ryanair model if lower costs are achieved through lower service standards and lower wage rates? In addition, we will explore the management of airline cost drivers. Holloway (1997) describes this as, in large part, the interplay between improved asset utilisation and increased employee productivity:

> Unit costs are influenced by the absolute level of input prices and by the productivity of inputs used. High productivity can go some way towards countering the adverse impact of high input prices, but the ideal is clearly to combine in a single production process both high productivity and low input costs (Holloway 1997, p.188).

Previous studies support the argument that factors such as the number of aircraft types in a fleet, the range of markets served, remuneration packages, the level of service, and traffic charges, all contribute to higher operating costs for airlines (Seristö and Vepsäläinen 1997, p.12). On the first of these variables for instance, evidence derived from Seristö and Vepsäläinen's study of 40 of the world's largest airlines shows that airlines with the most uniform fleet (Southwest, Singapore, Cathay Pacific) also have shown some of the best results in recent years. One reason for this is that:

> ...the higher the number of aircraft per aircraft type, the smaller the number of flight crew needed per one aircraft. This again would imply that the more

uniform the fleet of airline, the more efficiently the airline can utilise its pool of pilots (Seristö and Vepsäläinen 1997, p.17).

In addition to lower overall maintenance costs, a uniform fleet leads to savings in flight operations costs. Ryanair operates a single type aircraft fleet, comprising only Boeing 737 aircraft. Consequently, its overall employee per aircraft ratio is one quarter that of its traditional rival, Aer Lingus.[7]

Moreover, the company links employee salaries to performance, provides a basic, no frills service, and incurs the minimum in traffic charges. It therefore meets many of the criteria deemed necessary to bring about an authentic reduction in its operating costs.

Since 1995, Ryanair has managed to reduce costs annually in all areas of expenditure, with the occasional exception of personnel and depreciation.[8] Increases in depreciation reflect the increase in the number of aircraft operated by the company. It should also be noted that in parallel with a rise in overall operating expenses, Ryanair witnessed a significant increase in overall passenger numbers and in the number of routes served. The route network more than tripled between 1995 and 1998. Moreover, if we consider that during the period 1996 to 2001, Ryanair's annual number of passengers increased from 2.4 million to 7.4 million (Figure 6.2), and equate these numbers with the comparable annual operating expenses to get a rough average of expenses per passenger head, we can see that the airline has in fact succeeded in successively lowering its operating expenses.

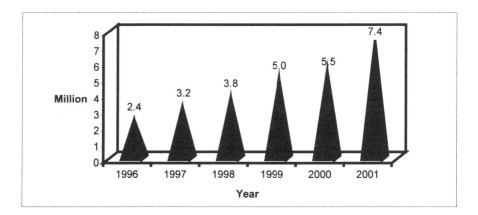

Figure 6.2 Ryanair passenger numbers, 1996-2001

Ryanair have experienced continuous improvement in their operating revenues and after-tax profit figures (Figure 6.3). This process has been ongoing since the company's restructuring and strategy reformulation at the beginning of the 1990s.

	Operating revenues	Profit after tax ‡
31/3/95	£86.1m	£12m
31/3/96	£110.1m	£13.4m
31/3/97	£136.4m	£21.4m
31/3/98	£182.6m	£30.2m
31/3/99	€295.8m	€57.5m
31/3/00	€370.1m	€71.6m
31/3/01	€487.4m	€104.5m

Figure 6.3 Ryanair operating revenues and profit margins *
Source: Ryanair annual financial results.

* All figures given for 1995-8 are in Irish punts. The value of the punt to the pound sterling was an average of 89p Irish to £1 sterling during 1998. All figures for 1999-2001 are in Euro. The value of the Euro to the pound sterling was an average of one Euro to 62p during 2001.
‡ Adjusted for the staff flotation bonus in 1997, which amounted to IR£1.3 million, net of tax; and for non-recurring gains in 2000.

Costs have fallen faster than yields within Ryanair, allowing profits to rise consistently. Expressed as a percentage of operating revenues (Figure 6.4), operating expenses declined steadily between 1994 and 1996 and increased only marginally in 1997, despite above average rises in personnel and maintenance costs (the latter costs being incurred as a result of the airline's acquisition of eight new aircraft during 1997/8). A similar pattern emerged during 1998-2001, with expenses rising slightly in 2000 due to the purchase of new aircraft.

1994 - 89.7%	1996 - 82.2%	1998 – 75.8%	2000 - 77.5%
1995 - 83.4%	1997 - 82.4%	1999 – 77.1%	2001 –76.9%

Figure 6.4 Ryanair's operating expenses expressed as a percentage of operating revenues

This translates into rapidly increasing operating profit margins in the same period, going from 10.3 per cent in 1994 to 17.6 per cent in 1997 to 35 per cent in 2001.

Ryanair has consistently brought about proportional cost reductions in two key areas of expenditures for most airlines – staff remuneration and marketing and distribution costs (Figure 6.5).

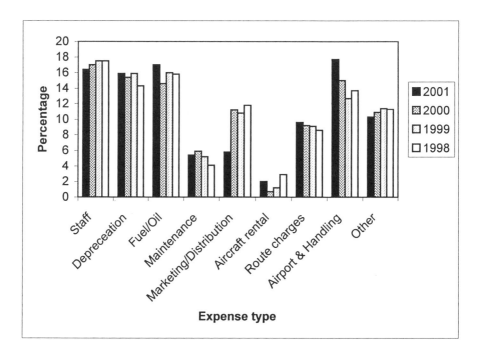

Figure 6.5 Ryanair breakdown of operating expenses, 1998-2001
Source: Data derived and interpreted from Ryanair financial results, 1998-2001.

* Year end 31 March.
** Expenses are expressed as percentages of Euros, not Irish punts, from 2000 onwards.

Staff costs increased in overall terms by 26 per cent in 2000/1, reflecting a 16 per cent rise in employee numbers to 1,467 and pay increases of 3 to 5.5 per cent. However, as a percentage of total operating expenses, staff costs have declined from 17.5 in 1998 to 16.4 per cent in 2001. Marketing and distribution declined from 11.8 per cent of total costs in 1998 to 5.8 per cent in 2000, decreasing by 33 per cent from 2000 to 2001. This large reduction resulted from an increase in the level of direct bookings via the internet, a 33 per cent reduction in the travel agent commission rate and the termination of the distribution agreement with Galileo, offset by a higher spend on the advertising of new routes and the Ryanair.com website. However, total operating expenses still increased by 31 per cent between 31 March 2000 and 31 March 2001, due to Ryanair's escalating activity across Europe and increased costs of depreciation, fuel and airport and handling charges. Route charges increased by 36 per cent in the 2000/1 period due to an increase in the number of sectors flown and an increase in the average sector length. Depreciation and amortisation increased due to an increase in the number of aircraft owned from 26 to 36 and the amortisation of capitalised maintenance costs. Fuel costs increased significantly due to a 29 per cent increase in the number of hours flown, combined with an increase in the average US dollar cost per gallon of fuel and the adverse impact of the strengthening of the US dollar to the Euro. Airport and handling charges increased by 54 per cent due to an increase in the total number of passengers flown, the adverse impact of the strength of Sterling to the Euro and increased airport and handling charges on some existing routes due often to the ending of fixed term charges agreements between Ryanair and some airport authorities. These costs were partially offset by lower charges on new European routes.

Furthermore, Ryanair has average load factors of 72.5 per cent (considerably higher than the estimated European average load factor of 64 per cent) and is driving yields down. The load factor measures the percentage of an airline's output that has been sold (Holloway 1997, p.437). In layman's parlance, it means basing an airline's financial strategy on the average number of seats sold per flight. This is distinct from yield management, which focuses on the average revenue generated per unit of output (seat) sold. As Ryanair CEO Michael O'Leary states, 'we do not manage yields, we manage the load factor...our budgets are based on driving costs down by x per cent next year' (Guild 1995, p.73). Managing load factors is not enough to ensure profitability. As Holloway illustrates, in 1993 for instance, Aer Lingus achieved a load factor of 70.4 per cent and failed to make a profit, whereas both British Airways and Cathay Pacific had passenger load factors of 69.9 per cent and 70.0 per cent respectively and both made a profit (1997, p.442). The issue is rather one of relating the average load factor to the break-even load factor. Improving this equation is the objective of every airline. Selling seats on flights must be combined with overall cost reductions if an airline is to be profitable. Table 6.1 illustrates that for Ryanair, the margin of difference between average load factor and break-even load factor has been consistently positive since the mid-1990s.

Table 6.1 Passenger load factors and break-even load factors compared (percentages)

	1995	1996	1997	1998	1999	2000	2001
PLF (passenger load factor)	76	73	72	70.5	71	71	72.5
BELF (break- even load factor)	72	68	64	59	57	56	54

* Passenger load factor is referred to rather than load factor as Ryanair does not carry cargo.

Furthermore, the gap between these two sets of figures has increased annually, allowing the airline further latitude in price-cutting and ensuring continued increases in absolute profit figures. Thus, although Ryanair may periodically experience declining yields, it also secures falling costs, suppresses its break-even load factor, and therefore consistently turns a profit. To date, costs have consistently fallen by more than sales, resulting in overall net profits. From the evidence, it is therefore apparent that Ryanair has a sustainable cost reduction strategy that is clearly achieving real results in terms of sustaining the company's price leadership strategy and ensuring profit maximisation.

Price leadership strategy: critical perspectives

A low price leader must, as Lynch argues, shave costs off of every element of the value chain (1997, p.487; Porter 1985). However, low cost alone does not provide competitive advantage. Competitive advantage can only be achieved in terms of a product or service that is seen by the user to have an advantage over the competition. Competitive advantage is therefore achieved through an organisation's output – its cost base being relevant only in so far as it may provide a means of achieving or improving that output. Porter (1985) added that it may be more useful to think of cost *based* strategies, the benefits of which (such as increased margins or low prices) can be used to achieve competitive advantage. Such a low cost strategy can have different manifestations. Johnson and Scholes (1997) describe these as:

(i)   The 'cheap and cheerful' strategy, dependent on low cost and low value-added
(ii) Reduced price strategy but with an emphasis on quality
(iii) Competitive prices with a better quality and more reliable product or service than rivals.

Porter argues that low cost firms usually sell a standard or no frills product or service and that such a firm will generally be an above-average performer in its industry, provided it can command prices on or about the industry average (1985, p.15). Ryanair pursues a strategy in line with option one, cheap and cheerful, with low operating costs and low profit margins. This latter variable is somewhat deceiving as profit margins are low when calculated as a percentage of revenue generated per passenger but are high when calculated as a proportion of total revenue generated. Ryanair believes that it is operating on more than mere operational efficiency. Senior management sources argue that cost reduction is more like a religion within the company. Every day, management thinks about how to reduce cost. An example is that Ryanair was the first airline in countries in which it operates to significantly reduce travel agent commission. They did this in the midst of their stock market flotation – a time when most companies would not be doing anything which might jeopardise their flotation.

Kay (1993) argues that in the European airline industry, costs are dominated by three main factors – labour, fuel, and capital costs. He further contends that:

Substantial differences in costs per unit of output can result from differences in the rate of fleet utilization (the proportion of potential flying time for which a plane is actually in the air) and in the load factors achieved in passenger carriage, since a flight costs much the same to operate whether there are empty seats on it or not (Kay 1993, p.294).

As Table 6.2 illustrates, Ryanair directly targets both labour and capital outlay for continuous cost reduction. Moreover, in striving to maximise aircraft utilisation, the company indirectly targets fuel expenditure for cost reduction.

Table 6.2   Where Ryanair cuts costs

1. **Secondary airports** (lower charges and less congestion means airline can increase punctuality rates and gate turnaround times).
2. **Standardised fleet** (lower training costs and cheaper parts and equipment supplies and maintenance costs).
3. **Point-to-point services** (direct, non-stop routes; through-service with no waiting on baggage or passenger transfers).
4. **Maximise aircraft utilisation** (fewer aircraft used to generate higher revenue; leads to higher passenger capacity and greater staff productivity).
5. **Cheaper product design** (no assigned or multi-class seating; no free food or drink).
6. **No frequent flyer programme** (costs money to manage and to implement).
7. **Non-participation in alliances** (code sharing and baggage transfer services lowers punctuality and aircraft utilisation rates and raises handling costs).
8. **Minimise aircraft capital outlay** (purchase outright used or new aircraft of a single type).
9. **Minimise personnel costs** (increase staff-passenger ratio; employee compensation linked to productivity-based pay incentives).
10. **Customer service costs** (outsource capital intensive activities, e.g. passenger and aircraft handling; increase direct sales through Internet site or telephone reservation system).
11. **Lower travel agent fees** (reduce associated travel agent commission, with the objective of moving eventually to total direct sales).

Taken together, these cost cutting principles form a very strong base for the success of a price leadership strategy. Emphasising factors such as fleet utilisation and aiming overall to maximise passenger load factors rather than yield ratios, Ryanair can reduce its costs per unit of output, along the lines previously advanced by Kay (1993). As mentioned earlier, Ryanair's objective is to fill as many seats as possible on every flight, rather than to achieve the maximum revenue per passenger on every flight. Its profit is therefore determined by high capacity and low profit margins, rather than low or standard capacity and higher profit margins, as with many conventional airlines.

It is often feasible to pursue a strategy of low price to achieve competitive advantage in an area such as air transport, where low price is important and a business has cost advantage over competitors operating in that segment (Johnson and Scoles 1997, pp.254-5). This is generally the case with Ryanair. However, as Barkin et al. indicate, 'a successful concept alone does not turn a low-cost competitor into a major threat' (1995, p.91). The critical issue is whether the low-fare airline can *sustain* its competitive advantage over time and gradually expand its operations. There are problems linked to the notion of sustainable price leadership, as it means having the lowest prices (and costs) compared with competitors over time. This is unlikely to be achieved simply by pruning costs – competitors can and will do that too. The question then is, how competitive advantage can be achieved and sustained – if at all – through price leadership. Market share advantage might be one possible answer. This provides a company with cost advantages through factors such as economies of scale and experience curve effects. There are different perspectives on what degree of advantage a company requires in order to sustain advantage over a long period of time. Buzzell and Gale (1987) argue that a firm with a high absolute market share may not have a high relative share because there may be a competitor who also has a comparable share. In developing strategy, it is dangerous to assume a direct link between relative market share advantage and sustainable advantage in the market because there is little evidence of sustainability: dominant firms do lose market share and others overtake them. We need only think of the fall from market grace of companies like IBM or TWA to substantiate this argument. Market share itself is not what is important but rather the advantage that it can bestow. Relative share advantage can give cost advantages but this requires a proactive and innovative management. Without this, advantage will be lost to competitors.

An alternative solution may be in product cost advantage: the product cost advantage enjoyed by LFAs such as Ryanair is more sustainable because traditional carriers have set certain service and quality standards which they would find difficult to abandon (Barkin 1995, p.92). The established customer base of many large airlines may not wish to do without in-flight meals, baggage transfer facilities, business class seating, and so forth. Process cost advantages may also be sustainable as established carriers often cannot emulate the high utilisation practices of their low-cost competitors. The example of Continental Lite illustrates this weakness among larger airlines. Established as the low cost subsidiary of US major, Continental Airlines, its market failure is generally accredited to its inability to emulate the product and process advantages of successful existing low cost competitors such as Southwest Airlines (Porter 1996).

All airlines – regardless of size – want to minimise costs (although not all wish to reduce prices). Identifying potential cost savings is the easy part of the analysis; designing the best way to implement cost reductions is the difficult part and varies from company to company. The important point to remember is that the main risks of pursuing a low cost/low price strategy are price war and low margins. It is therefore vital to be the cost leader and not just one of many (Johnson and Scholes 1997, p.251). Ryanair management are very conscious of this fact and are relentless in the pursuit of new and more efficient cost cutting techniques. Their approach continues to prove effective, as Ryanair remain the cost leader in European aviation.

Reconciling low cost strategy and European expansion

Whilst some commentators were initially sceptical that further expansion into Europe was the correct move for Ryanair, others believed that with the right routes, Ryanair would succeed (Guild 1995, p.73). Many routes across Europe still lack a low fare alternative to established competitors. Ryanair has proven that it can successfully expand markets to categories which are currently priced out of it or which use alternative modes of transport. Once the airline had established itself in the Irish-UK market, it was inevitable that it would seek new growth markets if it were to survive and prosper in the long term and truly be the 'Southwest of Europe'. This expansion of the airline's European route network began in earnest in 1997 with the launch of regular scheduled services from London Stansted to Oslo, Paris, Brussels, and Stockholm, and was consolidated in 1998 with services to Pisa, Rimini, Venice, Carcassonne (Toulouse), St. Etienne (Lyon), and Kristianstad (Malmo). This 'Europeanisation phase' was facilitated through the purchase of six additional B737-200 aircraft from Lufthansa, bringing the total fleet size to 20 by early 1998. The company subsequently added between two and four 737s per annum, 50 per cent of which catered for new route development. By the end of 2000, Ryanair had a fleet of 31 Boeing 737s. In mid-2001, the carrier cancelled an order with Boeing for new aircraft, as they failed to agree on a price. Instead, they turned to second hand planes, seeking to take advantage of the cutbacks in many established European carriers during 2001 by offering to buy up to 50 used Boeing 737s.[9] Drawing on its substantial cash reserves, Ryanair said that it needed no financing to take advantage of the aircraft glut in global aviation experienced in mid-2001. Savings could be made for the company as they cancelled orders for new aircraft with Boeing so as to buy second-hand aircraft at bargain prices from other airlines. Ryanair stated that it preferred planes between 7 and 14 years old and that it wanted delivery between 2002 and 2005. The extra aircraft would service Ryanair's anticipated 25 per cent growth during the 2002 to 2005 period.

Ryanair sources argue that there has not been a problem so far vis-à-vis their expansion into longer-haul routes. For instance, the 1997 launch of a two hour service between London and Stockholm proved so successful that the number of flights daily was rapidly increased from two to three. Moreover, a service from London to Oslo was launched on the strength of the success of the London-Stockholm route. These are countries where people traditionally have high expectations from airlines in terms of service. Ultimately though when Ryanair offers a much cheaper alternative to established carriers such as SAS or British Airways, most customers are happy to live with a no-frills service for two hours. At the moment, Ryanair believes it can get away with their approach on flights within a two hour radius of its main base airports. Southwest started that way and they are now up to journeys of five or six hours. Ryanair believes that for the time being, there is enough scope within the two hour catchment and will not expand beyond flights of two and a half hours duration.

There are some real dangers for low-fare carriers attempting to expand into longer haul markets. As Barkin et al. point out, the cost advantages accrued on short-haul, high traffic markets – low input costs and cheaper product and process designs – will weaken for longer haul markets (1995, p.93). In particular, the advantage gained through product or process design will lessen: passengers are likely to demand better in-flight service, more leg room, and so forth, when they are on a longer flight and the benefit accrued through fast turnaround is not as important. Overall, advantage through utilisation for instance, would be more difficult to sustain.

The creation of mainland European hubs

Following on easyJet's creation of European hubs at Geneva and Amsterdam, Ryanair selected Charleroi in Belgium in early 2001 to be Ryanair's first mainland European hub. The base at Charleroi continued the policy of flying chiefly to low cost secondary airports. It also signalled the beginning of the airline's European expansion plan, aimed at opening up the majority of Europe's routes to low fare competition.[10] Mainland Europe is expected to yield 40 per cent of the airline's traffic by 2004, compared with 20 per cent in 2000.[11]

By late 2001, Ryanair offered up to thirty flights a day from Charleroi to seven European cities – London Stansted, Glasgow, Dublin, Shannon, Carcassone, Pisa and Venice (Treviso). Four aircraft were allocated there and Ryanair invested more than $100 million in the Belgian base. Ryanair is the only scheduled airline operating services into and out of Charlerloi. The company aimed to increase the airport's total passenger traffic from 250,000 in 2000 to 1 million by 2002. Charleroi was selected initially as a hub over airports such as Hahn near Frankfurt, Skavsta south of Stockholm and Pisa.[12]

The final choice was determined by operating costs (landing charges, etc.), the ability of the airport to give a long-term commitment and the passenger catchment area and its growth potential. Charleroi was also selected due to its prime location and to give Ryanair the opportunity to target weak Belgian-based LFAs, Virgin Express, and the struggling – subsequently bankrupted – national carrier, Sabena.

The multi-hubbing approach also continues Ryanair's point-to-point strategy, resisting the temptation to pursue a 'hub and spoke' approach based on transfers and connecting flights. This is the first of four to five mainland European hubs that Ryanairs intends to develop by 2005/6.[13] The company aims to double total passenger volume to more than 14 million by 2004.

In a June 2000 Business Week article on European business leaders at the forefront of change, it was argued that Ryanair's CEO Michael O'Leary has a deceptively simple goal: to bring air travel within financial reach of more Europeans – and to make money at it. However, a note of caution emerges in a subsequent May 2001 Business Week special report on Ryanair, when it is argued that 'as O'Leary delves deeper into Europe, his strategy will be tested' (2001, p. 40). Reasons cited include deep-pocketed competitors such as Air France and Lufthansa, backed up by national governments; and a maze of different and complex labour and regulatory issues. However, Ryanair's CEO O'Leary responds to such negativism by arguing that first, Ryanair does not intend – in most instances – to compete directly with Europe's large flag carriers; second, LFAs mostly create new market space rather than taking customers from established airlines; and third, he is counting on the borderless appeal of low fares to win customers across Europe. On the issue of different labour and regulatory regimes, Ryanair's strategy is to negotiate with each airport individually and to work these variables into the equation.

Consistent successes and emerging market challenges

From the initial flotation of Ryanair in 1997 until August 2000, the market capitalisation[14] of Ryanair increased from €392 million to €3,185 million. A second share offering in early 2001 raised a further $135 million for the company and shares were valued at €1.60 each. The sale was four times oversubscribed by investors, who bought all 13 million shares on offer.[15]

2001 marked Ryanair's eleventh consecutive year of growth. The company realised a 35 per cent growth in passenger numbers (to 7.4 million) and a 44 per cent increase in net profit (to €104.5 million) for the 12 months ending 31 March 2001, despite difficult market conditions – including high oil prices and fears of economic downturn – and the negative impact of the foot and mouth crisis on travel into, within and between Ireland and the UK. Ryanair also found itself embroiled in disputes over landing and handling charges with the Irish airport authority, Aer Rianta. None of these problems appeared to hamper the airline's performance, as it once again performed beyond industry norms and market analyst expectations.

The year 2001 also witnessed the first serious challenge to Ryanair from another LFA. Moreover, this challenge was directed at the company's home base – Dublin. Go, the former BA low fare subsidiary, entered the Dublin-Edinburgh and Dublin-Glasgow markets from late September 2001. Ryanair's reaction was swift and decisive: in addition to its existing Dublin-Glasgow route, the carrier introduced its own Dublin-Edinburgh route almost three weeks ahead of Go. Introductory return fares from Ryanair on the new route started at £29.99 ($42), compared with Go's starting fare of £35. This was indicative of Ryanair's willingness and ability to under-price all competitors in order to maintain or extend their market reach.

Ryanair is well placed to ride out any recession in Ireland, the UK or mainland Europe as, unlike most of its low fare competitors, it has built up substantial cash reserves. Moreover, its business model is robust and likely to weather an economic slowdown better than most traditional carriers. Goodbody Stockbrokers, in a 2001 report on Ryanair, argued that the airline is the best strategically positioned airline to take advantage of the low fares market in Europe. The model is buoyed by market leading profit margins. For instance, in 2000-1, the company reported a 23 per cent profit margin, compared with an industry average of about three per cent. Finally, Ryanair could be a beneficiary of any slowdown as increasingly cost-conscious business and other passengers opt more often for LFAs.

Conclusions

LFAs have succeeded in revolutionising the European airline industry's price norms and costs structures. The leading industry shaker has been the independent Irish-based carrier, Ryanair. In emulating the strategy and improving on the cost reduction model pursued by the original LFA, Southwest Airlines, Ryanair has established itself as the most profitable company and a formidable competitor in the European air passenger market. This strategy has been premised on price leadership, a derivative of the cost leadership component of Porter's generic competitive strategy framework. The company initially employed a focused cost leadership approach, targeting specific, price sensitive customer segments. In essence, Ryanair found space (a new customer base) that wanted the stripped down product of air travel at bargain basement prices. Low prices could entice these customers to fly more frequently and to substitute air travel for other modes of transport. The strategy has evolved as the company has expanded, moving into the realm of overall cost leadership, with Ryanair becoming the lowest cost/price operator in the wider European airline industry. This strategy shift was largely demand-led, as business travellers and other seasoned flyers increasingly sought the lowest fare on particular routes.

Ryanair has pursued an authentic and highly successful cost reduction strategy. This has enabled the company to achieve low break-even load factors and high overall load factors. This consequently allows the airline to provide consistently low prices to its customers, whilst simultaneously sustaining high profit ratios. Ryanair's main cost reduction techniques include first, operating a standardised fleet; second, flying exclusively from or between secondary airports and establishing a secondary route dominance; third, operating a point-to-point service; fourth, offering a cheaper, no frills product (no seat classes or free food and drink); fifth, non-participation in restrictive alliances or expensive frequent flyer programmes; sixth, productivity-based pay schemes; seventh, an extreme focus on aircraft utilisation, leading to high load factors; eighth, reduced travel agent commission rates; and ninth, reduced customer service costs through outsourcing ground passenger and baggage handling for instance. Through emulating Ryanair's cost reduction practices and achieving similar low break-even load factors, European low fare and regional airlines can strengthen their market position and remain a viable competitive challenge to the larger, more established airlines.

Notes

1   Parts of this chapter have been reprinted from two of the author's journal publications on Ryanair. The first is *Long Range Planning*, vol. 32, no. 6, Thomas C. Lawton, 'The limits of price leadership: needs-based positioning strategy and the long-term competitiveness of Europe's low fare airlines', pp.573-86, 1999, with permission from Elsevier Science. The second is *The Journal of Air Transportation World Wide*, vol.5 no.1, Thomas C. Lawton, 'Flying lessons: learning from Ryanair's cost reduction culture', pp.89-106, 2000, with permission from the editor.

2   St£1 equals €1.59 at the time of writing and €1 equals a little less than US$1 (22 September 2001).

3   T. Hinthorne, Predatory capitalism, pragmatism, and legal positivism in the airline industry *Strategic Management Journal*, 17 (4), p.255, (1996).

4   Ryanair's low break-even load factor is attributable to its high passenger-per-mile yield, which is calculated by dividing the cost per passenger per mile by the revenue per passenger per mile.

5   Including a survey conducted by this author's research assistant at Stansted Airport during the summer of 1997.

6   Cited in 'Renegade Ryanair', Business Week,14 May, 2001, p. 38.

7   These statistics are taken from a Ryanair internal company document, 1997.

8   Ryanair's company accounts illustrate this fact.

9   This fact was reported by Charlie Weston in the *Irish Independent* newspaper on 7 August, 2001, p. 12.

10   This is based on a discussion between this author and Mr Sean Coyle, Ryanair's Commercial Director, Dublin Airport, 8 March 2001.

11   These figures were cited by Kevin Done in an article, 'British carriers eye some more markets', Financial Times, 11 May, 2001.

12   Although these three airports are likely candidates for Ryanair's intended next European hubs.

13   Interview with Sean Coyle of Ryanair, op.cit.

14   Defined by Morrell (1997) as the 'market share price per share multiplied by the number of shares outstanding'. Although it changes from day to day, market capitalisation is probably the most accurate and comprehensive measure of a company's worth.

15   Cited in Air Transport Intelligence news, 9 February 2001.

Chapter 7

The Contenders:
Competing Low Fare Carriers in Europe

Introduction

In Chapter 6 we focused on the leading LFA model in Europe: Ryanair's cost obsessed, lowest price, network expansion approach. Although the Ryanair model is financially robust and generates significant profits, there are alternative methods in the industry. In particular, easyJet's cost conscious, low price/friendly service, network intensifying method is distinct. The easyJet approach is popular with customers – especially small business people – and builds revenue at a steady pace. Other low fare market contenders are Go, Buzz and Virgin Express. A quasi-LFA, Basiq Air, emerged in 2001 but lags well behind the other players.[1] Figure 7.1 ranks the contenders relative to the market leader, Ryanair and in order of size based on number of aircraft operated.

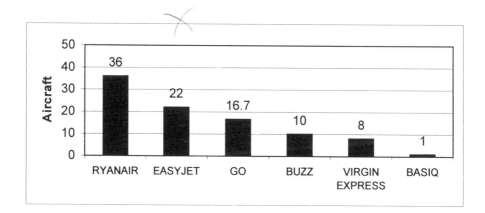

Figure 7.1 Relative fleet sizes of LFA contenders (August 2001)
Source: Company documents and websites.

Ryanair is significantly larger than all other LFAs in Europe, measured in fleet size. easyJet and Go both have reasonably sized fleets and are appreciably larger than the other low fare challengers. We proceed to examine each of these airlines, in order of fleet and route network size, consider their respective business models and compare each with other low fare strategies in Europe. Particular attention is given to Europe's second largest LFA, easyJet, and to the financial soundness and strategic logic of its particular business model. The other LFAs are subsequently examined and we consider how sustainable their individual business models and corporate strategies are – particularly when competing with the Ryanair or easyJet systems. Attention is also given to the reasons for the failure of low fare carrier Debonair at the close of the 1990s and the lessons that other low price carriers can learn from Debonair's demise. This leads us finally into a discussion of competing low fare business models in Europe and the challenges facing the market contenders if they are to successfully compete with traditional carriers and with each other.

The easyJet story

easyJet was founded in 1995 by Stelios Haji-Ioannou, a Greek-Cypriot entrepreneur with a background in the family shipping business. A £5 million investment by his father helped Stelios to lease two aircraft and hire a small, young staff to serve as reservation agents. Through its operating companies, easyJet Airline Company Limited and easyJet Switzerland S.A., easyJet provides high frequency services on short-haul and medium-haul point-to-point routes within Europe from its three airport bases at London Luton, Liverpool and Geneva. easyJet offers a simple, no frills service aimed generally at both the leisure and business travel markets at fares which are on average significantly below those offered by traditional full-service, or 'multi-product' airlines.[2]

easyJet's first flight was in November 1995 from Luton to Glasgow and was advertised for a one-way fare of £29. The flight was completely full, partly in response to the advertising campaign slogan, 'Fly to Scotland for the price of a pair of jeans!' Increasing demand soon led to new services from Luton to Edinburgh and Aberdeen. Over the next two years, Stelios raised a further £50 million in debt and equity to finance the company's expansion. The first new aircraft orders was placed in September 1997 when easyJet ordered 12 Boeing 737-300s. In October 1997, easyJet established a second hub at Liverpool, followed in March 1998 by the creation of its first mainland

European hub at Geneva. Its fourth hub was established in January 2001 when easyJet set up a base in Amsterdam.

In March 1998, easyJet Holdings Limited, at that time the corporate parent of easyJet UK, acquired a 40 per cent interest in a Swiss charter carrier, TEA Basel AG for a consideration of three million Swiss francs. During the course of 1998, TEA commenced scheduled services from Zurich and Geneva to London Luton under the easyJet brand. In April 1999, TEA changed its name to easyJet Switzerland S.A. and moved its headquarters from Basel to Geneva. In June 1999, easyJet Holdings Limited increased its shareholding in easyJet Switzerland to 49 per cent and secured an option to acquire the remaining 51 per cent, for an aggregate consideration of 2.4 million Swiss francs. Scheduled services from Geneva to Amsterdam and Nice commenced in July 1999. These were the first daily services entirely outside the UK on which easyJet had implemented its business model. As at 30 September 2000, the number of destinations served from Geneva had increased by four routes, including a daily flight from Geneva to Barcelona which is operated as a charter service to satisfy Swiss regulatory requirements.

easyJet's financial structure and cost reduction model

easyJet reported its first ever full-year profit in 1998, with a £2.32 million net surplus. The figure represented a swing of £5.6 million over the previous year, when easyJet made a loss of £3.27 million (Jasper 1999). easyJet's turnover for 1997/98 was £77 million, up 67 per cent from the £46.01 million of the previous 12 months, while the number of passengers carried grew 65 per cent to 1.72 million from 1.04 million. This profitability was achieved against a background of major expansion. During the 12 months the carrier added new routes from its two UK bases at Luton and Liverpool, and in March 1998 its holding company acquired Swiss carrier TEA Basel. By 2000, easyJet's annual revenue was over £263 million, with a net profit in excess of £22 million. The company carried 6 million passengers in the same year, on a fleet of 17 aircraft. The airline's average load factor continued to increase, rising from 70.8 percent in 1998 to 80.8 per cent in 2000.[3] The percentage of business travellers on easyJet continued to increase also and constituted more than 50 per cent of the total by 2001 (up from 36 per cent in 2000), according to easyJet CEO, Ray Webster.[4] He argues that this increase is due to easyJet's business model, based on high network density and frequency, which is attractive to business travellers.

In November 2000 the company was floated on the London Stock Exchange and valued at 310p per share. With 25.1 per cent of the carrier on offer, the sale raised £195 million ($279 million) for easyJet, valuing the company at £778 million. This was at about a 40 per cent discount to Ryanair, based on operating profit before depreciation (Baker 2000). The sale was ten times oversubscribed, despite occurring at a time of market volatility and negative sentiments towards airlines. Interestingly, shares were only made available to financial institutions. The company decided not to sell shares to the general public in the belief that thousands of small shareholders (probably customers) would be disappointed by receiving a very small share holding. By May 2001, easyJet shares were valued at 403.5p, down 7p on the previous month but still a significant premium on the 310p November 2000 float price. easyJet outperformed the FTSE all-share transport index by 35 per cent during its first six months of trading.

easyJet is able to provide value-for-money fares on a profitable basis by keeping unit costs low. This strategy does not necessarily mean taking the lowest-cost supply alternative. Rather, the carrier seeks sustainable efficiency improvements and unit cost savings, principally through seven distinct but interrelated cost reduction tactics.[5] These are, first, maintaining high aircraft utilisation, accomplished mainly by operating a young and reliable fleet, shortening aircraft turnaround times, extending the flying day, and investing in dedicated line maintenance and self-handling at London Luton. Second, eliminating all sales intermediaries between the customer and easyJet, other than airport sales desks (whether travel agents or other airlines), which means that easyJet does not have to pay commissions or CRS fees. This also simplifies back-office accounting and reduces staff costs. Third, focusing on sales via the Internet, which means that sales growth can be more easily accommodated without incurring significant additional costs. The company took its first Internet reservations in April 1998 and by March 2001 online sales had grown to account for 86.5 per cent of total sales. Fourth, adopting a single class, high density aircraft cabin layout offering 149 seats, the maximum permitted for the Boeing 737-300 and 737-700. Fifth, eliminating unnecessary service frills that, in easyJet's view, are not highly valued by the customer, such as complimentary in-flight catering, tickets and dedicated airport lounges. Sixth, using a simple business model, so that easyJet does not, for example, offer passenger connections, interlining, or freight services. Seventh, operating two similar variants of the Boeing 737 aircraft, thereby reducing training overheads and increasing operational flexibility; and eighth, establishing long-term agreements with many key suppliers.

In all of these cost reduction tactics, easyJet mirrors the approach of Ryanair. Differences do exist: for example, easyJet flies to many primary airports whereas Ryanair only flies to tertiary or regional airports. These differences will be discussed in more detail further on in this chapter.

The easyJet business model

easyJet describe their approach to customer service as a combination of 'professionalism and informality'. Although easyJet were originally modelled on US LFAs such as ValuJet and Southwest Airlines, there were some notable differences. For instance, Southwest offers a complimentary beverage and peanuts on its flights but easyJet offers nothing – except its in-flight magazine – for free. The organisational culture of easyJet is closely modelled on Southwest though. Teamwork and 'fun' are strongly encouraged and co-operation is considered essential. Chairman Haji-Ioannou and CEO Webster believe that easyJet's operational model could be copied but that their corporate culture could create a sustainable advantage that competitors would find difficult to emulate (Sull 1999, p. 23).

easyJet's strategy and business model[6] are based on six key strengths that the company believes support competitiveness, scalability and sustainable growth. First, a simple fare structure – easyJet only offers a single fare at any one time for a specific flight. This differs from a full service carrier such as BA, which will generally sell tickets in all fare classes simultaneously, each differentiated by progressively more restrictive fare conditions.[7] easyJet's pricing strategy is to offer value-for-money fares, although not necessarily the lowest fares for any given route. This fare generally increases in line with demand towards the date of the flight.[8] Second, low unit costs – easyJet keeps unit costs low by maintaining high aircraft utilisation, eliminating all sales intermediaries between the customer and easyJet (other than at some airport sales desks), focusing on internet sales, eliminating unnecessary service frills, operating a fleet of similar aircraft and establishing long-term agreements with many key suppliers. Third, strong branding – easyJet has established a strong brand in its key European markets, being the UK, the Netherlands and Switzerland. Fourth, commitment to customer service – safety is easyJet's first priority. easyJet also aims to provide a service consistent with its image: professional, friendly and informal. Fifth, a multi-base network – easyJet's network strategy is to provide dense point-to-point services on routes within Europe. The company believes that this strategy provides significant benefits, including reduced dependence on a single hub and the creation of local competitive advantages as a result of the size of easyJet at its bases and the frequency of its flights. Sixth, strong corporate culture – easyJet has a strong and coherent corporate culture, internally known as the 'orange culture', which the company believes helps substantially to motivate employees to implement easyJet's strategies.

This is a much more complex growth model that the Ryanair approach outlined in the previous chapter. easyJet's strategic vision is therefore to build an airline with sustainable profitability, based on seven core principles:

1. Yield managed fares
2. Modern and standardised fleet
3. High aircraft utilisation
4. Short haul services
5. No travel agents or tickets
6. Point to point service
7. No free food or drinks.

As we saw in Chapter 6, Ryanair also adheres to these principles. A significant difference is in the approach to profit generation: Ryanair focuses on maximising capacity and maintaining very thin profit margins per ticket sold, whereas easyJet focuses on maximising yield and gaining greater profit margins per passenger.

Contrasting the easyJet and Ryanair models

The main operational and strategic difference between easyJet and Ryanair is that easyJet focuses on building network density whereas Ryanair focuses on network expansion. Both airlines are now pursuing a multi-hub approach. The difference is that easyJet is aiming to increase the frequency of services from these hubs and consolidate its existing routes, whilst Ryanair consistently adds more routes from each hub. easyJet sources argue that their network strategy is very different from Ryanair as Ryanair is broadly hub and spoke, whereas easyJet operates more like a spider's web. easyJet will fly to a number of destinations from each hub. Their network development strategy is premised on three elements. First, adding routes between existing cities served ('joining the dots'); second, adding frequency onto existing routes; and third, ensuring that the network continues to grow by adding one or two new cities every year (either destination or base airport). This contrasts with Ryanair's network development approach which emphasises increasing the overall number of city pairs served rather than necessarily adding frequency on existing routes or joining up cities already within the network but not directly connected.

Ryanair has a lower cost base and higher operating profit margins than easyJet and could sustain itself for longer in the event of a downturn in the market or in its performance. The challenge for easyJet is to get higher margins despite having a higher cost basis. The easyJet model is more difficult to manage that the Ryanair model – it is not as simple. For instance, easyJet flies to many expensive airports but Ryanair sticks rigidly to the basic principles of the low cost model.

easyJet accept that they are different from other LFAs, particularly Ryanair. The core of this difference is on frequency of service: Ryanair's average daily departure per city is 5.5, compared with 9.1 for easyJet.[9] easyJet sources also acknowledge[10] that Ryanair have a very good cost base, so they can sell seats very cheaply. Ryanair does not aim to fill the aircraft first and foremost – their predominant focus is on cost.

Ryanair works to secure the lowest possible cost deal with airports, whereas easyJet fly into the major airports and hope people will pay higher yield for doing so. easyJet managers argue that not every aspect of the Southwest low fare model necessarily works in Europe and that they have amended the model. Ultimately, a LFA has to stick to a model but it does not have to be the Southwest/Ryanair model.[11]

So far, there has been little head-to-head competition between the two leading LFAs in Europe, except on the London-Glasgow route (but even here they operate from and to different airports).

In summation, easyJet differs from Ryanair in two principle ways: first, easyJet serves a number of major airports, which Ryanair avoids. Ryanair argues that increased revenue from business travellers does not justify the added costs and turnaround time. easyJet disagrees, placing more emphasis on gaining and retaining business travellers than their low fare rival. easyJet management contend[12] that high yielding business traffic will pay a little more for more convenient airports. Second, easyJet have never used travel agents and most of their sales are online. Ryanair's Internet sales are increasing steadily as a percentage of total sales but travel agents continue to be used for a proportion of ticket sales.

In addition to the impact of the 2001 US terrorist attacks on the world airline industry, the market challenges for easyJet in the years ahead are first, to continue to meet financial targets (this is particularly important for a newly listed airline); second, to continue to grow – the company's objective is to double in size in terms of capacity (22 to 44 aircraft, etc.) by May 2004; and third, to shift a lot of growth from London Luton to London Gatwick, prompted by a dispute with the airport authority at Luton.

Go

The Go story

In late 1997, British Airways (BA) announced its intention to launch a new airline with a hub at London Stansted and offering reduced service and low fares. 'Operation Blue Sky', as the project was initially called, aimed to put BA into direct competition with the low fare innovators, Ryanair and easyJet. An initial feasibility study conducted by Barbara Cassani, subsequent chief executive of the BA spin-off, predicted that the new airline could turn a profit in its third year of operations (Sull 1999, p. 31). This projection proved stunningly accurate. In June 2001, Go (as the subsidiary was named in early 1998), declared a small but respectable tax profit, compared to significant losses the previous year.

BA launched Go in part to stave off competition from Ryanair and easyJet, who were exerting pressure on BA to reduce its fare prices; and in part to have a presence in a potentially highly lucrative market. It soon became evident that the first part of this strategy was flawed. Instead of capturing its rivals' market share, Go caused mainstream customers to question the cost of BA's full-service fares.[13] The problem was that Go looked and felt too much like BA's short-haul services – minus the complimentary in-flight meal. Many passengers realised that this meal was not worth the often significant price difference between a Go and a BA flight.

When Cassani was appointed to head Go, there was no cash, no board approval (from BA) and no plan. Cassani, with the help of a number of other senior managers, spent from March to September 1997 drafting a business plan. An important basis for her plan was, according to Cassani, 'that this business needed to stand on its own and that it should be BA making a financial investment rather than starting a subsidiary'.[14] She emphasised the need to build the company from the ground up and requested (and received) an initial £25 million cash injection from the BA board. London Stansted was subsequently chosen as the initial operating base for the new airline, due to a competitive offer to provide facilities. Aircraft were leased from GE at an average cost of between $215,000 and $275,000 a month. The name of the airline took some months to emerge. Cassani and her team finally chose 'Go' because, in her words, it reflected a straightforward, modern and simple organisation that is for intelligent people who know what they want to do.

Deciding on the route network was the most important decision. As with their competitors, success or failure hinged on the selection of viable routes with growth potential. The first destinations chosen were Rome, Milan and Copenhagen.

Within three years, Go was financially viable. Go's key results for the year ending 31 March 2001 were very healthy. Revenues were £159.7 million, up 59 per cent on 2000. Pre-tax profits were £4.0 million, exceeding expectations of breakeven. Passenger numbers were also up, by 46 per cent to 2.76 million and load factors had increased from 63 per cent in 2000 to 72.5 per cent by 2001.[15]

Barbara Cassani, succeeded in a management buy-out of Go in June 2001, backed by the leading European venture capital company, 3i. The deal totalled £110 million and BA CEO Rod Eddington commented that this represented an excellent return on the initial 1998 investment of £25 million. BA received £80 million in cash and £20 million in vendor loan notes and will receive a further £10 million if Go is sold by 3i within five years. A 22.5 per cent share of Go's business is controlled by employees, with 19 senior managers investing in the company and all of Go's 750 staff being offered share options.

The business model

Go adopted a very similar strategy and business model to that used by easyJet. Emphasis is placed on frequency of service to new routes. The airline flies only Boeing 737's and has configured them with 148 seats. Go moved from an easyJet-type fare structure to a more traditional arrangement of a variety of fare types with different conditions. The top fare is 50 per cent of a standard full fare economy ticket on a traditional airline. It bypasses travel agents and sells direct to customers. No frills/free food and drink are offered in-flight. Go has tried to distinguish itself from easyJet and Europe's other LFAs by emphasising that they have raised the standards of LFAs.[16] The company believes that a LFA does not need to compromise on quality. They emphasise in particular punctuality and customer services. The Go approach is to go the extra mile for customers and when things go wrong, to be there for the customer. As a result, Go has won numerous plaudits for its high levels of customer service combined with low fares. For instance, in 2001, the company was voted 'best low cost business airline' in the Guardian travel awards and 'best low cost airline' in both the Business Traveller Awards and the Telegraph Traveller Awards.

Critical comparisons with other LFAs

A key differentiation between Go and its low fare rivals is on seat pricing. Go has a less complex pricing system than either Ryanair or easyJet. Its base price is often not as low as other LFAs but more seats are available at its lower rates than is the case with others. Moreover, its highest fare is usually lower than the highest fare of some rival LFAs. An example might be on the London to Nice route. In May 2001, Go started services on this route, in direct competition with easyJet. Go set a cap on its highest ticket price: £280 roundtrip for a fully flexible ticket. By comparison, easyJet's fares reached a high of £488 for a return ticket during peak times. The point that Go makes here is that they offer passengers more choice and better service because easyJet's lowest fares are often only available at unconvenient times, whereas Go's pricing system is more transparent and their lower fares are usually more readily available. Also, even at the lowest fares, passengers can change their travel plans for a fee. Go is therefore competing to Nice on price and on service.

An in-flight survey conducted by Go in April 2001 revealed that the most important things passengers liked about Go were its convenient departure airports, low fares/good value for money, the ease of online booking and the punctuality/reliability of Go's flights. UK Civil Aviation Authority figures for the first two months of 2001 show that out of London, Go was more punctual than easyJet, Ryanair, Alitalia, Bmi British Midland and Swissair (punctuality being defined as flights departing less than 15 minutes late).

Emerging scenarios

The LFA business is notoriously cut-throat and the narrow profit margins mean that there is little room for error. The failure of companies like People Express and Debonair will attest to this fact. Opinions are divided as to how Go may fare. The airline is much smaller than both of its main low fare rivals, Ryanair and easyJet (see Figure 7.1). Both rivals are also run by highly competitive entrepreneurs who are not averse to using aggressive tactics to gain and maintain customers. On the plus side, Go does have high brand awareness due to a successful marketing campaign and its original association with BA. Moreover, its majority owner – venture capital company 3i – have a proven track record of turning a profit from airline investments. A further advantage that Go possesses is its CEO, Barbara Cassani. Cassani is highly motivated and driven and is widely respected by her employees. Her four per cent equity stake in the post-BA organisation serves as an incentive to succeed. Some commentators have in fact argued that 'Go is Cassani – she raised the cash and it stands or falls on her ability to make it happen' (Rubython 1999, p. 36).

There are not too many similarities between Go and Buzz, aside from their origins. Their respective cultures and management structures are very different. There is a strong leadership style and profile at Go, Ryanair and easyJet. This is not the case at Buzz. As we will see further on in this chapter, this is all in stark contrast to the relationship between Buzz and its parent company, KLM.

In May 2001 Go created a second hub at Bristol International Airport in the south west of England. There are five million people within a 90 minute drive of Bristol, therefore the large catchment area was a major factor. Also, it is a brand new airport with significant growth potential. Finally, there is a very enthusiastic and supportive airport management at Bristol. There will be further Go hubs. Belfast has become a mini-hub, with services directly from Belfast to Glasgow. Italy and Spain have potential for future hubs.

Go appears to have positive prospects for further growth. Many observers believe that there is still market space in the UK and there is certainly market space across mainland Europe. Go is set to grow. It is not likely to become as big as Ryanair in the foreseeable future but it could definitely compete with easyJet for the number two position in the European LFA sector. By their very size, the nature of their fleet, route network and core customer markets, easyJet are a close competitor. The battle is on for second place in the future (vis-à-vis easyJet) and for third place now (vis-à-vis Buzz).

Buzz

The Buzz story

Buzz was launched by KLM UK in 1999. It appeared to be a defensive response by a major European flag carrier to the growing success of Ryanair, easyJet and Go. Not so, according to KLM UK's chief executive, Floris van Pallandt. He argued that the move was 'not a defensive measure, more of an opportunity'.[17] He justified this stance by pointing to market research that predicted UK low fare passenger number would increase from 5.4 million in 1998 to 15 million by 2003.

The business model

Buzz looks to differentiate itself on service quality, which the airline believes will reap benefits over time. The carrier aims to attract business travellers through a combination of price, frequency, schedule and convenient airports. The Buzz model is therefore a hybrid, with lower costs and prices than traditional airlines but more emphasis on service quality than other LFAs. According to the airline's publicity material, the Buzz idea is simple: it is a low-cost airline that believes in treating people as individuals. What does this mean in practice? Buzz believes that people want different things from an airline, at different times. This means that on occasion customers want extra services such as an in-flight meal and at other times they simply want a cheap flight without frills. Buzz offers a choice on many extras: onboard food and beverages, business lounge access and fast-track service can all be availed of for an extra charge. The carrier's management consider the main factors attracting passengers to fly with Buzz are:

A. Low prices.
B. Convenient schedule.
C. Airports that are relatively convenient in terms of proximity to destination cities.
D. Adequate procedures for dealing with problems when they occur.
E. The passenger is provided with an opportunity to purchase goods.

As with all LFAs, price is paramount, with the other factors serving more to encourage repeat custom. Buzz has a core number of users (mainly business people) because of the geography of their Stansted base. They supplement this with a number of price-conscious customers. Buzz's average revenue per seat is higher than both easyJet ad Go.

The VFR market is very important for LFAs. In addition, the expatriate market has huge potential. In particular, Buzz targets British expatriates living all or part of the year in countries such as France, Italy and Spain. Research carried out by the company on the Dordogne region of France for instance found significant market potential based on British people with homes in that region.

Buzz initially offered two types of fares, as Go does. The first was called the 'Done Deal' and was the cheaper of the two fare types. Only return tickets were available and the passenger had to be away for at least two nights. Tickets could not be exchanged or refunded. The second fare option was called the 'Open Deal'. This was more expensive but very flexible. One-way tickets were available and reservations could be changed without charge. In February 2001, Buzz abandoned this pricing system, arguing that it was too confusing and irrelevant as the airline discriminated only by demand and not by customer segment in its pricing. In its stead, Buzz introduced a simple one-way fare structure, each fare type split into several yield classes. This is virtually identical to the easyJet system and has proven successful in helping to raise volumes and yields.[18]

Destinations served from London Stansted tend to concentrate on the French and German markets. This is indicative of LFA's tendency to focus on certain country markets. Go and Ryanair both focus on the UK-Italy and UK-

Scandinavia routes for example, whilst easyJet predominantly serves the UK-Spain and UK-Switzerland routes. Buzz's most direct route competition from other LFAs comes from Ryanair (to France and Germany) and it also competes directly with Go on the London-Milan route.

As with easyJet, Buzz appears to contradict one of the basic premises of the low fare model, i.e. to always fly to secondary or tertiary airports. Baker argues that 'Buzz has broken one of the rules for other low-cost airlines by targeting primary hubs' (2000b, p. 19). Buzz sources respond by arguing that they have been able to negotiate good deals with these airports. This does not take account of other cost-inflating factors in serving major airports though, such as the impact of traffic congestion on turnaround and on-time departures. However, Buzz management argue that they fly to major city airports such as Paris Charles de Gaulle and Frankfurt International only when they can maintain a high level of productivity and where they have a substantial number of customers willing to pay more for the convenience of the airport. In all other places, Buzz already has or is in the process of moving to cheaper secondary airports.

Buzz has been heavily criticised for its choice of aircraft, the Bae 146 regional jet. This aircraft is more costly to operate and service than the Boeing 737 favoured by other LFAs. It also has a more restricted seat configuration – generally having a maximum capacity of 110, as opposed to a maximum of 148 seats on the Boeing 737. This fleet was inherited from KLM uk but is being gradually phased out and replaced by Boeing 737 aircraft.

Buzz also has pre-assigned seating. This prevents a free-for-all when boarding the plane and the airline argues that it is more convenient for many passengers, particularly older or infirm passengers. A negative aspect of this policy is that it slows turnaround time: passengers tend to board at a more leisurely pace when their seats have been allocated in advance. In part as a result of this policy, Buzz's average gate turnaround time is 35 minutes and can be as high as 45-50 minutes at their more congested airports (compared with 20-25 minutes maximum for Ryanair). This means that Buzz cannot achieve the same daily aircraft utilisation rates as the leading LFAs in Europe. Buzz respond that punctuality is more important and point to easyJet's declining punctuality in 2000/1, precipitated by efforts to achieve a 15 minute turnaround time at their Luton hub.

Writing in 2000, Aviation analyst Chris Avery of JP Morgan commented that 'there appears to be no fundamental change in the cost base between KLM uk and Buzz'. Buzz sources respond that this is simply not the case. It is correct to argue that the cost of fleet or pilot contracts has not (yet) changed. Buzz does have the wrong aircraft at the wrong cost, so this is a valid criticism. Its fleet contains a number of Boeing 737-300s (the standard LFA aircraft) but most of its aircraft are the more costly Bae146 jets. This problem will work its way out if the system as the fleet modernisation process continues. However, in many other ways the cost base has been transformed. First, the distribution cost has changed dramatically. The no frills, direct sales approach of Buzz means that the airline can reduce costs significantly compared to KLM uk. These savings occur through the elimination of tickets and of complimentary services such as an in-flight meal, as well as a shift towards online sales and the resultant disintermediation of the travel agent. Second, Buzz avails of fewer services at airports than did KLM uk. Its more rapid turnaround time means that it spends less time than its predecessor at the gate. Third, Buzz operates (mostly) to and from cheaper airports than did KLM uk. Fourth, productivity is now higher. Crew are flying more hours and the number of daily aircraft operations has increased. Buzz does also accrue some cost advantages by working off the KLM 'platform'. Initial start-up costs were lower as a consequence. Nonetheless, a major cost shortfall remains between Buzz and its LFA rivals.

Critical comparisons with other LFAs

Buzz management admit that there is not much difference between Buzz and Go: Buzz is simply 'low price with a veneer of quality'.[19] Two factors which do distinguish Buzz a little from its rivals are first, airport location (Stansted is preferred by many customers over easyJet's Luton hub); and second, frequency of service (which is generally superior to Go's). Quality equates to simple extras such as assigned seating. The linkage with a parent company such as KLM raises the expectations of passengers.

Buzz management[20] draw on Ryanair as a role model for cost focus, secondary airports and irreverence; and easyJet as a role model for innovation, brand strength and network intensity. They concede that they cannot replicate Ryanair, as the Irish carrier is simply too far ahead on cost advantage. They cannot replicate easyJet as it is too far ahead in terms of brand image and awareness. Buzz's main competitors are thus traditional airlines.

Buzz has been compared with the ill-fated Debonair, particularly given its targeting of both business and leisure passengers. Buzz responds that, unlike Debonair, its 'pay-as-you-go' policy for the extras that business travellers may want (such as access to a business lounge) ensures that costs are kept under control and differentiates it from Debonair.

The Buzz model is similar to Go in that considerable emphasis is placed on customer service and individual choice. In this respect, it is a variation on the easyJet model. However, Buzz's cost structure appears to be considerably less robust than either Go or easyJet and it is in danger of market straddling by trying to be both a low price and high quality provider. As discussed in previous chapters and further illustrated in Chapter 8, a market straddling position is generally unsustainable over a period of time. Buzz management are aware of this challenge and it is fair to say that that their business model is evolving and becoming even more cost and price focused.

Emerging scenarios

Buzz does have an image problem and has received more bad press that is deserved. The company is perceived as less interesting than other LFAs, in part because it lacks the charismatic figurehead that easyJet and Ryanair both possess and in part because it is not perceived as an obvious champion of the consumer. On the market competition between Go and easyJet, a Buzz spokesman believes that the Go product is better (e.g. Go's punctuality record in superior) but that Go is fighting on easyJet terms. A service ethos is important. The Buzz spokesman has admiration for Ryanair but, over time, the price-based model might be difficult to sustain as service and customer satisfaction matter, particularly for repeat custom.

Buzz has no plans yet to develop a multi-hub approach as its low rivals have done but management concede that it is likely to happen. As 35 per cent of Buzz's business is non-UK originating, so the market potential does exist.

Buzz sources visualise key future developments at the airline as first, a unified aircraft type; second, at least one new aircraft hub; and third, productivity levels closer to easyJet and Ryanair. However, by September 2001, Buzz was experiencing difficulties, as the hoped-for fleet upgrade from Bae 146 to Boeing 737 or Airbus 320 planes had failed to materialise. This was seen by industry observers as a significant blow to the airline, as the Bae 146 aircraft are more expensive to operate and have a lower passenger capacity than either the 737 or the A320. The airline dropped its London to Vienna route due to low yields, as the level of business traffic fell significantly below projections. Industry commentators noted that KLM's long term commitment to the low fare subsidiary was questionable (Baker 2001, p. 24). Nonetheless, few analysts or media commentators appear to acknowledge that the Buzz organisation and product is developing and becoming more focused. Learning from Ryanair, Buzz is endeavouring to use more cheap airports; taking example from easyJet, it is operating only high frequency business routes to major airports. Moreover, Buzz receives high satisfaction ratings from customers, as evidenced in its ranking in surveys by leading British publications such as *Holiday Which?* magazine and The Guardian's *The Observer* newspaper. This leads us to conclude that Buzz has the right product but has not yet developed the right business model – although this is evolving. The question is whether or not Buzz will be able to complete its transformation before it loses the support of KLM.

Virgin Express

The Virgin Express story

Virgin Express began life as a charter airline in February 1992, operating under the name of EuroBelgian Airlines (EBA). In late 1994, responding to further EU deregulation of air transport, EBA began scheduled services between Brussels and Barcelona and Vienna and Rome. In April 1996 the Virgin Group bought a 90 per cent stake in the Brussels-based EBA for approximately $60 million and purchased the remaining 10 per cent the following year. The airline was renamed Virgin Express. Virgin Express built on the established five city service of EBA and moved from a dependence on charter business to scheduled services.

Jonathan Ornstein, a former senior executive at Continental Express in the US, led the new management team.[21] The new focus was on rapid growth. The company's initial success was based on four core strengths: low operating costs, the Virgin brand, a very experienced management team and a steady revenue stream from its charter service and Sabena agreement (Sull 1999, p. 31). The latter strength turned out also to be a weakness. Rival LFA executives argue that Virgin Express's fundamental strategic misjudgement occurred in October 1996 when the airline formed a block-space agreement with Sabena on the Brussels-Heathrow route.[22] This agreement was extended in March 1997 to cover routes from Brussels to London Gatwick, Rome and Barcelona and was subsequently extended further as the airline's network expanded. The agreement worked as follows: Sabena purchased a fixed number of seats on each Virgin Express flight (usually around half of capacity) and then resold these to its own business and economy class passengers. Sabena paid Virgin Express to provide full business and economy class service to its passengers. Each flight was designated with both a Sabena and a Virgin Express code and flight number (CAA 1998, p. 128). Sources within Virgin Express argue that it was not a mistake to go into an alliance with Sabena. Money from this arrangement helped to 'pay the bills' and in many ways actually served as a financial lifeline for Virgin Express.

However, the Sabena deal also cost money, as Virgin Express does not operate to secondary airports because the high proportion of business travellers on its flights would be inconvenienced by such routings. Although this further undermines the low fare model, Virgin Express would agree with easyJet that you have got to serve your market. Business travellers are not going to make a 110km bus trip from Torp to Oslo, as Ryanair passengers must when they fly to the Norwegian capital. This does not square with the Southwest model either, as Southwest goes to where the public want to travel. Also, charges at secondary airports will go up eventually.

The business model

The Virgin Express business model is a confusing mix of orthodox and unorthodox LFA principles. As with leading LFAs, Virgin Express does not issue tickets, offers no extras such as free newspapers or executive lounges and operates a homogenised fleet of Boeing 737s. Unlike other LFAs, Virgin Express offers a complimentary snack (although not a hot meal) and dual cabin service and operates to major airports. Virgin Express's fares system is a tiered structure of one-way fares with different conditions attached.

Company sources[23] argue that the Virgin Group wanted to set up a European airline but it was not really intended to be a LFA. Lower prices than the majors were an objective but these were not meant to be the lowest prices. The idea was to build on the Virgin Atlantic model and tender the middle product – offering a quality service at affordable prices. Virgin essentially aimed to extend the Virgin Atlantic model into a short-haul, intra-European model. The belief was that a vacuum existed between the likes of Aer Lingus and Ryanair and easyJet and BA. Astute companies like Bmi British Midland have taken advantage of this market space and it is also where Virgin Express sees itself best placed.

The key mistake of the business model was to buy EBA and take on board its baggage. Virgin Express should have been an offshoot of Virgin Atlantic or a pure start-up.

Emerging scenarios

For the nine months ended 30 September 2000, total revenues at Virgin Express rose one per cent to Euro 227.8 million. Net losses totalled Euro 27.5 million. Results reflected increased capacity, offset by higher fuel and aircraft ownership expenses. Continuing losses forced Virgin Express in 2000/1 to begin restructuring its operations. The airline closed down its Irish operation based at Shannon and reduced its unprofitable charter activities to focus on its scheduled business. The restructuring paid some immediate dividends: Virgin Express cut its 2001 first quarter losses to €0.8 million from €3.8 million the previous year. Operating costs dropped 24 per cent on the previous year. The load factor was up by nearly nine points to 74.4 per cent (rising to as high as 90 per cent for the second quarter of 2001). However, scheduled passenger numbers were down by 11 per cent in the second quarter of 2001, to just over 600,000.

What factors lie at the core of Virgin Express's persistent lacklustre performance and financial woes? 'Unless you've got a very good product, no one will buy it', argues one industry source.[24] Richard Branson bought EBA against all advice. He inherited all of the cost structures and union regulations of EBA. Belgian employment laws are extremely complex and onerous for companies. For instance, PRSI contributions are 30 per cent, employees must be given meal vouchers and if staff are not able to take 70 per cent of their vacation in the summer, they must be given 25 per cent more salary. Virgin Express (Ireland) was established to reduce operating and social costs. Due to JAR regulations in Europe, the new operation was effectively a separate airline. All of the airline's aircraft were put on the Irish register, all pilots were officially employed in Ireland, and so forth. Employing staff in Ireland meant that the airline could circumvent much of the social restrictions in Belgium as social laws in Europe are based on where you are officially employed. However, in undertaking this policy, turmoil emerged in Belgium as the fear of job losses led to labour unrest at Virgin Express's Brussels operations. Richard Branson subsequently signed a 5 year employment guarantee with the Brussels workers. This meant that when cutbacks became necessary due to Virgin Express's losses, these resulted at the airline's Irish division rather than the Belgian operations. This was not necessarily justifiable on purely economic grounds.

Some other LFA executives[25] contend that because Virgin Express has been a sub-service carrier for Sabena, it was never able to compete with the Belgian flag carrier. Also, it bought its aircraft at the top end of the cycle, burdening it with more aircraft debt than most other LFAs. These factors, together with its choice of expensive and congested airports, explain Virgin Express's problems.

Managers at other LFAs[26] argue that Virgin Express has not built a profile or a network or offered fares that are as competitive as other LFAs. Also, the firm is not sufficiently concentrated. It offers both full fare and low fare on the same aircraft and as discussed in previous chapters, such a market straddling approach cannot work successfully.

Industry sources[27] also reason that the airline's very high Belgian cost base is certainly a problem. Also, they reiterate the point that the passenger sharing deal with Sabena and the related route deal has proven highly restrictive for Virgin Express. Finally, although trading on the Virgin name, Richard Branson never seemed to give Virgin Express his public support, which may have undermined the brand.

Basiq Air: a genuine LFA contender?

Transavia Airlines, an 80 per cent-owned subsidiary of KLM, carries over 3.5 million people to sun and snow destinations each year. Transavia is largely a charter operator but approximately 30 per cent of its flights are scheduled. Under the Transavia banner, KLM launched a new service in late 2000 called 'Basiq Air', claiming that research indicated that there was strong demand in the Dutch market for the sort of low fares available in the UK and US. Industry sources[28] comment that Basiq Air equals Transavia, without the free food and that it would make sense to adopt a multi-hub approach for Buzz rather than to create a different brand for the Dutch market. easyJet accuses KLM of setting up Basiq Air in direct response to easyJet's hub development in Amsterdam. Claims were made by easyJet that an internal KLM memorandum spoke of the need to stop the growth and development of easyJet and to make sure that the newcomer would not be able to secure a solid position in the Dutch market. It cannot be coincidental that Basiq Air commenced operations one month before easyJet launched its Amsterdam hub and that its routes mirror those of easyJet. To confirm this argument, Peter Legro, Transavia Chief Executive, stated at the time of Basiq Air's launch that there was 'no time to wait any longer. We know the competition has eyes on our market...The European airline business has become a price-driven market in which there is no room for sentiment'.[29]

The defining principles of Basiq Air differed from Transavia and borrowed from the LFA model existing elsewhere in Europe. In particular, Basiq Air operates only Boeing 737-300 aircraft, online bookings are encouraged and the level of extra, in-flight service is decided by the individual customer and accrues extra charges. Initial routes served were Amsterdam and Rotterdam to Nice, Barcelona and Malaga. In-flight food and beverages are a la carte and luxury goods such as jewellery and perfume are also available for purchase. In-flight goods can be purchased at discounts of up to 20 per cent, as Basiq Air absorbs the VAT on flights within the EU. Initial flight prices from Amsterdam and Rotterdam to Malaga started at $52 one-way – less than half the lowest price charged by Transavia on its scheduled services. Speaking at the launch of the Malaga route, Transavia President Peter Legro stated: 'the low-cost, no-frills concept clearly appeals to our passengers.

Malaga is therefore expected to be just as successful as Nice and Barcelona' (Dunn 2001a).

As with Buzz, the sustainability of the Basiq Air business model must be called into question and would undoubtedly experience problems were it not for KLM's patronage. Moreover, Basiq Air's fleet size (Figure 7.1) indicates that it is not a serious competitive challenger within the European LFA market. Basiq Air's integration into Buzz can only be a matter of time.

Learning from the demise of Debonair

The rise of Debonair

The rapid demise of Luton-based Debonair continues to be a spectre hanging over Europe's LFAs. Debonair was founded by Franco Mancassola, a veteran of the airline industry, with 25 years of management experience in US companies such as Continental Airlines, World Airways and Discovery Airways. Debonair commenced operations at London Luton Airport in June 1996 with six Bae 146-200 planes (with 96 seats per aircraft). The company launched services to Munich, Dusseldorf, Copenhagen, Madrid, Newcastle, Rome and Barcelona. Debonair's strategy was to create a series of hubs that would allow passengers to move between several European cities using the same carrier.

Debonair's one-way fares were structured on a four-tier basis, with prices increasing in line with demand. A ticketless reservation system allowed passengers to book directly using Debonair's loyalty card. Passenger booking details were kept on computer, allowing Debonair to provide a personalised service and offer a free flight for every ten booked. Unlike easyJet, booking could also be made on Debonair flights via travel agents. Also, in contrast to easyJet and Ryanair, complimentary beverages and light snacks were offered on Debonair flights.

Debonair commenced operations with the philosophy 'lower fares with minimal restrictions and no compromise on comfort' (Sull 1999, p. 26). As Debonair's CEO Mancassola stated, 'Debonair was designed to offer high quality service at extremely competitive fares'. Debonair targeted business travellers and attempted the impossible strategy of combining high levels of comfort/service with low fares (Porter 1996; Lawton 1999). Its fleet of Bae 146-200s were in fact partly chosen because they were considered the quietest passenger jets available and therefore suited Debonair's emphasis on comfort and business passengers. However, the downside was that they also proved considerably more expensive to operate and had a smaller seat capacity than the Boeing 737, favoured by other LFAs.

The fall of Debonair

Debonair's problems first became evident less than a year after its inception, with the discontinuation of two routes (Luton-Newcastle and Barcelona-Madrid) in early 1997. Management cited insufficient demand as the reason. In 1998 Debonair announced a pre-tax loss of £5.5 million for the first six months. The financial situation worsened from there, with the airline finally declaring bankruptcy in 1999.

Sull (1999) points out that inexpensive fares, more legroom and quiet jets were three of Debonair's key selling points to business travellers, who made up 58 per cent of the airline's passengers. The problem with this approach is that it was not sustainable from a cost perspective. As the Ryanair model outlined in Chapter 6 illustrated, low fares and operating profits can only be sustained in tandem if operational costs are minimised and flight capacity is maximised. Contrary to Sull's (1999) argument, operational efficiency and a reconciliation of the price/service equation cannot be achieved simply through concentrating on point-to-point markets, operating a uniform fleet, concentrating service costs in the UK and subcontracting functions such as maintenance and check-in. On the first point, Debonair's route network was point-to-point but the airline also encouraged passengers to fly from point-to-point and then on to another point. This could result in delays and customer dissatisfaction as it builds an interlining expectation in the minds of passengers. Furthermore, Debonair's 'bus stop principle' simply did not make economic sense. The strategy of operating a single service from London to Munich, Munich to Perugia and Perugia to Rome does not work because the related costs are too high. Much of the fuel cost associated with a flight is expended on the takeoff and landing of the aircraft, thus rendering the Debonair approach extremely fuel intensive. Fuel costs are a large part of an airline's total cost base and passenger numbers on each leg of the flight did not offset the extra costs caused by higher fuel consumption.

On the second point, uniformity of aircraft is important in order to minimise maintenance and crew training costs. However, it must be a uniform *and* cost efficient/revenue maximising fleet. The Bae 146 is a much more costly airplane to operate than the Boeing 737. It also has a significantly lower seat capacity (96 seats on a Debonair Bae 146-200 aircraft, compared with 149 on an easyJet Boeing 737-300). Sull's other points are valid but inadequate. As we have seen in Chapter 6, LFA success is premised on a much more extensive and rigorous adherence to cost reduction than was evident at Debonair.

Also, as is apparent at Virgin Express, Debonair's brand positioning was confused, particularly towards the end of the company's existence. It could not decide whether it was a LFA or a business airline and the resultant confusion and service contradictions severely damaged its cost base. Moreover, Debonair never succeeded in building adequate market awareness or customer recognition.

The challenge ahead: which model for Europe?

easyJet management forecast a number of key competitive challenges ahead. First, intensifying competition between LFAs, as price and frequency further squeeze the yield and core markets (e.g. the UK) reach maturity. A highly publicised example is the competition between easyJet and Go on the London-Nice route. Although Go is highly price competitive on this route, easyJet maintains significantly greater frequency – the main differentiating factor between the two LFAs. A second example is the competition offered by Basiq Air to and from easyJet's Amsterdam hub. Basiq Air is, in effect, a branch of Transavia, KLM's low cost charter airline. Its routes mirror those of easyJet and its inception coincided almost exactly with easyJet's creation of an Amsterdam hub. easyJet claims not to be too perturbed by Basiq Air as it lacks the efficient cost base of easyJet.

Second, is the problem of managing high growth rates. LFAs are locked into 20-25 per cent compound growth rates, which brings enormous pressure to bear on the airlines to deliver such abnormally high growth figures each year. Linked to this is the risk of over-capacity.

Third, controlling the cost-base during the transition from start-up to established company. Renegotiating initial contracts can prove problematic as airports and other suppliers generally seek to raise their prices once an airline shows a profit. Wage inflation also occurs during this period.

Fourth, the threat from charter airlines is real and some are attempting to make the transition to offer scheduled 'seat-only' services. Although charters offer lower cost per ASK, they also have drawbacks relative to LFAs (see Chapter 3 for further details).

Both easyJet and Ryanair experienced conflicts with their base airport during 1999-2001. Cost underlined both disputes. In easyJet's case, the airline witnessed a near four-fold increase in its landing charges at Luton after its initial five year contract ended. This meant an increase from a charge of £1.57 per departing passenger agreed within the terms of the initial contract, to £5.50 under the interim agreement negotiated in early 2001. This fee was confirmed for 20 years from October 2001. The Chief Executive of London Luton Airport defended these price increases, arguing that the new charges were economically sensible and viable and were still below the airport's normal tariff. This view was not shared by easyJet and the airline's future at Luton came into question.

The Ryanair model is much easier to manage than the easyJet model. It will ultimately reach its market limits but this is a long way off. Both models will survive but the Ryanair approach is favoured by financial analysts.

Conclusions

Several key points of differentiation between Europe's LFAs emerged in this chapter. Clear distinctions exist on issues such as customer service emphasis and approach, route network and airport strategy and methods for ticket pricing and sales. The LFA model is not monolithic – alternatives to the Ryanair model have emerged, particularly in service quality, route structure, and even fares themselves. How viable these alternative models are remains to be seen but the success of easyJet (and increasingly Go) indicates that there are more ways than one to be a low fare success story. Despite this fact, one important fact remains: airlines should ensure that an emphasis on cost reduction remains at the core of their strategies and that they do not deviate too much from the main elements of the Ryanair/Southwest model discussed in Chapter 6.

Of the airlines examined in this chapter, easyJet and Go stand out as the best prospect for future expansion and success. This is due to their respective dynamic management teams and charismatic leaders, satisfactory cost bases, quality images and growing brand awareness. Go remains a long way behind Ryanair and easyJet and in competing directly with Ryanair on Dublin to Scotland routes from late 2001, Go's cost reduction model and market appeal will be tested.

Among the others, Buzz and Basiq Air are largely unknown quantities in terms of performance figures, as this data is not publicly available. However, there is evidence to suggest that both would be in serious financial trouble without the backing of their parent company, KLM. The Buzz business model is improving and, given time, might well prove profitable. The issue is whether it will be allowed to transform and consolidate before KLM withdraw their support. Virgin Express has undergone significant restructuring but its business model remains fundamentally flawed. It straddles the business class and low fare markets, ensuring that economy customers expect good prices but costs must remain high if the business customer is to receive the service that he/she requires.

Notes

1   It also appears likely that Basiq Air will be folded into Buzz during 2002 as part of KLMs overall restructuring process.
2   This information is derived from the easyJet Shares Prospectus issued on 15 November 2000, p. 11.
3   easyJet's average passenger load factor is significantly higher than Ryanair's. However, easyJet's break-even load factor is considerably greater than Ryanair's which means that Ryanair achieves better profit margins.
4   Ray Webster, writing in easyJet's Interim Report, 31 March 2001.
5   Data derived from easyJet Shares Prospectus 2000, ibid., pp. 13-14.
6   Ibid., pp. 8-9.
7   These issues were clarified in an interview conducted by this author with Mr Trevor Metson, Fares Manager at the UK Civil Aviation Authority, 18 May 2001.
8   easyJet has in fact moved from a range of four yield classes to thirteen, with a much greater spread of fares, particularly at the top end (interview with CAA official, ibid.).
9   Data derived from a presentation delivered by Nigel Fanning of easyJet.
10   Interview with Toby Nicol, easyJet Corporate Communications Manager, June 2001.
11   Interview with Toby Nicol, easyJet's Corporate Communications Manager, June 2001.
12   Ibid.
13   Jeff Randall 'BA gets back on course now Go has finally gone', Sunday Business, 17 June 2001, p. 18.
14   Barbara Cassani cited in Tom Rubython's 1999 article in *EuroBusiness*, p. 37.
15   Taken from a Go press release, 14 June 2001.
16   This discussion is in large part based on an interview conducted by this author with Go's public relations manager, London, May 2001.
17   Floris van Pallandt cited in Colin Baker (2000) 'KLM uk sets off for low cost growth', *Airline Business,* February, p. 19.
18   This information was provided to this author in a correspondence from a Buzz manager, 27 September 2001.
19   Based on a discussion with a Buzz manager, Stansted Airport, 21 May 2001.
20   Ibid.
21   Mr Ornstein subsequently left the company and became CEO of US regional, Mesa Air Group.

21 Airline executives at Ryanair, Buzz and Go concur that Virgin Express's decision to enter into alliance with Sabena was a serious business error and has undermined the airline's strategy and structure ever since.
22 Interview conducted by this author with an ex-Virgin Express manager, August 2001.
23 Ibid.
24 Interview conducted by this author with Ryanair's commercial director, March 2001.
25 Interview conducted by this author with Go's public relations manager, June 2001.
26 Interview conducted by this author with a senior Buzz manager, May 2001.
27 An anonymous source within the LFA industry
28 Peter Legro cited in the Financial Times, 'KLM challenges easyJet on no-frills routes', 22 November, 2000.

Chapter 8

Trans-Atlantic Lessons

Introduction

The US is the largest commercial air transport market in the world, with the biggest airline companies and the greatest variety of regional and low fare carriers. In addition, the US was ahead of other countries in liberalising the air transport market. Moreover, Southwest Airlines, the original and much copied LFA, is US-based and focused. As such, it is worth examining the US industry and market in comparative context with the EU. This chapter begins by examining the development of the US airline industry in the post-deregulation era. This is followed by an evaluation of the Southwest model and the essence of its success. Finally, the more recent wave of US LFAs are examined, particularly the strategies and structures of prominent new entrants such as JetBlue, Vanguard and AirTran.

From deregulation to consolidation: the development of the US airline market

Gudmundsson states that from 1978 to 1989 approximately 88 jet-operating airlines (scheduled, charter and cargo) were formed in the US, of which 83 failed (1998, p.217). Another 164 airlines were planned but never even got off the ground. Since the deregulation of US commercial aviation in 1978, a total of 120 airlines have gone bankrupt. In the decade and a half after liberalisation of the industry, 34 carriers began new, primarily scheduled, passenger services. Of these, only one – America West – survived and grew into a major scheduled, low cost company (but not without going into and out of Chapter 11 bankruptcy in the process). All other newly formed scheduled carriers went bankrupt within a few years (with the exception of high-income carrier, Midwest Express).[1] These included Pacific East, Pacific Express and American International (founded in 1982 and bankrupt by 1984); Hawaii Express (founded in 1982 and bankrupt by 1983); Air One (founded in 1983 and bankrupt by 1984); and Northeastern (founded in 1983 and bankrupt by

1985). Other prominent start-ups lasted a few years longer but ultimately disappeared. These included Midway Airlines (founded in 1979 and bankrupt by 1991), Braniff (founded in 1984 and out of business by 1989) and People Express (founded in 1981 and acquired by Texas Air in 1986). New carriers have tended to fall prey to predatory pricing by major airlines and their own poor planning and inefficiencies. As Barkin et al. comment, 'traditional carriers have faced low-cost competitors not once but twice, successfully beating them off in the early 1980s only to see a resurgence a decade later' (1995, p. 87).

The second round of LFAs in the US emerged in the 1990s. 27 new scheduled airlines were founded between 1992 and 1995 alone. These varied in size and nature from the likes of Frontier Airlines (commenced operations in mid-1994 and based out of Denver) to ValuJet (founded in late 1993 and based in Atlanta) to Reno Air (started in mid-1992 and based in Reno, Nevada). The new entrants of the 1990s had several advantages over their predecessors that emerged in the wake of airline deregulation. Two important advantages were first, many markets were uncontested; and second, public sources of capital were plentiful (Schultz and Schultz 2000, p. 90). A third advantage was the ability to take advantage of the surplus capacity that resulted from aggressive fleet expansion in the late 1980s and depressed demand for air travel in the early 1990s (Barkin et al. 1995, p. 88). The downturn of the early 1990s forced many airlines out of business or caused them to cut back on staff. This allowed new entrants to acquire aircraft and people at low cost. More than 650 jet aircraft were for sale or lease at the end of 1992, which was about three times as many as in the late 1980s. Also, in excess of 50,000 airline industry employees had lost their jobs in the 1990-92 period and were therefore in search of work.

The new entrants also benefited from active government support. Unlike the Reagan and Bush administrations, the Clinton Administration actively sought to assist new airlines in navigating through regulatory barriers and in staving off the predatory behaviour of larger, established carriers (Schultz and Schultz 2000, p. 91). In all, more than 100 start-up airlines sought approval to fly in the 1992/3 period. This is despite the fact that the years 1990-3 were the worst in the history of the US civil aviation business (Schultz and Schultz 2000, p. 89). One such new entrant was Morris Air, which began scheduled services in 1992. Morris Air owed much of its subsequent success to cost cutting innovations and to its discipline in filling a well-defined market niche (Schultz and Schultz 2000, p. 87). The company's innovations included the pioneering of ticketless travel, later to become a LFA norm. An example of Morris Air's success was that in 1993, it achieved an operating cost per available seat mile (ASM) of 6 cents, compared with

Southwest's figure of 7.03 cents and an industry average of 10.5 cents. Although Morris Air was subsequently sold to Southwest, the sale did net a sizeable profit for its shareholders.

Despite success stories such as Morris Air, many of the second round LFAs also ran into problems or went out of business. John Ash, managing director at Global Aviation Associates in Washington D.C. argues that this is because 'the vast majority are ill-conceived from a strategic point of view and inadequately financed'.[2] In addition, many of the new entrants found it difficult to compete once the cost of aircraft and personnel began to rise again. The ValuJet crash in 1996 caused further turbulence in the low fare sector of the market and the after shock was felt especially hard by the less resilient start-ups. Many of the new entrants failed also because of insufficient revenue. Some gained the traffic and decent load factors with low fares but not enough revenue to make them profitable (Nuutinen 1996a, p. 9). This illustrates the danger of pricing too low – particularly at below cost level.

The major US airlines responded to the LFA onslaught of the 1990s in a different way than a decade earlier: this time around most of the major carriers established low fare subsidiaries to compete directly with the new entrants (as well as to challenge the growing market strength and route expansion of the original LFA, Southwest). The first to do so was Continental, with the creation of Continental Lite in 1993. In line with LFA norms, Continental Lite lowered fares, eliminated free meals and business/first class cabins, increased departure frequency and reduced gate turnaround time. However, Continental Lite was an unmitigated failure, as it straddled both the low fare and full fare markets (Porter 1996). Unlike established LFAs such as Southwest, Continental Lite operated as both a point-to-point and a hubbing carrier in many markets. This meant that its turnaround time was increased due to interlining. Also, costs remained higher than low fare competitors because Continental Lite operated a mixed fleet and sold most tickets via travel agents.

United Airlines was next to respond, launching Shuttle by United. This offshoot was unlike most LFAs though, offering frills such as a business class section, assigned seating and hot meals. United Shuttle engaged in fierce competition with Southwest Airlines on the US west coast. It later withdrew from some of these competitive markets and concentrated on its Los Angeles and San Francisco hubs, providing a feeder service for its longer haul flights from these airports. The organisation's performance subsequently improved (Nuutinen 1996b, p. 10).

Delta Airlines launched Delta Express in October 1996, operating a fleet of Boeing 737-200 aircraft and initially linking Orlando with eight cities in the

Midwest and Northeast United States. Delta Express offered a hybrid service: advance seat assignment, free snacks and frequent flyer programme participation but no first class, hot meals or other frills (Nuutinen 1996b, p. 8). The pricing structure for Delta Express was simple: 14 and 21 day advance purchase tickets started as low as $59 on long-haul routes. As with LFAs, the aircraft cabin was also reconfigured to accommodate more seats (12 more than on Delta's 737s). In addition, Delta Express sought a 70 per cent higher daily utilisation of its aircraft – 12 hours, compared to Delta's 7 hours. The introduction of Delta Express caused considerable problems for many smaller carriers operating on north-south routes. Airlines affected included American TransAir, AirTran, Spirit, JetTrain and, to a lesser extent, Southwest. Orlando-based AirTran was one of the worst hit carriers and subsequently pulled out of three markets – Nashville, Providence and Hartford – because it believed that its single daily flights could not compete with high-frequency services introduced by Delta Express to these routes (Nuutinen 1996b, p. 9). The aggressive competition introduced by Delta Express weakened AirTran to the point where it became a target for takeover. This subsequently occurred when ValuJet management bought out AirTran. However, Delta Express has failed to undermine the low fare leader, Southwest, which remains more profitable on seven out of eight routes where the two carriers compete. The only route where Delta retains a (slight) profit lead is Raleigh-Orlando and Southwest is relatively new to this route. It may soon overtake Delta Express on this route too.

In mid-1998, another major – US Airways – launched MetroJet as its response to low fare competitors. MetroJet began by offering low fare services to four destinations from its base at Baltimore, Maryland. Both Southwest Airlines and Delta Express had begun to erode US Airways east coast territory. MetroJet operated Boeing 737-200 aircraft with 118 economy class seats. As with LFAs, MetroJet does not offer a business or first class section and the in-flight snack consists of a soft drink and bag of peanuts. MetroJet continues to compete but struggles to succeed. On almost all routes where it competes with Southwest, Southwest remains the profit leader.

Instead of keeping Southwest and other LFAs in-check – if not driving them out of business – the low cost experiments of airlines like Continental and United have mainly caused problems for other majors. Continental Lite did serious damage to USAir while United Shuttle drove all of United's high cost competitors out of California (Nuutinen 1996a, p. 6). These low fare offshoots of the majors damaged some LFAs – such as the original AirTran and Spirit. However, the more robust LFAs – primarily Southwest – remained largely unscathed. Furthermore, in the wake of the September 2001 crisis, Metrojet, Delta Express and United Shuttle services were all significantly reduced,[3] whilst Southwest made no changes to its schedule. Other prominent LFAs, such as JetBlue and AirTran, added new services to fill the vacuum left by cutbacks at Metrojet and Delta Express.[4]

The contemporary policy environment for LFAs

In 1996, the US Department of Transportation (DoT) declared that:

> the rapid growth and competitive success of low-cost, low-fare airlines has reduced the cost of flying for Americans by $6.3 billion over the past year…these low fares have encouraged more people to fly, stimulating growth in the aviation industry and the economy.[5]

According to a 1996 DoT study of the LFA impact on the aviation market, LFAs have had a substantial part to play in the growth of the industry. The study showed that in the early 1990s, the total number of passengers in markets with low fare carriers tripled, while the number of passengers without access to low fare carriers fell. By the mid-1990s, almost 40 per cent of passengers within the US were flying in markets where a low fare competitor existed, compared with under 15 per cent in 1988.

LFA executives such as Joe Leonard, Chief Executive of AirTran Airways spend significant time in Washington D.C., lobbying, testifying and otherwise pressuring policymakers and legislators (Field 2001b, p. 42). The primary objective of this lobbying is to improve airport access for smaller and new entrant airlines, particularly at slot-controlled hubs such as Washington Reagan National Airport. Companies like AirTran claim some success in these efforts. For instance, the airline directly attributes its entry into the limited access market of New York La Guardia Airport to the political lobbying efforts of its chief executive.

The US government is taking some – albeit cautious – steps to respond to this lobbying by airlines and to support new entrants. AIR-21 legislation earmarks slots for new entrants but real infrastructure constraints may limit the full impact of this legislation. The effect of AIR-21 does appear to be nominal. For instance, at Washington National Airport, the legislation created 24 new slots that were awarded to specific carriers on specific routes. LFAs such as AirTran argue that not enough slots were dispensed and that they alone would need ten times the number of slots allocated at Washington National (Field 2001b, p. 43). On a positive note, LFA executives acknowledge that AIR-21 does require airports to produce plans to encourage competition before they can raise departure fees or qualify for certain federal grants.

The DoT has made pronouncements on competition and warned the majors that it will be monitoring the business to ensure that large carriers do not engage in predatory behaviour. The DoT did in fact bring an antitrust suit against American Airlines for its predatory practices against SunJet, Vanguard and Western Pacific. This was the first predatory pricing case brought in many years.

US regional airlines: low fare competitors or a different market segment?

The US Regional Airlines Association (RAA) define a regional airline as one operating short and medium-haul scheduled services connecting smaller communities with larger cities and connecting hubs and operating 19 to 68 seat turboprops and 30 to 100 seat regional jets. This definition is similar to that advanced by the European Regions Airline Association in Chapter 3. The two primary issues distinguishing a regional airline from a LFA are first, LFAs serve 'dense' routes, i.e. routes between two major population centres; and second, LFAs usually operate a standard 148 seat Boeing jet aircraft and, unlike regionals, would never operate an aircraft with a capacity of less than 100 passengers.

As of mid-2001, there were 97 regional airlines in the US, serving 678 commercial airports and carrying approximately 85 million passengers during 2000 (up from 78.1 million in 1999). This is a 49 per cent increase on the 1995 figure and more than double the total number of passengers carried by regionals in 1990. The total fleet size of the US regional airlines is more than 2,000 and of these, 18 per cent are regional jets and the remainder are turbo props of various sizes and type. The average age of the fleet is 8-9 years, significantly lower than the average age of larger airline fleets.

Interestingly, 50 code-sharing agreements exist between regional and major airlines and these account for the majority of passenger numbers. In 1999 for instance, 97 per cent of regional airline passengers travelled on code-sharing regional airlines. The reasons varied but included the perceived safety assurance of a regional being in a code share with a major and the convenience of interlining directly to a regional destination. The RAA have found that around 65 per cent of regional airline passengers are business travellers. Also, most prefer code-sharing regional and major airline partners to have adjacent gate areas.

A major constraint on the growth of regional carriers is the lack of airport capacity in the US, particularly at the larger hubs. This is bolstered by the limitations on the air traffic control system and the increased regulatory cost burden. Industry and FAA growth predictions for 2005 are for passenger numbers to reach 104 million, revenue passenger miles to grow to 31 million (from 20.8 million in 1999) and aircraft fleet to increase to 2,500. The proportion of regional jets is also predicted to increase significantly (fuelled by passenger's dislike of turboprop), representing about 50 per cent of the total fleet in 2005 and carrying approximately 70 per cent of passengers.

The US regional airline industry experienced significant growth during the 1990s and into the early 21st century. Most of this expansion occurred independent of the low fare sector, as regionals and LFAs tend to serve different markets. This reinforces the European findings detailed in Chapter 3 of this book.

Southwest Airlines: the original of the species

Commencing service in 1971, with three Boeing 737-200 aircraft and flights to Houston, Dallas, and San Antonio, Texas, Southwest Airlines has grown to become the fifth largest US airline, flying over 50 million passengers a year to more than fifty cities around the US Some analysts predict that Southwest will become the largest domestic carrier by 2005.[6] Southwest became a major player in 1989 when it exceeded the billion-dollar revenue mark. The company was the only major US airline to make net and operating profits during the first three years of the 1990s, when the US airline industry experienced a significant downturn in growth and sales revenue. Southwest is the US's only major short haul, low fare, high frequency, point-to-point carrier.

Since 1990, the US airline industry has witnessed the collapse of such prominent airlines as Pan Am, Eastern and Midway, as well as continual financial problems at large airlines like Continental and TWA. Profitability became a goal rather than an actuality for many carriers. Airline debt in the US reached $36 billion by the mid-1990s. During this entire period Southwest continued to expand and turn a profit. The company continued to experience traffic growth of up to 36 per cent annually. Its stock performed formidably, trading at twenty times earnings, compared with an industry norm of half that figure. Moreover, Poor and Moody gave it the highest credit rating in the business (Freiberg and Freiberg 2001, p. 5).

Southwest was built to meet the needs of the short-haul, point-to-point customer and this remains the primary focus for the airline. As a result, approximately 70-80 per cent of Southwest's passengers fly non-stop, in sharp contrast to a hub-and-spoke carrier, which concentrates on connecting traffic. Southwest avoids 'costly and complicated' interlining arrangements with other carriers. Evidence of Southwest's non-reliance on hubs can be found in the fact that its capacity is spread throughout the US Unlike hub-and-spoke competitors who have large concentrations of flights at a couple of hub cities, Southwest has 45 per cent of its capacity in the western US, 25 per cent in the East, 16 per cent in the Midwest and 14 per cent in Texas and surrounding states.

The average age of Southwest's aircraft in December 2000 was 8.2 years and aircraft utilisation was 11 hours and 18 minutes per day. With only 57 cities and less than 10 per cent of the domestic market, Southwest still has significant opportunities to expand its route system in both new and existing cities.

Southwest Airlines serves price and convenience sensitive travellers. The essence of its strategy is in the activities: choosing to perform activities differently or to perform different activities than rivals. For instance, Porter provides evidence that Southwest tailors all its activities to deliver low-cost, convenient service on its particular type of route. Through fast turnarounds at the gate of only fifteen minutes, Southwest is able to keep planes flying longer hours than rivals and provide frequent departures with fewer aircraft (1996, p.64). Southwest does not offer meals, assigned seats, interline baggage checking, or premium class of service. Automated ticketing at the gate is thought to encourage some customers to bypass travel agents, allowing Southwest to avoid their commissions. A standardised fleet of Boeing 737 aircraft boosts the efficiency of maintenance.

Southwest has staked out a unique and valuable strategic position based on a tailored set of activities. On the routes served by Southwest, a full service airline could never be as convenient or as low cost (Porter 1996, p.64). Collins and Porras argue that genuinely successful companies understand the difference between what should never change and what should be open for change, between what is truly untouchable and what is not (1996, p.66). Southwest is an example of such a company, regularly innovating and constantly differentiating itself from the competition but resisting the urge to tamper with the fundamental features of their strategy formula.

Southwest's rapid gate turnaround, which allows frequent departures and greater use of aircraft, is essential to its high-convenience, low-cost positioning. This is achieved in part due to the company's well-paid gate and ground crews, whose productivity in turnarounds is enhanced by flexible union rules. The bigger part of the answer lies in how Southwest performs other activities. With no meals, no seat assignment, and no interline baggage transfers, Southwest avoids having to perform activities that slow down other airlines. It selects airports and routes to avoid congestion that introduce delays.

The Southwest model is not necessarily easily transferable. As we saw earlier in this chapter, Continental and United Airlines both attempted to copy the Southwest model for their low-cost US subsidiaries. They were able to duplicate the route structure and other observable and quantifiable elements but they failed to emulate the Southwest culture (or organisational capabilities) – the key to its success (Couvert, 1996, p.61).

Williams describes Southwest Airlines and its CEO Herb Kelleher as a 'master scale orchestrator' (1998, p. 41). By this he is referring to a management style that benefits from economies of scale but requires organisational capabilities that go beyond size for the sake of size. In using the orchestra metaphor, Williams refers to how the four sections of a symphony orchestra (string, bass, percussion and woodwind) are difficult to master individually, yet world-class orchestras achieve excellence and balance across all sections simultaneously (1998, p. 21). The simple point is that excellence is more than the sum of its parts. So it is with Southwest Airlines. Its orchestration – or balancing – of volume growth, product design, process improvement and organisational learning illustrates how elements of a scale orchestra best fit together in a service business.

A consistent market share of at least 60 per cent on virtually every airport route pair it serves is evidence of Southwest's short haul dominance (Freiberg and Freiberg 2001, p. 6). It is the US industry productivity leader in the following respects (Freiberg and Freiberg 2001, p.7):

- Workforce; services twice the number of passengers per employee as any other airline (annual average of 2,400 passengers per employee).
- More daily departures per gate.
- More productive hours out of an airplane.
- Lowest cost per ASM (compared with equivalent aircraft stage lengths).

Southwest has always been known as a maverick and an innovator in the US airline industry. When it introduced permanently low fares in the early 1970s, it went against the basic premise of the industry that this would reduce revenue. It also challenged the underlying presumption by most carriers that only two market segments existed: those who could afford to fly and those who could not (Freiberg and Freiberg 2001, p.28). Southwest introduced a simple two-tiered pricing structure – peak and off-peak – that eventually became standard practice for many airlines. They introduced even lower prices for seats on off-peak flights so as to fill as many seats as possible. This practice meant that their revenue generation was based on a system of maximising capacity rather than yield – a revolutionary approach in the airline business of the 1970s.

The Southwest strategy is not market share led. Rather, the company focuses on keeping costs down in order to increase profitability. The low costs lead to low fares that in turn translate into increased market share. Herb Kelleher believes that this is where many airlines have gone wrong – emphasising market share before cost reduction. He underscores this point with the simple statement that:

Market share has nothing to do with profitability…Market share says we just want to be big; we don't care if we make money doing it.[7]

As with Ryanair and other genuine LFAs, Southwest is willing to forego ostensibly lucrative routes if they are likely to disproportionately increase its costs. For example, although Chicago's O'Hare Airport to New York's La Guardia is a dense air corridor with many frequent flying business travellers, Southwest will not attempt to enter due to the increased landing and related airport charges that would be incurred, as well as the adverse impact on aircraft turnaround time (and therefore utilisation) that would result from serving such congested airports. Similarly in Europe, Ryanair would not contemplate serving airport such as London Heathrow, Frankfurt International or Paris Charles de Gaulle for the same reasons. A key explanatory variable in the success of LFAs emerges here: by focusing on profitability rather than market share, companies such as Southwest (and Ryanair) have been willing to forego dense, often high yield routes that might distort their cost reduction model. This constitutes what Porter (1996) describes as the willingness to make hard choice and strategic trade-offs in order to maintain a successful strategic position in your market or markets.

In 1973, Southwest was the first company in the airline industry to introduce a profit-sharing plan for employees. Nowadays, all Southwest employees become participants on the 1 January following their date of employment. The company invests 15 per cent of its pre-tax operating income into its profit sharing plan. A minimum of 25 per cent per employee must be reinvested in Southwest stock. This means that approximately 12 per cent of the company is owned by its employees (Freiberg and Freiberg 2001, pp. 99-100). Profit sharing serves two important purposes. First, it increases employee morale and loyalty to the organisation. Second, it can translate into increased productivity and consequently, reduced costs and increased revenue. This policy has since been mimicked in Europe by airlines such as Ryanair and Go.

Southwest place considerable emphasis on corporate culture as a vital ingredient in their success. Freiberg and Freiberg argue that culture is the glue that holds any organisation together, encompassing beliefs, expectations, norms, rituals, communication patterns, symbols, heroes and reward structures (2001, pp. 144-5). Strategy and culture are inextricably intertwined at Southwest, serving to reinforce the distinctive capabilities of the company.

Southwest's performance highlights

Table 8.1 Southwest Airlines consolidated highlights

	2000	**1999**	**Change**
Operating revenues	$5,649,560	$4,735,587	19.3%
Operating expenses	$4,628,415	$3,954,011	17.1%
Net income	$625,224*	$474,378	31.8%
Net margin	11.1%*	10.0%	1.1 pts.
Revenue passenger miles	42,215,162	36,479,322	15.7%
Available seat miles	59,909,965	52,855,467	13.3%
Passenger load factor	70.5%	69.0%	1.5 pts.
Number of employees	29,274	27,653	5.9%

Source: data derived from Southwest Airlines Co. Annual Report 2000.

Dollars in thousands except per share amounts
*Excludes cumulative effect of change in accounting principle of $22.1 million ($0.04 per share).

As Table 8.1 illustrates, the year 2000 witnessed an increase in revenue passenger miles (RPMs) and a resultant 3.6 per cent increase in passenger revenue yield per RPM. The increase in passenger yield was partly due to an 8.2 per cent increase in average passenger fare, partially offset by a 4.6 per cent increase in average length of passenger haul. The increase in average passenger fare was due to fare increases combined with a higher mix of full fare passengers. The increase in RPMs exceeded a 13.3 per cent increase in available seat miles (ASMs), resulting in a load factor of 70.5 per cent, up 1.5 per cent on the previous year (Figure 8.2). The increase in ASM resulted primarily from the net addition of 32 aircraft during 2000.

Excluding fuel costs, operating expenses per ASM decreased 2.6 per cent in 2000. Salaries, wages and benefits per ASM increased slightly, as increases in productivity in several areas of operations were offset by higher benefit costs and increases in average wage rates.

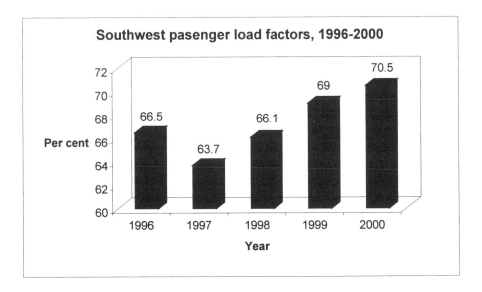

Figure 8.1 Southwest passenger load factors, 1996-2000
Source: data derived from Southwest Airlines Co. Annual Report 2000 and miscellaneous
Southwest website data.

At the end of 2000, Southwest operated 344 Boeing 737s and provided services to 58 airports in 29 states. Southwest has the lowest operating cost structure in the US airline industry and consistently offers the lowest and simplest fares. The company also has one of the best overall customer service records. The year 2000 was Southwest's 28th consecutive year of profitability and ninth consecutive year of increased profits. This occurred despite a surge in oil prices from $11 a barrel in 1999 to a high point of $37 a barrel in 2000. Southwest managed to suppress unit costs, excluding fuel, by 2.6 per cent. Southwest estimate that they provide approximately 90 per cent of all low fare airline competition in the US.

Southwest – the customer service leader

In 2000, for the fourth consecutive year, *Fortune* magazine named Southwest one of the top five 'Best Companies to Work for in America'. Fortune magazine also again named Southwest the most admired airline in the US. Frequent customers receive Rapid Rewards wherein after purchasing and flying eight roundtrips, a customer receives a roundtrip ticket valid for travel anywhere on the Southwest system for up to a year. There are no restrictions on the awards and few blackout dates around holidays. Flight credits can also be earned through purchases with several car rental and hotel partners as well as through the use of the Southwest Rapid Rewards Visa card. In 2000, Inside Flyer magazine placed Southwest's Rapid Rewards programme first in the Best Customer Service, Best Bonus Promotion and Best Award Redemption categories.

Southwest was also number three in 2000 (and number one in 1999) in the National Airline Quality Rating study conducted annually by aviation experts at the University of Nebraska and Wichita State University (see Chapter 5 for further details).

Of the major airlines in the US, Southwest scores best in measures of customer satisfaction. In the year ended 31 December 2000, the DoT received 0.47 complaints per 100,000 customers boarded on Southwest. This compared to 5.30 per 100,000 for United Airlines and 3.54 for American Airlines for example.

Southwest argues that its success (measured in terms of profitability and customer satisfaction) is due to the following:

- low fares
- few restrictions
- generous frequent flyer programme
- high frequency service
- wide range of destinations
- young, all jet fleet
- total 'trip time' (both on the air and ground) kept to a minimum
- convenient airports
- point-to-point service
- quick and simple ticketing, boarding and seating procedures (non-assigned)
- high standards of reliability (measured in terms of on-time performance, few flight cancellations and low levels of mishandled baggage, etc.)
- caring, friendly, fun-loving customer service.

Is Southwest unassailable?

Southwest's impeccable record for on-time performance suffered a setback during the 1998-2000 period. Its monthly on-time performance dropped considerably relative to its peers. Southwest was still scoring quite high but instead of ranking first or second, it was regularly ranking sixth, seventh and even eighth (Flint 2000, p. 48). The key reasons for Southwest's relative slump in on-time performance were at first difficult to discern. However, it then became apparent that problems began when Southwest expanded significantly on the East Coast of the US, adding six cities in that region between January 1997 and May 1999. More weather challenged airports together with increased congestion (and the related air traffic control problems) and more problematic ground handling unions, seemed to be hampering Southwest's high utilisation/rapid turnaround time model. However, Southwest's Chairman Herb Kelleher downplayed these explanations, arguing instead that Southwest's rising average load factor and unwillingness to 'artificially stretch its block times' (i.e. the time its aircraft spend at the gate) precipitated the decline in on-time performance (Flint 2000, p. 48). More people on the average flight inevitably slows the turnaround time. Maintaining the same time allocation per flight segment when competitors are increasing theirs also serves to disadvantage Southwest in performance tables. Goldman Sachs analyst Glenn Engel added another factor to the equation: annual industry cancellation rates during the 1999-2000 period averaged three per cent, compared with less than one per cent at Southwest. This indicates a trade-off, with Southwest willing to suffer more late departures instead of increased flight cancellations.

PaineWebber analyst Sam Buttrick, speaking about Southwest, states that: 'I've spent the best part of the last decade trying to find its soft underbelly, whether such-and-such is justified and what could go wrong. I've pretty much come up empty-handed.'[8]

The new breed of low fare competitor: JetBlue Airways

...the most impressive airline of its kind since Southwest Airlines began operations...(Avmark Aviation Economist, November 2000).

In examining the new crop of LFAs in the US, one stands out as being particularly well planned, structured and financed. JetBlue Airways is ahead of the competition, having turned a profit within six months of its launch and expanding at a steady pace from its New York base.

David Neeleman, a man with a proven track record in the LFA business, founded JetBlue Airways in 1999. Neeleman was founder and CEO of Morris Air between 1984 and 1995[9] and subsequently played a role in the establishment of WestJet Airlines, the leading Canadian LFA (see Chapter 9). JetBlue attracted media and investor attention from the outset. It had $130 million in start-up financing, the largest capitalisation in history of any start-up airline. It also had a fleet of 10 new 162 seater A320s, an attractive pricing policy and experienced LFA management (several of whom previously worked for Southwest Airlines). Most notably perhaps, JetBlue claimed to be 'New York's new hometown airline', establishing its base at New York's

Kennedy International Airport. Deprived of low fare stimulus after the demise of People Express, air traffic from the New York region stagnated during the 1990s. Traffic at the three New York airports accounted for 10 per cent of all US domestic boardings in the mid-1980s. This figure had fallen to five per cent by the end of the 1990s. An opportunity beckoned for a LFA entrepreneur like David Neeleman: New York had huge, previously exploited market potential; it was abused by the major airlines through high pricing; and it was only served in a peripheral fashion by the low fare leader, Southwest (Solon 2000, p.4).

Kennedy was chosen above New York's other airports due to its gross under-utilisation during most hours of the day because of its heavy proportion of international flights (Shifrin 2000, p.42). Most of New York's domestic flights operate from LaGuardia or Newark airports. The appeal of New York is obviously the large and highly mobile market. There are 18 million people in the New York metropolitan area. Added to this is New York's attraction as a business and tourist destination for people from many other regions of the U.S. JetBlue management believe that these factors outweigh the high landing fees and facilities rentals at New York. Moreover, they argue that the reasonable costs at other airports in their system offset the costs accrued in New York. This approach differs from the Southwest model, in not serving secondary airports. However, it does equate with the approach of low fare carriers easyJet and Buzz in Europe. The JetBlue approach is further evidence that deviations from the Southwest/Ryanair model appear tenable, particularly if the purpose is to attract the low end of the business market.

Surface access to JFK International is problematic at present, being further from Manhattan than La Guardia or Newark and more expensive to get to by taxi. This is being addressed however, as a light rail system is being built which will link JFK directly to the New York subway system and to the Long Island rail network.

JetBlue's management team pay close attention to the lessons learned from People Express Airlines, which operated low fare services from a Newark hub between 1981 and 1986. People Express expanded rapidly in the first half of the 1980s by using its low fare, no frills concept on routes abandoned or little served by the major carriers. It thrived until the major airlines retaliated by using their yield management systems to sell spare capacity at equally low fares. People Express responded by trying to expand and over-extended itself. It incurred massive losses and was acquired in 1987 by Texas International (Barkin et al. 1995, pp. 87-8).

JetBlue has five fares on each route: 14 day or 7 day advance booking (with the option of peak or off-peak rates) and a more expensive fare that can be purchased on the day of departure. All fares are priced on a one-way basis with no requirement for a Saturday night stay over. Overbooking is avoided as all bookings must be accompanied by credit payment within 24 hours. All tickets are non-refundable but passengers who cancel their flights will receive a one year credit for future flights (minus a $25 rebooking charge).

Pricing is highly competitive. For instance, in early 2001 JetBlue offered one way fares from New York to Orlando ranging in price from $70 to $199. This compared with fares from Delta Airlines on the same route ranging from $70 to $584.

There were several reasons for JetBlue's selection of the Airbus 320 aircraft ahead of the standard LFA aircraft, the Boeing 737-700. CEO Neeleman argued that it was a difficult decision but the A320 was selected for three reasons: first, it allowed for 24 more passengers than the Boeing 737; second, it also offered more legroom for passengers than competing economy class cabins;[10] and third, it burns less fuel than the 737 (Shifrin 2000, p. 43). By mid-2001, JetBlue had a fleet of 10 aircraft, with the intention of growing to 40 by 2005. An option for 42 more aircraft will come into play in 2004.

As already witnessed with the choice of New York's JFK Airport as its base, JetBlue is not afraid to deviate from the tried and tested Southwest model. It goes further in trying to distinguish itself through service innovation:

> JetBlue is low-price and all coach, like Southwest Airlines, yet hip and sassy, like Virgin Atlantic (Time, 2001).

This fits with JetBlue's strategy aimed at the frugal yet style-conscious consumer. JetBue has furnished all of its aircraft with leather seats, enhancing passenger comfort. This costs twice as much as fabric but is more durable. Also, passengers can access 24 live TV channels for free from the individual monitors in each seatback. Oversized overhead storage bins allow passengers to fit suitcases and roll-on bags more easily. Finally, there is more legroom (a generous 32 inch seat pitch) and a slightly wider seat bottom than on the Boeing 737. This is particularly important on the longer flights such as the five hour coast-to-coast service. As is standard for LFAs, there is no free in-flight meal but beverages and snacks are provided at a charge.

JetBlue is ticketless, which translates into administrative savings. Furthermore, more than 40 per cent of JetBlue's tickets are currently sold online. This percentage is well below the rates for Ryanair and easyJet in Europe but significantly higher than the US industry average. Unlike Southwest, JetBlue has pre-assigned seating. This also contrasts with Ryanair but coincides with the policies of both Go and Buzz. A JetBlue innovation is that passengers can select their own seats via the Internet by clicking on a diagram of the JetBlue aircraft, with available seats appearing in green. The absence of pre-assigned seating is one of the major complaints from frequent travellers on Southwest, as it can make it difficult for families or business groups to fly together.[11]

JetBlue is concerned with efficiency: it plans to operate 12 flights a day from each gate at Kennedy and aims at a turnaround time of 30 minutes (slightly more than Southwest's 20 minutes). All flight and ground crew are taught the 'one minute rule': the airline expects there to be just one minute between the time that the last passenger disembarks and the first passenger boards for the next flight (Shifrin 2000, p. 43). A double jet bridge system is operated to speed the process and flight attendants use handheld vacuum cleaners to tidy the aircraft as passengers disembark.

JetBlue needs to keep costs at under seven cents per seat mile if it is to remain on a par with Southwest. A breakeven load factor of around 50 per cent is required.

How did JetBlue get into JFK? According to Dirk Kronemeyer, head of e-business at Buzz, JetBlue 'harnessed the political process and the demand of passengers for low fares' to achieve its commercial goals. With effective lobbying, JetBlue was awarded 75 slots at JFK, to be phased in over three years. The poor service reputation of JFK, combined with a decade of over-pricing and market stagnation in the New York air travel market, meant that jetBlue attracted some influential political support. This included Rudolph Giuliani, Mayor of New York City, New York State's Governor Pataki and both of New York's US senators.

JetBlue announced on 23 May 2001 that Long Beach Airport in southern California would be its second base of operations, with 27 daily departures to as many as 15 cities by 2003. JetBlue's first service, to New York's JFK, commenced at the end of August 2001.[12] Long Beach has a chequered history is terms of attracting and losing airlines, due to the noise restrictions governing the area. This has been a growth obstacle for larger airlines such as America West and American Airlines. This is not a hindrance for JetBlue, as it uses only new A320 aircraft. JetBlue were attracted to Long Beach due to its under-utlilisation and its proximity to both Los Angeles and Orange County. Long Beach, former home to the commercial aircraft operations of McDonnell Douglas, has a catchment area of more than 6 million people, five runways and limited commercial services (Shifrin 2001, p. 15). Long Beach's noise sensitivity means that the number of daily departures from the airport is limited to 41. JetBlue was awarded all 27 slots that were not being used.

In terms of competition, JetBlue plans to avoid direct competition with Southwest, which offers services from Islip on Long Island, New York, about 40 miles from Manhattan (Zellner 1999, p. 8).

JetBlue's recipe for success[13]

For JetBlue, emulation of the Southwest approach was a given, as Neeleman had done in the past with Morris Air: 'Like Ryanair's Michael O'Leary, Neeleman believed that there as no shame in following a successful model, adapted to local conditions' (Solon 2000, p. 4). However, as we have already seen, the New York-based carrier does deviate from the model (e.g. operating to and from some major airports and offering pre-assigned seating) and has introduced a number of service innovations such as leather seats, more legroom and larger overhead bins. Neeleman argues that there are four main reasons for the failure of most airline start-ups in the US in the post-deregulation era. These are: (1) weak management teams, often consisting of people who had failed at established carriers; (2) bad business plans, often basing the airlines in markets too small to support operations of significant scale; (3) inadequate equity financing; and (4) fleets of old, second-hand aircraft, subject to reliability problems and high maintenance costs.

Neeleman addressed the first problem by recruiting a seasoned management team with relevant experience of low cost airline operations and the New York regional market. On the issue of business planning, the JetBlue management team launched a suitably modified version of the Southwest model, aimed at a very large and overpriced market with significant traffic stimulation potential.

Service is point-to-point with all flights originating or terminating at JFK. JetBlue points out that although 'Southwest claims to be a point-to-point operator, it offers significant through-plane service frequencies and operates de facto connecting hubs with high service frequencies at Baltimore, Nashville and Kansas City' (p. 5).

JetBlue was profitable within six months of operation, a remarkable achievement in an industry used to long lead times before reaching profitability. It turned its first profit in August 2000, as had been project in its financial plan. It is highly unusual for a start-up airline to move into the black so rapidly. On the strength of this performance, JetBlue obtained a further $30 million in equity capital, bringing total commitments to $160 million.[14] David Neeleman's comments: 'my philosophy is that you can never have too much cash in the airline business...' (p. 6). In making this point, Neeleman has learned from the lesson of People Express and other bankrupt low fare start-ups. These were often driven out of business due to under-capitalisation that left them incapable of surviving protracted price leadership battles with established carriers.

The fourth key element of survival and success in JetBlue's strategy is the acquisition of new aircraft. JetBlue management view the standard start-up practice of acquiring used Boeing and other aircraft as false economy. In their view, reliability and low maintenance costs easily outweigh minimal first cost. Moreover, new aircraft instil a sense of trust among passengers in the safety of an untried new airline. Again, the acquisition of new aircraft is common practice for Southwest.

As with Southwest, a key element of JetBlue's business model is to stimulate traffic. A key difference from the Southwest business model is JetBlue's emphasis on taking frequent flyer business traffic from conventional competitors. An important element of this objective is the reward mechanism. Like Southwest (but unlike Europe's LFAs), JetBlue has a loyalty or 'appreciation' programme for its frequent flyers. This entails the award of a (restricted) free flight ticket to passengers upon the purchase of a set number of trips.

In its first six months of operations (February-August 2000), JetBlue maintained very impressive operating statistics. Overall on-time performance was 80.25 per cent (within 15 minutes of schedule) and the passenger load factor was 71.6 per cent. The airline had carried 500,000 passengers by early September 2000. By mid-2001, the load factor had risen to around 80 per cent, compared with a US industry average of 68.4 per cent:

> …JetBlue appears likely to be a successful variation on the Southwest theme. It is still early days but this airline looks like a long-term winner (Solon 2000, p. 7).

Interestingly, JetBlue does not set a maximum flight duration as is the case – unofficially – for many European LFAs. It offers several direct coast-to-coast services, many of them being overnight 'red eye' flights. For example, JetBlue departs from Oakland, California before midnight, arriving at New York's JFK airport before 8am the next morning.[15] One way fares on these routes range between $99 and $299. The lowest fare is some 62 per cent below conventional carriers' cheapest regular advance purchase prices. Not surprisingly, load factors have been very high.

Southwest Airlines view David Neeleman as a genuine market threat, with Southwest Chairman Herb Kelleher describing Neeleman as 'a genius'. So much so that upon leaving Southwest in the mid-1990s, Neeleman was obliged to sign a five year non-compete agreement. During this period Neeleman had ample time to work on and refine his plan for JetBlue.

In early 2001, JetBlue was voted the US's number two economy airline in the Zagat Airline Survey. The number one economy airline in the 2001 survey was Midwest Express, which offers business-class service at full coach fares. In the survey, in which more than 30,000 fliers participated, JetBlue outscored all the major airlines. The survey covers 70 domestic and international airlines, and surveyors rated airlines separately for 'comfort', 'service' and 'food'. JetBlue ranked second in the 'service' and 'comfort' categories and tied fifth in the 'food' category, despite the fact that the carrier serves snacks rather than meals. 'This Zagat rating is a great achievement for JetBlue,' said David Neeleman, CEO of JetBlue. 'To be voted the country's number two economy airline by the people who fly us means that we're doing exactly what we set out to do when we launched a year ago – that is, bringing humanity back to air travel by offering passengers low fares, great customer service and friendly staff.'[16]

The DoT received a total of five complaints about JetBlue in 2000, which equals approximately 0.5 complaints per 100,000 enplanements. By comparison, the ten largest carriers averaged nearly six times this number, with 2.98 complaints per 100,000 enplanements through 2000. It also compares favourably with 0.47 complaints per 100,000 for industry leader Southwest. Furthermore, JetBlue recorded a total of 2.7 mishandled bags per 1,000 enplanements through 31 December, compared to an average of 5.29 per 1,000 enplanements for the ten largest carriers in 2000.

AirTran Airways: putting their troubles behind them?

Another contemporary success story has been Orlando-based AirTran Airways. AirTran emerged from the ruins of ValuJet, the prominent LFA that went out of business after the 1996 crash of its McDonnell Douglas DC-9 in the Florida Everglades with the loss of 110 lives. Using funds acquired in the pre-crash public flotation of ValuJet, management bought the failing AirTran Airways and adopted this name for the organisation. Surplus cash was used to purchase a new fleet of Boeing 717s and to weather three years of losses, totalling $278 million. For several years, AirTran shunned large-scale media attention, seeking instead to rid itself of association with the ValuJet brand in the minds of the travelling public. By 2001 AirTran was again profitable and eager for publicity (Field 2001, p. 42). The turnaround was aided by Boeing who, in 2000, helped AirTran to reduce some of their $230 million debt. Boeings's assistance was due to the fact that AirTran was a critical launch customer for Boeing's 717 aircraft. In the same year, the airline realised a record net profit of $47.4 million on total revenue of $624.1 million. This was a 63 per cent increase on the previous year's net earnings of $29.1 million (on total operating revenue of $503.8 million). Revenue passenger miles increased by 19 per cent from 3.5 billion in 1999 to 4.1 billion in 2000 and traffic numbers increased from 6.5 million to 7.5 million during the same period. Moreover, revenue per available seat mile (ASM) increased 16 per cent to 10.3 cents. Finally, load factors increased, rising from 63.5 per cent in 1999 to 70.2 per cent in 2000.[17]

By mid-2001, AirTran recorded its ninth consecutive quarter of profits. For the second quarter of 2001, traffic grew by 17.8 per cent, an increase of 15.9 per cent in capacity. Load factor for the second quarter increased by 1.2 points, to 74 per cent, compared to 72.8 per cent in the second quarter of 2000. For the first six months of 2001, RPMs rose 23.9 per cent on a 17.5 per cent increase in ASMs and load factor rose 3.8 percentage points, to 72.3 per cent from 68.6 per cent in the first six months of 2000. AirTran has also won a reputation for safety, earning six consecutive annual Diamond Awards from the Federal Aviation Administration for excellent in maintenance training. AirTran's main competitor, Delta Airlines/Delta Express, in comparison, struggled during the same period, incurring losses for the first time in several years.

As with all LFAs, a significant competitive threat to AirTran comes from aggressive price matching or undercutting by large traditional carriers. In mid-2001, AirTran's largest competitor, Delta Airlines, began to match AirTran's prices and ticket flexibility on flights from Atlanta – a core hub for both Delta and AirTran. UBS Warburg airline analyst Jamie Baker warned that this could expose as much as 40 per cent of AirTran's revenue base to Delta discounts and risks undermining AirTran's healthy profitability.[18] A similar response was evoked from US Airways when AirTran began services between Pittsburgh and Philadelphia, two key US Airways hubs.

Despite these market threats, AirTran retains some significant advantages. Its Boeing 717s aircraft are fuel efficient and still relatively young and not in need of major repairs. AirTran has 22 717s in service, out of a total fleet of 58 planes. This figure is due to increase to 52 by early 2002, as AirTran phases out its Boeing 737 and DC-9 planes. The airline retains options and purchase rights on 48 more 717s through until 2005.

A problem looming with AirTran is the possibility that it will begin to straddle markets (Porter 1996) through its intended business class product.

With 12 business class seats and 105 coach seats, the 717 can accommodate coach passengers who wish to upgrade for a $25 fee per flight segment. Air Tran tends to target business customers who are small business owners or managers. In part recognition of this service, AirTran was named the best low fare airline for both 1998 and 2001 by *Entrepreneur* magazine. The magazine's Editorial Director, Rieva Lesonsky, stated that:

> AirTran Airways meets all of our criteria for an award-winning airline by offering low fares, easy business class upgrades and policies that never require a round trip purchase or Saturday night stay – all amenities that business travellers require.[19]

Further indications of AirTran's market straddling efforts to be both a low fare and a high quality service provider include:

- advanced seating assignments
- frequent flyer programme
- full participation in travel agents computer reservation systems.

Also, the airline has 4,000 employees in total, which is a very high staff-customer ratio, compared with LFAs such as JetBlue or Ryanair. All of these variables illustrate AirTran's deviation from the cost structures and strategic priorities of successful LFAs.

To date, these LFA deviations do not appear to have detrimentally affected AirTran. In August 2001, AirTran's holding company moved from the American to the New York Stock Exchange, signalling the low fare carrier's rapid rise towards major carrier status (Sobie 2001a). All US majors are already traded on the New York Stock Exchange (NYSE), but most regional and national carriers are traded on the smaller American or NASDAQ exchanges. Along with Midwest Express, however, AirTran will be only the second national or regional carrier to trade on the NYSE. All other publicly traded carriers in this category – including American TransAir, Atlantic Coast Airlines, Frontier Airlines, Hawaiian Airlines, Mesa Airlines, Mesaba Airlines, Midway Airlines and SkyWest Airlines – are listed on the American or NASDAQ exchanges.

Nonetheless, a question mark must remain about the company's future performance, given its lack of rigour on constant cost reduction and its efforts to be both a low price and a business class operator. This market straddling approach inevitably leads to failure, as the Debonair example in Chapter 7 and the Continental Lite example earlier in this chapter illustrated.

Vanguard Airlines: the problems of market straddling

Having examined a number of low fare success stories – both old and new – we now turn to an airline that has a more varied record. As with the likely impending problems at AirTran, we argue that Vanguard's problems have been caused by its market straddling strategy, due to the company's efforts to be both a low fare and a high quality provider.

Incorporated in 1994, Kansas City, Missouri based Vanguard Airlines provided jet services to 14 cities across the US. The airline claims to offer low fares with no advance booking requirements, advanced seating assignment and extra legroom. In 2001 it operated a fleet of nine Boeing 737s and four Boeing MD-80 aircraft. Interestingly, Vanguard is transitioning away from the 737s and towards the MD-80s, actually returning 737-200 planes to the lessors upon taking possession of the MD-80s. This strategy is set to continue through 2002-3. As we have seen in previous chapters, these aircraft are not normally used by LFAs as their operational costs and seat capacity are not considered adequate. Vanguard offers some competition to JetBlue, primarily on the New York-California routes. Passengers cannot fly direct though, having to stop first in Kansas City when travelling from New York City (La Guardia Airport) to San Francisco.

Vanguard has experienced some significant problems. It posted a net loss of $2.7 million for the second quarter of 2000, which rose to a net loss of $6.8 million for the second quarter of 2001. Total operating revenues for the second quarter of 2001 decreased by 20 per cent to $30.2 million from $37.6 million in the same quarter of 2000. This is despite realising a reduction of 11 per cent in total operating expenses, from $40.1 million to $35.8 million during the same periods. The airline's losses have also increased despite an increase in its monthly load factor. Load factors increased by a significant 10.6 points between June 2000 and June 2001, rising from 61.5 per cent to 72.1 per cent (clearly putting them in the LFA category on this measure). Furthermore RPMs increased by five per cent at Vanguard, from 271.6 million to 284.1 million. Capacity decreased by 11 per cent though, going from 441.4 million ASMs in the second quarter of 2000 to 393.9 million ASMs during the second quarter of 2001.

This is evidently a mixed record but rising losses and declining revenues do signal trouble. What factors can we identify as the root cause of Vanguard's poor performance? One explanation comes from Scott Dickson, Chairman, CEO and President at Vanguard. He says that:

> The second quarter [of 2001] was a transition period for Vanguard...The quarter continued and intensified the reconfiguration of our route system to operate longer-

haul flights, saw the airline transition to Sabre as its host reservations system and brought the introduction of MD-80 series aircraft into our fleet. These changes had a significant adverse impact on revenues and expenses during the second quarter.[20]

Going into more detail, Vanguard management argue that the airline's route restructuring (moving into longer haul, lower frequency routes) has increased certain costs and undermined revenue generation. They emphasise that this will change as they consolidate the new routes and build their reputation in these areas.

A further explanatory factor in Vanguard's woes appears to be the airline's very high breakeven load factor. Vanguard's breakeven load factor (BELF) for the three months ended 30 June 2001 for example, was 89.2 per cent. This compares with a BELF of 66.2 per cent for the same period in 2000. By comparison, Europe's leading LFA, Ryanair, achieves an average BELF of 54 per cent. The importance of maintaining a low BELF – certainly lower than your overall load factor – was emphasised in previous chapters. In the case of Vanguard, their BELF in mid-2001 was 17.1 per cent higher than their actual load factor. This differential translates into substantial losses for an organisation and is unsustainable over a period of time.

All of the above factors are undeniably important and do help to explain in part the travails of Vanguard. However, it is only when we undertake a larger, strategic analysis that we can identify the carrier's core dilemma. Applying the strategic positioning model developed in Chapter 6, it becomes apparent that Vanguard is straddling markets, trying to be both a low fare and a business class operator. The crux of the problem is that the airline markets itself as a low price carrier but combines this with a business class service on its flights (the business class cabin is called 'SkyBox'). It is impossible to make money with the resultant BELFs and the Vanguard data proves the point that market straddling clearly does not make business sense.

An ominous note emerges in Vanguard's interim financial statement of 30 June 2001, presented to the US Securities and Exchange Commission. It is pointed out that for the six months ended 30 June, 2001 and the year ended 31 December 2000, the company incurred a net loss of $18 million and $26 million respectively. The airline also had a working capital deficiency and stockholders deficit at 30 June 2001 of approximately $41 million and $25 million respectively. The statement goes on to say that 'these conditions raise substantial doubt about the Company's ability to continue as a going concern' (2001, p. 8). Although Vanguard was seeking to raise additional capital, there was no assurance that it would raise enough to fund ongoing operations. If this were the case, Vanguard would have to cease operations.

Other 'lower' fare airlines

There are other airlines within the US that may lay claim to the low fare title or have been identified as such by industry commentators. These include Denver-based Frontier Airlines, serving 22 cities with a fleet of 28 aircraft (mostly Boeing 737s), which describes itself as 'an affordable fare airline'; and Sun Country Airlines, based out of Minneapolis, offering 'friendly service and good value for customers'[21] and flying only Boeing 737s. While these airlines compete largely on price and meet many of the LFA criteria embedded in the Southwest model, they deviate in certain important ways. The most common deviation is that they offer a full service to passengers and usually have both economy and business class cabins on each flight. Many of these carriers were adversely affected by predatory behaviour by the majors and the US economic slowdown in 2001. As with AirTran, Frontier Airlines saw its profits erode as a result of increased competition from major carriers, which have slashed fares to offset steep declines in business traffic. The weakening US economy further undermined Frontier's profits (Sobie 2001b). Frontier's chief operating office, Jeff Potter, commented:

> Like the rest of the industry, we have experienced the impact of a slowing economy and a highly competitive marketplace…However, we are pleased that we have been able to maintain profitability during this economic downturn given that the current softening economy coincides with our Airbus transition and the increased costs associated with that transition (Sobie 2000b).

The industry crisis of late 2001 heralded further problems for many of the lower fare airlines in the US. Frontier Airlines was forced to cut nine per cent of its workforce and 3.2 per cent of its daily flights. Smaller LFAs with weaker market profiles fared even worse:[22] Spirit Airlines cut its schedule in half after the 11 September attacks; Vanguard Airlines reduced its schedule by 20 per cent; and Sun Country posted losses for the eighth consecutive quarter, with no end in sight to its cash haemorrhage.

Conclusions

Freiberg and Freiberg (2001) argue that the essence of Southwest's success is 'discipline'. Since its inception, Southwest has relentlessly adhered to its low cost/low fare strategic vision and operational model. Comparing this with the European context, only Ryanair appears as focused and disciplined as Southwest in adhering rigidly to its low cost/low fare model. However, as we saw in Chapter 6, there are some fundamental differences between the Southwest and the Ryanair model, particularly on the issue of customer service (as we defined it in Chapter 5). Of the US low fare new entrants since the mid-1990s, JetBlue appears best placed to challenge Southwest in the future. However, questions must be raised about its cost base, which is not as low as Southwest's due to their use of some more expensive airports, less dense aircraft seat configuration and loss of turnaround time because of pre-assigned seating. All of the US LFAs were adversely affected by the New York and Washington D.C. airplane crashes of September 2001. Those best able to survive this and similar calamities possessed the largest cash resources. This emphasises the necessity to maintain a constant and rigorous focus on cost reduction and profit generation. In this regard, no US company has yet come close to matching Southwest.

Notes

1   Midwest Express was in a different category as it focused on high yield traffic and avoided low cost/low fare operations.
2   John Ash cited in Jones (1996) 'Baby boomers', p. 22.
3   Industry analysts also indicated that Metrojet and United's Shuttle were in fact being phased out.
4   Marilyn Adams 'Discount airlines see better odds as others slash flights', USA Today, 26 October, 2001, pp. 3A-B.
5   This is according to a study titled *The low cost airline service revolution*, released by the US Department of Transportation in April 1996.
6   These include Darryl Jenkins, Director of the Aviation Institute at The George Washington University in Washington D.C., cited in Marilyn Adams (2001), op. cit.
7   Herb Kelleher, CEO of Southwest Airlines, cited in Freiberg and Freiberg (2001), NUTS!, p. 49.
8   Cited in Joan M. Feldman (2000) 'IT, culture and Southwest', Air Transport World, No.5, p. 46.
9   Morris Air was bought by Southwest Airlines in 1993, netting Neeleman a profit of 20 million. Neeleman remained in charge of Morris Air, running it as a Southwest clone, until his departure in 1995.
10   A relatively generous 32 inch pitch and one inch of extra seat bottom width per passenger compared with the Boeing 737.
11   This argument is advanced in an Avmark Aviation Economist article on JetBlue's corporate strategy, November 2000, p. 5.

12 Ralph Olsen writing about Long Beach Airport in Airliner World, August 2001, p. 81.

13 A significant portion of this section is drawn from a corporate strategy analysis in Avmark Aviation Economist, November 2000. This was based on interviews with senior management at JetBlue, including the CEO, CFO and Head of Marketing and Sales.

14 JetBlue's equity capital was garnered from some of the most seasoned investors, including George Soros's Quantum Fund ($40 million) and the Chase Capital unit of Chase Manhattan Bank ($20 million).

15 The time is adjusted to account for the fact that California is three hours behind New York.

16 Taken from a press release on JetBlue's website, dated 20 March, 2001, www.jetblue.com

17 Data derived from AirTran's 2000 annual report.

18 Quoted in David Field, 'Back in the limelight', *Airline Business*, 2001, p. 44.

19 Quoted on *Business Wire*, 1 May, 201, www.businesswire.com/webbox/bw.050101/211212616.htm

20 Scott Dickson is quoted on the Vanguard Airlines website, www.flyvanguard.com

21 This is according to Sun Country Airlines CEO, Bill La Macchia, in the welcome introduction to the 'About Us' section of the airline's website, www.suncountry.com

22 Marilyn Adams 'Discount airlines see better odds as others slash flights', USA Today, 26 October, 2001, pp. 3A-B.

Chapter 9

The Global Emergence of Price-Based Competitors

Introduction

Beyond Europe and the US, LFAs have developed in a number of countries across the globe. Canada and Australia have been at the forefront, with countries as far apart as Japan, Brazil and South Africa also experiencing the challenges and opportunities of low fare competition. This chapter examines the Canadian and Australian contexts in some detail, charting the structures and strategies of companies like WestJet, Impulse and Virgin Blue and examining the response of incumbent airlines to these new market entrants. In both countries, the airline industry has undergone major restructuring, in no small part as a result of the competitive dynamics unleashed by the LFAs. The chapter concludes by looking briefly at some of the other countries around the world – particularly in Latin America – where LFAs have emerged and considers their experiences and prospects.

Low fare airline competition in Canada

During the 1999 to 2001 period, Canadian air transport went through a protracted transformation. The 1999 takeover of Canadian Airlines by its main rival Air Canada prompted a degree of market vibrancy never before witnessed in Canadian aviation (long used to a market carefully controlled and co-ordinated by government). Charters converted to scheduled services and start-ups flourished (Knibb 2001b, p. 101). By the first quarter of 2001, the shake-up had run its course. By mid-year, all of the start-ups had gone. A spate of mergers and acquisitions resulted in three significant competitors left standing in the Canadian market. Air Canada remained by far the largest, a status confirmed by its acquisition of Canadian Airlines. Canada 3000 had also grown through acquisition, subsuming both Royal Airlines and CanJet to become a major force in Canadian aviation. WestJet emerged as the third significant pan-Canadian competitor. Unlike now defunct Canadian start-ups such as CanJet, Roots Air and Greyhound Airlines, WestJet succeeded in growing organically and achieving progressively higher net earnings on a year on year basis.

WestJet will be discussed in more detail in the next section of this chapter. First, a word about CanJet, a LFA that appeared promising at its outset but failed to survive for long on its own. CanJet was set up in the summer of 2000 as the low cost airline for I.M.P. Group of Halifax, Nova Scotia. I.M.P. Group is one of Canada's largest aerospace, general aviation and flight management companies and also owns Execaire, the largest executive jet charter company in Canada. CanJet's market focus was eastern and central Canada, setting Winnipeg and St. John's as the two cities on the western and eastern extremities of its market scope. I.M.P. executives believed that its extensive maintenance facilities – located at all of the main airports in eastern Canada – would ensure that CanJet had the lowest costs of any Canadian airline. This was reinforced by an experienced management team, many of whom had run I.M.P.'s Air Atlantic for 15 years.[1] Less than one year later, former charter airline Canada 3000 bought CanJet for seven million Canadian Dollars (C$) in stock, marking the second major acquisition in a short space of time by the largest domestic competitor after Air Canada. So, what went wrong at CanJet? Unconfirmed reports indicated that CanJet was losing about C$2 million a month before its acquisition. The carrier was embroiled in a legal dispute with Air Canada, which was before the federal Competition Bureau. CanJet accused the national carrier of predatory pricing on routes where they were in direct competition. Moreover, CanJet commenced operations just as the market began to experience a downturn because of the flagging North American economy. It never had time to establish itself in good times and to build up sufficient customer loyalty and cash resources to sustain it during hard times.

CanJet management appeared positive about the acquisition, with the chairman and CEO of parent group I.M.P. commenting that the two companies would be in a better position to compete as a team. This sentiment was echoed by Canada 3000 president, Angus Kinnear, who stated that the mergers were necessary to create a national alternative to Air Canada, which controlled 80 per cent of the market.[2] The enlarged Canada 3000 was in a position to capture up to 30 per cent of the Canadian market. However, learning from the mistakes of Canadian Airlines, Canada 3000 aim to avoid consistent direct competition with Air Canada.

At the outset in mid-2001, the combined entity (also including Montreal-based Royal Airlines, acquired in March 2001) had revenue of more than C$1 billion, 4,400 employees and a fleet of 40 aircraft. Despite these substantial figures, the airline was only one tenth the size of Air Canada. Nevertheless, industry commentators[3] argued that the merger was advantageous for the industry, preventing a vigorous competitive rivalry that was likely to weaken all three of the original airlines. Also, it created a credible competitor to Air Canada in the wake of the Canadian Airlines takeover by the national airline. Although small, Canada 3000 appeared to be better managed and financially more robust than Canadian Airlines had been during its final years as an independent company. Time would tell.

WestJet Airlines: the successful growth of a low fare alternative

The third main competitor in the Canadian airline industry is a LFA Calgary-based WestJet Airlines. The idea behind WestJet emerged in the mid-1990s, when a small group of cost conscious businessmen in western Canada realised the need for a low fare airline on key routes such as Calgary to Vancouver. Tim Morgan of Morgan Air, together with Calgary businessmen Clive Beddoe, Donald Bell and Mark Hill, believed that the potential market was not just in western Canada but ultimately right across the country. They began to examine successful low fare airlines in the US, including the ubiquitous Southwest Airlines and smaller operations such as Morris Air. David Neeleman, then president of Morris Air and later founder of JetBlue, was asked to advise the Canadians on their business plan. He subsequently became the fifth member of the WestJet Airlines founding team.[4] Initial capital was raised swiftly from other Calgary businesspeople. The airline came to life during the summer of 1995, as its corporate offices opened in downtown Calgary. Its first aircraft were purchased that November and in January 1996, further capital was raised from retail and institutional investors. This allowed WestJet to commence operations in February 1996 as a low cost, low fare, short-haul airline, serving markets in western Canada with a fleet of three Boeing 737-200 aircraft. The initial city-pairs served by WestJet were Vancouver, Calgary, Kelowna, Edmonton and Winnipeg. Since then, the airline has expanded to serve other western Canadian cities such as Victoria, Regina, Saskatoon, Thunder Bay and Prince George.

WestJet met a major business goal when it completed its Initial Public Offering of 2.5 million common shares in July 1999. The capital raised was primarily used to finance fleet expansion and to build new corporate offices and hangar facilities for the company in Calgary.

By 2000, WestJet was ready to go nationwide with its successful formula of low costs, low fares and frequent flights, usually between uncrowded secondary airports (Knibb 2000a, p. 16). The carrier began its pan-Canadian expansion plans in early 2000, with the opening of a service to Hamilton, Ontario. Hamilton is an attractive airport due to its low costs, lack of congestion and relative proximity to Toronto, which is 45 miles away. The airline subsequently set out to build Hamilton as its eastern hub. Moncton, New Brunswick and Ottawa were added to WestJet's eastern network during 2000.

By July 2001, WestJet served 17 Canadian cities with a fleet of 23 Boeing 737-200 aircraft.[5] The company's operating performance continued to improve on previous years (Table 9.1). Operating revenue grew by 47 per cent to C$205.1 million during the first six months of 2001. Net earnings increased by 20.9 per cent, from C$11.6 million during the first half of 2000 to C$14.1 million from January to July 2001. This growth in profits occurred despite an increase of 14 per cent in the cost of fuel. Capacity, measured in available seat miles (ASMs), increased by 58.3 per cent during the first half of 2001and revenue passenger miles (RPMs) grew by 55.1 per cent. Diluted earnings per share also climbed, from 26 to 30 cents during the same period. These figures indicated rapid market acceptance of WestJet's added capacity. The airline's load factor also improved during the 2000/1 period, rising from 72.9 to 73.3 per cent. Further cost efficiencies are likely to occur as the first half of 2001 also saw an increase in average stage length from 420 to 438 miles, resulting in decreased cost per ASM (down 2 per cent). [6] The phased introduction of the new Boeing 737-700 series aircraft is likely to realise further cost reductions for WestJet.

Table 9.1 WestJet operating highlights, 1998-2000

	2000	**1999**	**1998**
Load factor	72.9%	70.8%	69.7%
Revenue per passenger mile (Canadian cents)	22.7	21.3	18.2
Revenue per available seat mile (Canadian cents)	16.5	15.1	12.7
Cost per passenger mile (Canadian cents)	19.6	18.7	17.3
Cost per available seat mile (Canadian cents)	14.3	13.3	12.0

Source: Data derived from WestJet Airlines Ltd. *Expanding Horizons,* Annual Report 2000.

Not content to rest on its laurels, WestJet continued its expansion strategy. In September 2001, the airline announced the opening of a new service between Hamilton and Sudbury, Ontario from December of that year. One-way fares on the new route were due to start at C$79. This marked the airline's eighteenth destination within Canada. As with all airlines, the events of 11 September in the US had an impact on WestJet. However, as with Southwest and Ryanair, WestJet's cash resources and business model were resilient enough to ensure that the Canadian carrier weathered the subsequent industry downturn.

Comparing WestJet with Air Canada and Canada 3000

Fare prices are a significant first point of comparison between Canada's main airlines. This is particularly true for tickets purchased on the day of departure. For example, in mid-2001 WestJet's highest fare from Vancouver to Calgary was C$213. Air Canada's full fare on the same route was double the price.[7] Also, at the lower end of the price sale, Air Canada imposes more restrictions than WestJet, e.g. obligatory Saturday night stop-over, advance purchase rules and the sale of return tickets only.

WestJet is conscious of not deviating from its Southwest-style strategy of building frequencies to established destinations and cautiously expanding its route network, rather than developing a sprawling but low frequency route map (Knibb 2001b, p. 102). Some commentators[8] argue that the low fare carrier has actually favoured route expansion over building frequency but on the whole it has managed to maintain a balance. This organic growth strategy contrasts with the acquisition-led approach of its two main rivals, Air Canada and Canada 3000. Also, Canada 3000, best known in the past as both a charter and low price scheduled carrier, has moved away from low fare nuances with the addition of a business class service. In so doing, the carrier is directly targeting the business traveller and competing with Air Canada for this profitable market.

Canada 3000 has ambitions to become an international alternative to Air Canada. This includes interlining with foreign airlines and participation in global alliances. As Knibb (2001b) points out, there is an obvious gap in the Oneworld alliance with the demise of Canadian Airlines and Canada 3000's membership in the American Airlines loyalty programme would indicate that it is leaning towards this partnership. WestJet, by comparison, has no international ambitions, beyond possibly some trans-border services to the US during the next few years. WestJet simply wants to maintain its status as Canada's most profitable airline and the 'Southwest of the north'.

When we examine key operating statistics for the three main competitors (Table 9.2), it is clear that although WestJet is by far the smaller airline in terms of passenger traffic, fleet size and so forth, its profit margins on operating revenue is substantially higher than both of its larger rivals (10.1 per cent compared with just over 1 per cent for Air Canada and 1.2 per cent for Canada 3000). This ratio compares favourably with US low fare leader, Southwest Airlines, which achieved a profit margin of 11.1 per cent in 2000. Europe's low fare leader, Ryanair, remains well ahead of both, with a margin of 21.5 per cent in 2000.

Table 9.2 Comparative statistics for Canada's three largest airlines (2000)

	Air Canada	Canada 3000	WestJet
Passenger traffic *(RPKs billion)*	68.5	9.8	0.3
Seat capacity *(ASKs billions)*	95.3	11.6	0.9
Domestic market share	73%	13%	14%
Fleet size	375	36	23
Destinations	150	100	18
Employees	40,000	4,400	1,700
Revenue	C$7.9 billion	C$0.8 billion	C$0.3 billion
Profit	C$82 million	C$9.6 million	C$30.3 million

Source: Reproduced from Knibb (2001b) *Canadian challengers*, p. 104.

* C$1 = US$1.55

Analysis by HSBC Securities and others reveals that Air Canada's dominance in the domestic market is not as unassailable as it may appear. On Canada's 15 busiest routes for instance, Air Canada has a 61 per cent market share. Its overall market share is higher because of its almost total control of secondary routes, many of which it is required by the government to serve for socio-political reasons. These routes are avoided by the likes of WestJet and Canada 3000 as they are too small to produce much if any profit. Air Canada is dominant in eastern Canada. However, on transcontinental routes, it controls only slightly more than half of the market, whilst in western Canada, its share falls below 50 per cent.[9] Competition from WestJet and Canada 3000 has clearly eroded Air Canada's dominance in certain market segments and geographical areas. Whilst WestJet is targeting price sensitive travellers and the western provinces, Canada 3000 is pursuing the business traveller and is strong on transcontinental, eastern Canadian and international routes. Although both companies remain a long way behind Air Canada in sheer scale and scope, they are succeeding in making inroads into some of its core markets.

Air Canada's low fare spin-off

In mid-July 2001, Air Canada's CEO Robert Milton, announced that the country's pre-eminent airline would enter the low fare market:

> Air Canada want to compete in the low cost market because that is where the customers want to go and where there is money to be made (Robert Milton, CEO of Air Canada, 2001).[10]

Air Canada had to first strike a deal with pilots unions so as to clear the way for its entry into the low fare business. Such an agreement was necessary to allow a no frills subsidiary to operate with more flexible labour terms and working conditions.[11] The pilots were concerned that they should remain Air Canada employees and retain all associated benefits. Air Canada's decision to start its own LFA signalled an end to a previous agreement it had with Skyservices Airlines to run a jointly owned discount carrier. Air Canada's pilots opposed this deal, arguing that it violated their contracts. Air Canada preferred to maintain the support of its pilots above the Skyservice deal, a fact acknowledged by Air Canada CEO Milton. The termination of the Air Canada-Skyservice alliance signalled the end to Roots Air, a short-lived LFA launched by Skyservice. The move came as Air Canada found itself under increasing market pressure from Canada 3000 and WestJet, both of which were gaining larger market share through offering lower fares. Also, economic slowdown in North America during 2000/1 precipitated a contraction in the high yield business traveller market, traditionally where Air Canada makes most of its profit.

Air Canada reported a seasonally adjusted basic loss of C$279 million in the fourth quarter of 2000. This represented the largest basic quarterly loss ever for Air Canada.[12] The poor performance indicated the malaise within the national carrier and led to restructuring initiatives among senior management. Air Canada's move into the low fare market appears to have been prompted particularly by a slump in business travel – long the primary income stream for the airline. A further reason was the changing regulatory environment, specifically the US-Canada bilateral agreement that liberalised cross-border aviation between the two countries. This precipitated a growth in the number of (primarily US) regional airlines flying north-south on routes such as Ottawa to Washington D.C., and further eroded Air Canada's route dominance and operating revenue. 'Air Canada Lite', as it became known in the industry, was announced in mid-2001, with the projected transfer of 20 Boeing 737-200 aircraft from the main fleet to the discount subsidiary (Knibb 2001a, p. 20). In October 2001, the low fare subsidiary was officially named 'Tango' and commenced services on 1 November. No minimum stay or advance purchase were required for Tango tickets and all tickets were electronic. In addition to routes within Canada, Tango offered some cross-border services to the US (primarily between Toronto and Montreal and a number of cities in Florida). Based in Vancouver, Tango signified Air Canada's intention to take on WestJet and Canada 3000 in the region where they were inflicting most damage on Air Canada's business. In an apparent managerial coup, Air Canada secured former WestJet chief executive, Stephen Smith, to run the low fare carrier. Air Canada's chief executive, Robert Milton, commented that Smith's appointment would provide the low fare subsidiary with the strategic vision and leadership needed to survive and flourish in the low fare sector.[13]

A potential regulatory impediment exists for Air Canada. Canadian competition law prohibits an airline from matching rival fares if they fall below its own costs. This means that in order to offer low fares, Air Canada's low fare offshoot will have to ensure even lower costs. This could prove difficult, particularly given that Air Canada's highly unionised – and expensive – employee structure limits its cost flexibility from the outset. Analysts doubt that Air Canada can genuinely match WestJet's costs (Knibb 2001b, p. 104).

It is generally accepted that the Canadian aviation market was not big enough for two competitors when the two – Air Canada and Canadian Airlines – were competing in much the same fashion for precisely the same markets. However, the more recent stratification of the market and consolidation of a serious low fare competitor would indicate that two, if not three, airlines should be able to compete, survive and perhaps even turn a profit.

Low fare airlines in Australia

In the year 2000, two LFAs entered the Australian market, posing a direct challenge to the nationwide duopoly of Qantas Airways and Ansett Australia.

It signified the first serious challenge in almost a decade to the incumbents and industry commentators speculated on their response (Knibb 2000b, p. 76). Australia was seen as ripe for low fare competition, with many industry analysts[14] arguing that fares were more expensive on a cost-per-km basis than in the US or Europe. The new competitive dynamics emerged from a combination of international airline alliances and acquisitions, as well as a policy shift in Canberra. On the first, the Air New Zealand (ANZ) takeover of Ansett was approved by the Australian government in June 2000, which fulfilled the conditions for Singapore Airlines (SIA) to buy into ANZ. This in turn ended SIA's flirtation with Virgin's proposed Australian start-up, leaving the Virgin Group to go it alone in the Australian market. On the second point, as with Canada, the Australian government was hesitant to make the transition from a policy approach that privileged two carriers, through a lacklustre deregulation process and ultimately to lifting the cap on foreign ownership (Knibb 2000b, p. 76). In moving to this later policy position, the Australian government were, in effect, accepting that deregulation had failed. Significant criticism was indeed levied at the way in which the government handled the deregulation of Australian air transport, initiated in 1990. For instance, controversy still surrounds the failure of the post-deregulation Compass start-up carrier, with allegations that the government failed to prevent predatory behaviour by Ansett and Qantas (still part state owned at that time). Also, little was done to break up the control that these two airlines had over Australia's regional carriers and the preferential agreements that they had with virtually all of the country's travel agents. In effect, deregulation occurred without any attempts being made to wrest control of the infrastructure and distribution system from the incumbents – a point noted by Gerry McGowan, chairman of 2000 new entrant, Impulse Airlines.[15] This began to change in the mid-1990s when a new government introduced an airport privatisation programme. This programme included the provision that airport bidders must provide terminal space for new entrants. This was followed in the late 1990s by the previously mentioned decision of the Australian government to remove the cap on foreign ownership of domestic airlines. Richard Branson's Virgin Group had been interested for some time in establishing a presence in the Australian market but was only lukewarm about doing so in partnership with another organisation. The 1999 legislation meant that it could establish its own airline, on its own terms.

Virgin Blue

Virgin Blue was founded in mid-2000, as a wholly owned subsidiary of the Virgin Group. The carrier launched its first route between Brisbane and Sydney and leased five Boeing 737-400s from Virgin Express. The new airline flew straight into a fare war and the highest jet fuel prices in a decade (Thomas 2000b, p. 74). It was further hampered by regulation; Australia's Civil Aviation Authority initially refused approval to fly Brisbane-Sydney, forcing Virgin Blue to defer the service and to refund approximately A$150,000 in advance bookings. This gave rival LFA, Impulse Airlines, (see next section) a market opportunity and they promptly announced a Brisbane-Sydney service, starting at A$33 one way for Internet bookings. This was the lowest ticket price ever seen in Australia and was less than one-tenth the price of a Qantas or Ansett ticket on the same route (Thomas 2000b, p. 74). Nonetheless, both incumbents matched this bargain price, as it had done with all other low fares offered by Impulse. When Virgin Blue was finally permitted to enter the Brisbane-Sydney market on 31 August 2000, it offered introductory one-way fare of A$48 but by this time the marketing momentum had been lost.

The airline's growth strategy is focused on underserved markets away from crowded and slot constrained airports and where there is traffic growth potential. For example, the Brisbane-Adelaide route was seen as one such prospect. This was a relatively thin route but had potential with the VFR market in particular.

Virgin Blue is expected to make losses for three or four years. As Virgin Group Chairman Richard Branson argued:

> If you offer over 50% of your seats at under A$100, you can't expect great profits. And we're not looking for great profits.[16]

The company posted a modest A$518,962 operating profit in its first 7 months of operation. The net result after abnormal items for the 16 month reporting period from incorporation to 31 March 2001 was a loss of A$10.8 million. Management were satisfied with this performance as the operating profit came ahead of schedule and was earned despite the Australian dollar's record low, high jet fuel prices and extreme competitive pressures.

A total of 641,113 passengers were carried up to 31 March 2001 with load factors averaging more than 74 per cent. This load factor compares very favourably with LFAs elsewhere in the world. For example, in the same period Southwest Airlines achieved an average load factor of 70.5 per cent, Ryanair reached 72.5 per cent and WestJet attained a 72.9 per cent average.

In July 2001, Virgin Blue finally entered the Sydney-Melbourne route, Australia's busiest business route. This sent a clear signal (primarily to Qantas) that Virgin Blue intended to build loyalty amongst corporate travellers.

In September 2001, Virgin Blue reaffirmed that it would remain committed to a low fare strategy, despite the demise of Ansett and the chance that Australia would return to a duopoly situation, with Qantas and Virgin Blue as the only two national carriers.[17] The low fare carrier also rejected a A$250 million offer to be bought by Air New Zealand.

On 31 August 2001, one year after commencing operations, Virgin Blue management announced that the company had positioned itself as a profitable long-term player in the domestic market.[18] Virgin Blue said that its low-fare strategy was working despite the fact that all carriers were suffering from a weak Australian dollar, which raised US dollar-denominated costs such as fuel purchasing.

Impulse Airlines

The Australian regional airline, Impulse Airlines, launched itself into the low fare market in June 2000. At that time, Impulse was Australia's fifth ranking regional carrier, had no debts outstanding, made a profit margin of eight per cent on passenger routes and had a breakeven load factor of 48 per cent. Revenue had increased by 20-25 per cent per annum in the late 1990s and Impulse had achieved a consistent record of operating profit.[19] In short, this was a healthy airline going into the low fare business. The New South Wales-based airline launched low price, single class services initially on the Brisbane-Melbourne-Sydney triangle, which is one of the densest air corridors in the word and accounts for about 38 per cent of Australia's domestic market.[20] Impulse leased five Boeing 717-200 jets to begin these services. Although Impulse management argued that such aircraft best met their passenger demand and comfort, they lacked the capacity of the standard LFA aircraft, the Boeing 737 (about 117 seats on the 717 versus up to 148 for the 737). More importantly, Impulse's route network was extremely competitive and ensured that Impulse would compete directly with the two majors, Qantas and Ansett. Direct competition with large, established carriers is normally avoided by LFAs, particularly during the early stages of their development, so as to minimise the likelihood of predatory behaviour. Impulse's network strategy was fundamentally flawed from the outset as they pursued well served, established, high yield markets rather than trying to develop under-utilised routes neglected by the majors.

Impulse managing director, Gerry McGowan, stated that Impulse aimed to provide a 'friendly, cheerful, hospitable, no-nonsense country-style service'.[21] Interestingly, the Impulse strategy was one of low frills and not one of no frills. No free meals were provided to passengers but complimentary tea or coffee and newspapers were provided. The seat pitch was also generous by low fare airline standards, being 32 inches compared with 30 inches on Virgin Blue's Boeing 737s. These service deviations from the low fare model outlined in earlier chapters resulted in a higher cost base for Impulse and were likely to have been a contributory factor in the firm's loss of autonomy. Moreover, the airline would offer no-conditions fares at half of Ansett's and Qantas' published economy rates. For instance on the Melbourne to Hobart route (launched in April 2001), Impulse's fully flexible economy return fare was AUS $172, compared with average prices of AUS $299 for traditional airlines on that route. As with LFAs in Europe, more than 65 per cent of Impulse's total ticket sales were generated online. Impulse created two hubs for its low fare operations – one at Mascot, New South Wales and one at Canberra, the federal capital. The carrier operated both Boeing 717-200 jets and a regional turboprop fleet of Beech 1900D, 19 seater aircraft.

In May 2001, Impulse announced details of what it called a 'long term commercial relationship' with Qantas Airways. Under the terms of the agreement, Impulse would continue to operate both interstate and regional air services but would cease operations on the major trunk route markets of Sydney-Melbourne and Sydney-Brisbane. In essence, this meant that Impulse was withdrawing from operating scheduled services in Australia under its own brand. The full terms of the bilateral agreement were: first, Impulse contracted to Qantas its eight Boeing 717 and 13 Beechcraft 1900D aircrafts, complete with pilots and cabin crew. Second, Impulse began to operate services for Qantas, under the Qantas brand and livery, to primarily leisure destinations such as Gold Coast. Third, Impulse began to operate new services for Qantas to regional airports not previously served by Qantas. Fourth, Qantas loaned funds to allow Impulse to buy back its institutional shareholders shares and provide working capital.

Senior management at both Qantas and Impulse claimed that the agreement resulted directly from the increasingly competitive conditions in both Australia and the world aviation market. Under the agreement its founders, Gerry and Sue McGowan, own Impulse. The demise of Impulse leaves Virgin Blue as the only independent LFA in the region. Why did the deal happen? Impulse was cash strapped and Qantas agreed to bail them out. Also, speculation had abounded for some time that Qantas would launch its own low fare subsidiary. In order to do so, it would first have to remove the competition. Also, as mentioned earlier, Impulse deviated from and actually never fully subscribed to the low fare model of Southwest/Ryanair/WestJet. This was particularly evident in their 'low frills, not no frills' approach mentioned previously and in their network strategy, which emphasised dense, high yield markets and brought them into direct conflict with the major carriers.

Comparing and contrasting Impulse and Virgin Blue[22]

Both LFAs followed a very similar operational structure and market strategy. The points of similarity included:

- High daily frequency services on the Brisbane-Melbourne-Sydney triangle
- Stage lengths of under 2 hours
- Low fare, single class service with limited frills (the 'flying bus' approach)
- Similar fleet size
- Emphasis on enlarging the market pie rather than on acquiring the incumbents' shares.

Despite these parallels, some notable difference also existed between the two LFAs. These were:

- Culturally, the airlines were very different. Impulse emerged from a country background, with a cautious approach to national growth. Virgin Blue evolved from a global organisation noted for its flair and innovation.
- Impulse's chairman, Gerry McGowan, was averse to lawsuits, preferring to take his complaints to the Australian Consumer and Competition Commission. By contrast, Virgin Blue has a 'fighting fund', a non-capital reserve set aside to pay for litigation against Qantas and Ansett if they engage in predatory behaviour.

It may be significant that neither of the two Australian low fare new entrants was a genuine start-up. Impulse evolved into a jet operator after operating as a regional carrier in south-east Australia for eighteen years previously. Virgin Blue is a division of the global Virgin Group, which includes two other airlines. For Impulse, this meant that it had time to build up the required infrastructure – always a problem for genuine start-up airlines. In the case of Virgin Blue, it successfully traded off the Virgin brand name to secure initial market capitalisation of A$30 million and to lease A$540 million worth of aircraft from the outset.

According to Air Canada CEO, Robert Milton,[23] Impulse and Virgin Blue entered the Australian market ostensibly to increase competition and benefit consumers (as well as to make money of course). Instead, their market entry led to a damaging price war that seriously weakened Qantas and forced both Ansett and Impulse out of business.

Return to a duopoly?

Ansett ceased operations on 14 September 2001, two days after ANZ gave up on its subsidiary and called in administrators (Ionides 2001). Sources within ANZ argued that Ansett was being purposefully liquidated as part of a proposal made to the Australian Government seeking underwriting to keep parts of its struggling Australian subsidiary alive and convert its remnants into a low-fare carrier known as 'Ansett 2'. Under the proposal, Air New Zealand would liquidate the existing Ansett airline companies and form a new airline (Ansett 2) which would, in its initial form, seek to be a value-based airline with a similar cost base to Virgin Blue but which provides much broader network coverage, nationally and regionally, across Australia. At the same time, Qantas announced plans to create a low fare subsidiary, reviving the name 'Australian Airlines' (a company it merged with in 1993) for the start-up venture.

The outcome remains to be seen at the time of writing. ANZ's problems and effective renationalisation in October 2001 appeared to cast doubts over the plans for Ansett 2 but Star Alliance partner, Singapore Airlines, expressed an interest in running the low cost operation with or on behalf of ANZ. What was clear was that by late 2001, Australia had returned to a duopoly status in the national market. However, the market was now divided between the national carrier, Qantas, and a LFA, Virgin Blue. Virgin Blue assured its customers that it would not abandon its low fare strategy, even if it were only one of two airlines covering the country. There is no indication that it will change its position in the near future. The real issue is whether or not it will be able to maintain its independence in the face of a much larger and aggressive competitor.

LFAs in the rest of the world

Liberalisation in the Asia Pacific region

In the wider Asia Pacific region, air transport liberalisation has met with mixed results. We have already discussed the Australian situation and alluded to the New Zealand context (one of the first countries in the world to privatise the national flag carrier and embrace airline liberalisation). However, genuine efforts have also been made in India and Japan to deregulate air transport and stimulate competition. Ionides (2000b) points out that elsewhere in Asia, other countries have also publicly embraced liberalisation: Singapore, Malaysia, Taiwan, South Korea, Brunei and Pakistan all have open-skies air service agreements with the US. In Taiwan and South Korea, liberalisation measures in the late 1980s and early 1990s spawned the birth of carriers that are now major players in their countries air service sectors, both domestically and internationally. In Thailand, the domestic market has undergone deregulation and new private players are looking to expand, while Indonesia has witnessed the emergence of a large number of new entrants, following government moves to allow more competition. Ionides (2000b) further illustrates that in India, Pakistan, Bangladesh, Nepal, the Philippines and Malaysia, domestic markets underwent varying forms of deregulation in the early-to-mid-1990s and, despite some glitches, passengers have generally come to experience much greater choice in domestic travel. Even The People's Republic of China has been opening up its air transport market and foreign investment is being encouraged, while in Hong Kong, restrictions barring more than one locally based airline from operating on a particular route have been eased. These moves have been long overdue in a region that has been resistant to change in the airline sector.

In early 2000, Japan finally underwent complete air transport liberalisation, freeing up fares and routes within its domestic market. Analysts argue that the size and nature of the Japanese air transport market mean that Japan is not likely to experience the dramatic post-deregulation competition and industry shake-up witnessed in the US after 1978 or in the EU from the mid-1990s. Nevertheless, a number of new, low cost entrants emerged in Japan. Skymark Airlines, founded in 1998, was the first new airline in Japan for 35 years. The carrier was backed by discount air ticket broker, HIS. After a two year struggle with Japan's Ministry of Transportation over issues such as the carrier's refusal to agree to minimum fares, Skymark was finally allowed into the market. Its initial fares were half those charged by the established carriers (Japan Airlines, Japan Air Systems and All Nippon Airways) on the Tokyo to Fukuoka route.[24] Such significant price undercutting was a new development in the Japanese airline business. Skymark's founder, Jun Okawara, acknowledged that the company was modelled on US low fare leader Southwest Airlines.[25] Skymark floated on the Tokyo Stock Exchange in May 2000, selling 5,000 shares (seven per cent of the total) and raising US$7 million.

A second low fare competitor emerged shortly after Skymark. Hokkaido International Airlines – better known as Air Do – commenced operations in December 1998. Air Do launched its first service on the busy Tokyo-Sapporo route. It was backed by Hokkaido-based business concerns.

Both low priced competitors suffered financially in the inevitable price war launched against them by the incumbents (Jeziorski 2000). The price war eventually forced Skymark off of the Osaka-Sapporo and Osaka-Fukuoka routes from June 2000 but the carrier did increase services between Tokyo and Fukuoka from three times to six times daily from 1 July 2000, following the accreditation of six new slots at Tokyo's Haneda airport, where it is based (McMillan 2000).

Fair Inc. became the third new airline to start operating in Japan post-deregulation, offering services in early August 2000 between Sendai and Osaka's Kansai airport. Fair Inc. was founded by Jun Okawara, founding vice chairman of Skymark. Fair Inc. began passenger operations on the one route with a single Bombardier CRJ Series 100. The aircraft was purchased from Lauda Air and was joined by a second at the end of 2000. The carrier also ordered two CRJ200s directly from Bombardier for delivery in 2002 (Ionides 2000a). The new carrier is backed financially by computer firm Japan Digital Laboratory.

A point worth noting is that all of the new entrants received support from established carriers. Skymark and Fair Inc. received help from ANA while Air Do received help from JAL.[26]

Skymark Airlines reported an improved operating loss of ¥676 million ($5.5 million) for the first half ended 30 April 2000, compared with ¥1.7 billion a year previous (Fullbrook 2001). Net loss also improved, to ¥759 million from ¥1.73 billion for the six months ended 30 April 2000. Tough competition pushed revenue down, however, to ¥6.32 billion from ¥6.39 billion. In August 2001, having agreed to lease a third Boeing 767-300, Skymark announced that it would launch services between Tokyo and the southern Japanese city of Kagoshima from April 2002.

Latin America and South Africa

Outside of Western Europe, the US, Canada and the Asia Pacific region, the LFA story is yet largely untold. Reasons abound as to why this is the case. Regulatory restrictions and the dominance of state-owned carriers are probably the primary constraints. Although airline liberalisation is now the accepted norm in many OECD countries, it has not yet dissipated to most of the world's nations. Competition among carriers – particularly competition based on price – remains limited to those states that have embraced air transport deregulation.

Despite this situation, LFAs have emerged or are emerging in a number of countries outside of those already discussed in this book. Many commenced operations in 2001, indicating a global trend, possibly spurred by the success of European and US LFAs. The Latin American region is the other main area where LFAs have emerged. This was advanced by the 1997 open skies agreements signed between the US and six Central American countries. Other countries followed, including Chile and Argentina in 1999.

In Chile, Aerocontinente Chile was launched as a low fare affiliate of Peruvian airline, Aero Continente. This company ran into problems in mid-2001 when it was grounded for a number of weeks following allegations that it served as a front for the laundering of drug money (Wagland 2001a). It was relaunched in early September 2001 but faced serious unrest among its workforce, most of who had not been paid since July of that year.

In Brazil, Gol Transportes Aéreos, emerged in 2001 as Brazil's first LFA. Despite launching during one of the worst years ever for the Brazilian airline industry, the new carrier fared better than most (Flores 2001). It flew more than one million passengers during its first six months of operation (January to July 2001) and was operating at a slight profit by mid-year. The airline recorded a load factor of 78 per cent in July 2001, well above the Brazilian industry average and on a par with LFAs elsewhere in the world. As Flores (2001) emphasises, Gol's enviable financial track record is basically ascribed to the carrier's diligent attention to maintaining a lean and efficient operation – in contrast to the country's other carriers. Gol operates a fleet of Boeing 737-700 aircraft, projected to total four by late 2002.

· Perhaps the most prominent LFA to emerge in Latin America was Mexico's Transportes Aeroes Ejecutivos (TAESA). Taesa was founded in 1988 as an executive charter service. It expanded into commercial services in 1991, using low fares to challenge the two major carriers, Aeromexico and Mexicana. Its innovations included selling airline tickets at booths within supermarkets. By the late 1990s, Taesa was Mexico's third largest airline, carried over two million passengers per annum and flew to 21 destinations in Mexico and four in the US. A crash in November 1999, resulting in 18 deaths, brought a tragic end to the Taesa phenomenon. Ticket sales fell by 18 per cent in the two weeks immediately following the crash. Former employees argued that the carrier had held back on maintenance for the airline's ageing fleet.[27] Government investigators who inspected Taesa planes after the crash found a series of irregularities and incidents. Consequently, in the wake of the crash senior aviation officials convinced the Mexican government that the airline should be grounded, pending an official investigation. The investigation, conducted by the Mexican Communications and Transportation Secretariat, found 69 operational and administrative faults at Taesa.[28] Although the airline tried to respond to and comply with all of the requirements that emerged from the investigation, they were unable to do so due to mounting financial problems. Debts of US$400 million, combined with a lack of new investors, forced the airline into bankruptcy in early 2000. Taesa's market exit heralded the return of a near monopoly in the Mexican domestic market, as Mexicana and Aeromexico are jointly owned.

The Taesa case, as with the ValueJet case in the US, emphasises the centrality of safety to all airlines and the need to ensure that cost reduction efforts are tempered when it comes to maintenance and safety checks. This is especially pertinent for LFAs, which usually lack the financial resources needed to overcome the operational and brand damage caused by a fatal crash.

In South Africa, Comair, BA's franchise carrier in that country, launched a domestic discount carrier called Kulula.com. Commencing operations in mid-2001, the new carrier launched its first service between Cape Town and Johannesburg. Bert van der Linden, Comair's commercial director, said that the new carrier is aimed at passengers who until now could not afford to fly and have previously used ground transport (Birns 2001). The new venture must maintain a 65 per cent load factor if it is to make money. It surpassed this figure during its first month of operations, achieving a load factor in excess of 80 per cent. In line with standard LFA practice in Europe and the US, Kulula does not offer in-flight service, food, business class, pre-seating, frequent flyer programme, flight changes or refunds for cancellations. Most bookings are taken directly, via telephone or the Internet. About 60 per cent of seats are sold at the lowest fare of Rand (R) 400 single, with the highest fares double that amount.

South African Airways (SAA) retaliated against Kulula by dropping some fares on certain flights to R1 or R2 below Kulula's lowest fare, although there are many conditions attached. However, unlike Kulula's onboard no-frills services, the SAA flights will offer a meal service and frequent flyer points (Dunn 2001b). South African competition authorities dismissed previous accusations of predatory pricing by SAA.

Conclusions

The global economic liberalisation process of the late 1990s was linked inextricably with the emergence of LFAs in many countries. Markets were deregulated and competition stimulated in previously oligopolistic sectors such as commercial air transport. In countries like Japan, new entrants emerged for the first time in many years. In Canada, the turn of the century witnessed a major shake-up of the old order, with a series of mergers and acquisitions resulting in the emergence of Air Canada and Canada 3000 as the country's two largest airlines. The third player was WestJet, the highly successful and rapidly growing LFA from Calgary. The success of WestJet, paralleled by serious financial problems at Air Canada, precipitated the launch of Tango, Air Canada's low fare offshoot, in late 2001. At the time of writing, it is too soon to comment on Tango's market performance or long-term prospects. However, lessons from the US industry indicate that it is difficult – if not impossible – to successfully embed a LFA within a traditional carrier's cost structures.

Similarly, the Australian airline business experienced considerable change and vigorous competition in the late 1990s and early 2000s. The market entry of two LFAs, Impulse Airlines and Virgin Blue, heralded a price war that led in large part to the demise of Ansett, Australia's second largest carrier. Market leader Qantas fought back, ultimately acquiring Impulse and reducing the competition to a straight conflict with Virgin Blue. At the time of writing, these market dynamics remained in flux. Qantas appeared likely to launch its own low fare subsidiary and Ansett was being revived in a new low cost guise by its New Zealand owners, with some assistance likely from Singapore Airlines. In both cases, as with Air Canada, there is a high probability that significant strategic and financial difficulties will emerge. As we have seen in previous chapters, the low price subsidiaries of full fare airlines are generally fraught with problems and rarely result in profitable ventures.

Notes

1 This was reinforced in a press statement released by IMP Group on 6 April 2000, www.impgroup.com/news/Apr6_00.htm
2 Angus Kinnear was quoted in an online Canadian business site called 'Canoe', 28 March 2001. www.canoe.ca/AirMergers/mar28_can3000canjet-cp.html
3 Professor Fred Lazar of the Schulich School of Business at York University, cited in an online article at Canoe, on air mergers in Canada, ibid.
4 David Neeleman stepped down from the Board of Directors of WestJet in 1999 to concentrate on his own ventures, primarily the establishment of JetBlue.
5 WestJet began to phase in the next generation 737-700 aircraft during the second quarter of 2001.
6 Data derived from a WestJet press release announcing 2001 second quarter results, 1 August 2001.
7 This price differential was conveyed to the author in correspondences with Mr Lian Qiu, vice president for network strategy and planning at Air Canada, September 2001.
8 This was commented upon by Mr Lian Qiu, ibid., in a correspondence with this author.

9   Research conducted by Ted Larkin, aviation analyst at HSBC Securities, cited in Knibb (2001b), 'Canadian challengers', p. 104.
10 Mr Milton was speaking at the Aviation Management Education and Research Conference (AMERC), Montreal, 17 July 2001.
11 Cited in Keith Damsell 'Air Canada pilots strike deal for discount airline', Globe and Mail, 21 July 2001.
12 Data obtained from Statistics Canada, the official Canadian Government statistical agency, 6 June 2001.
13 Robert Milton cited in Sobie (2001) 'Former WestJet chief to run Air Canada's low fare carrier'.
14 These include Peter Harbison, managing director of the Centre for Asia Pacific Aviation, quoted in Ian Thomas (2000a) 'Branson unsettles Australia', p. 39.
15 Quoted in David Knibb (2000b) 'Australian test match', p. 77.
16 Richard Branson, cited in Ian Thomas (2000a) 'Branson unsettles Australia', p. 39.
17 This point is made by Virgin Blue CEO, Brett Godfrey, on 11 September 2001, on the Virgin Blue website, www.virginblue.com/news2001.html
18 Taken from the Virgin Blue website, www.virginblue.com/news2001.html
19 Mattias Killian ' The twin-engined Cockatoo', Airliner World, August 2001, pp. 52-3.
20 Paul Phelan 'Impulse confirms June start for cut-price 717 services', Flight International, 18-24 April 2000.
21 Cited in Mattias Killian ' The twin-engined Cockatoo', Airliner World, August 2001, pp. 52-9.
22 This analysis is drawn from David Knibb's article, 'Australian test match', Airline Business, August 2000, p. 79.
23 Robert Milton was speaking at a conference luncheon hosted by the Molson Business School of Concordia University, Montreal, 17 July 2001.
24 This is the second densest air route in the world, after the Tokyo to Sapporo route.
25 Mr Okawara was cited in a Financial Times article, 'Quiet revolutionary takes to the Japanese skies', 2 September 1998.
26 This support undermines the LFA credentials of these new entrants.
27 Data derived from Airwise News bulletin dated 23 November 1999, www.news.airwise.com/stories/99/11/943363313.html
28 Airwise News, ibid., December 23 1999.

Chapter 10

Epilogue:
The Way Ahead for Low Fare Airlines

Long-term success in this high growth area depends on one's ability to maintain low cost and efficient operating practices, establishing a long term record of sustained profitability, and above all maintaining a disciplined and controlled rate of annual growth. It is this combination of features which has enabled Ryanair to uniquely replicate the Southwest model successfully in Europe.

(David Bonderman, Ryanair Chairman, 2000).

Mr Bonderman's analysis summarises the essential determinants of a successful low fare business model. To achieve it requires a ruthless and relentless focus on cost cutting and increased operational productivity, combined with an ability to generate and maintain a cash surplus and a cautious but steady fleet and route network expansion. The mastery of these techniques has made Southwest and Ryanair industry leaders and rendered them virtually unassailable in their respective markets. There are no secret or nonreplicable elements of the Southwest/Ryanair approach: the key is to have the drive, discipline and desire to be the lowest cost service provider and the lowest priced airline in the market. Other approaches do exist and these have also proven successful. Most notably, easyJet has a proven record of profitability and market growth, despite not being the lowest cost or price provider. However, easyJet also does not realise the sizeable profit margins of its main low fare rival, Ryanair. For instance, in 2000 easyJet realised a net profit of £22 million on operating revenues of £263 million (8.4 per cent). By comparison, Ryanair achieved a £65.3 million net profit on revenue of £304.6 million (21.5 per cent).

This chapter has three main objectives. First, it briefly summarises the comparisons between the different LFA models in Europe. Second, it discusses price leadership strategy and the lessons that can be learned by other airlines and other industries from LFAs. Third, it assesses LFAs in times of crisis and attempts to explain why leading LFAs such as Southwest and Ryanair fared so well relative to traditional carriers after the industry, market and societal calamities of September 2001.

Competing low fare models

Some commentators[1] argue that the choice of LFAs in Europe can be broadly divided into two groups: the cheapest and the lowest frill (Ryanair and easyJet); and the lifestyle sellers with a little more finesse (Go and Buzz). This dichotomy is broadly accurate. Virgin Express is notably absent from this list, possibly because it is seen by many as falling between the two groupings.

Several key points of differentiation between Europe's LFAs emerged in this book. Clear distinctions existed on issues such as customer service emphasis and approach, route network and airport strategy and methods for ticket pricing and sales. The LFA model is not monolithic – alternatives to the Ryanair model have emerged, particularly in service quality, route structure, and even fares themselves. How viable these alternative models are remains to be seen but the success of easyJet (and increasingly Go) indicates that there are more ways than one to be a low fare success story. Despite this point, one important fact remains: airlines should ensure that an emphasis on cost reduction remains at the core of their strategies and that they do not deviate too much from the main elements of the Ryanair/Southwest model discussed in Chapters 6 and 8.

A key difference between Europe's two largest LFAs, Ryanair and easyJet, is their approach to profit generation. Profit margins per ticket sold are usually low for Ryanair. Instead of seeking to extract the maximum revenue per passenger, Ryanair emphasises the lowest operating costs and cost per passenger kilometre in the industry, as well as a consistently high load factor. By ensuring a significant margin (usually 15-18 per cent) between the breakeven and the passenger load factors, Ryanair is able to generate the highest net profits in the business. The easyJet model has a wider span between its lowest and highest fares and clearly targets high yield business passengers on many routes. As a result, global surveys of airline passenger yields for 2000[2] ranked easyJet fourth in Europe with a revenue passenger-km (RPK) of 8.65 cents, up 5.2 per cent on the previous year. This puts easyJet just below full fare carriers British Airways, Alitalia and Air France in terms of passenger yield. Ryanair is also in the European top ten for passenger yield but its RPK decreased by 11.2 per cent in 2000.

A three-pronged strategy framework for price leaders

1. Adopting a viable strategic position

In establishing itself as a price leader within a given industry (in this case airlines), a company must first construct a viable strategy framework. This has three components, the first of which is 'positioning'. Positioning is a means of locating an organisation in its environment. In this context, strategy is the mediating force between organisation and environment, between the internal and the external context. Strategy thus becomes a focus for resource concentration. As positioning, strategy encourages us to look at how firms find their market positions and protect them in order to meet, avoid, or subvert competition (Mintzberg 1998, p.20). Needs-based positioning (Porter 1996) – targeting the needs of price sensitive customers for instance – comes closest to conceptualising LFAs source of strategic positioning. A focused competitor, such as Ikea in household retail, Direct Line in motor insurance, or Ryanair in airline travel, thrives on groups of customers who are overpriced by more broadly targeted competitors. Strategic positioning is usually described in terms of customers. US low fare pioneer, Southwest Airlines, serves price and convenience sensitive travellers for example. A successful positioning strategy necessitates hard choices in terms of customer focus: choosing not to concentrate on attracting business passengers, for instance. Southwest has staked out a unique and valuable strategic position based on a tailored set of activities. On the routes served by Southwest, a full service airline could never be as convenient or as low cost. The Southwest model is not easily transferable. Continental and United Airlines both attempted to copy the Southwest model for their low-cost US subsidiaries. They were able to duplicate the route structure and other observable and quantifiable elements but they failed to emulate the Southwest culture or organisational capabilities, the key to its success (Couvret, 1996, p.61).

2. Leveraging organisational capabilities

Once a position is established, competitive advantage is secured by leveraging capabilities that cannot readily be emulated by rivals. Quality, efficiency, innovation and customer responsiveness can all be building blocks to competitive advantage.

Distinctive capabilities are generated from organisational resources. Resources may be tangible, as in the case of human and technological assets, or they may be intangible, as in the case of reputation, market information, and knowledge. The most important company resources in strategy development are architecture, reputation, and innovation (Kay 1993). These contribute to the distinctive development of a company's strategy and differentiate a company's resources from its competitors. Architecture is seen in terms of a distinctive structure of relationships either within the corporation (between management and workers) or between it and its suppliers or customers. This is something that is not so readily copied and forms the bedrock of a company's unique organisational capabilities. Reputation allows an organisation to communicate favourable information about itself to its customers. Reputations are difficult to create and are not easily emulated.

Building on the work of Collis and Montgomery (1995), Couvret (1996) argues the need to adopt a resource-based view of the company, recognising that an airline's routes are its main asset. He further argues that organisational capabilities are an important source of competitive advantage for airlines. Ultimately, the primary physical source of advantage in a successful airline is the combination of its route structure and its corporate history and culture. Also, for service sector companies such as airlines, key capabilities derive from human resource management and customer services. Long-term competitive advantage is fabricated upon the relationship that exists between the company, its employees, and its customers, as well as the reputation that is built on the basis of reliability and quality of service.

3. Reconceiving the value equation

A third stage in developing a strategy framework for low price competition is to pursue a route that will revolutionise the terms of competition within a given industry. Companies such as Ryanair, easyJet, Go and Buzz have taken the route which Hamel (1996) termed, 'reconceiving a product or service', through radically improving the value equation. This refers to improving an industry's ratio of price to performance or put simply, offering better value for money. Through revolutionising this ratio and offering the customer a 500 per cent rather than a 50 per cent improvement, a company can force a reconception of a given product or service. This is essentially what Europe's LFAs have done, becoming so-called 'value revolutionaries' (Hamel 1996) in the process. This correlates with Kim and Mauborgne's concept of 'value innovators', wherein a company refuses to take its industry's conditions and norms as given, preferring instead to pursue market innovation through making quantum leaps in value (1997, p.105). LFAs have relentlessly pursued this strategy, targeting the mass air travel market and offering unrivalled value for money. They have served as value innovator on both secondary routes, dominated by charter carriers, and primary routes, controlled by large established airlines. Prices dropped, the markets grew, and firms like Ryanair and easyJet experienced high growth and sustained profitability.

LFA performance in time of crisis

Traditionally, airlines have had severe difficulties coping with a sudden steep decline in revenue as they are capital intensive companies and need to maintain a network, with all the associated fixed costs.[3] For most airlines, the gap between the breakeven and the actual load factor is small, so even a drop of a few percentage points in traffic can result in an operating loss. Moreover, an airline's product – passenger seats – is a perishable item: if it is not used on any given flight it cannot be used again and a company loses the associated revenue. Zorn (2001) argues that LFAs are more resilient than traditional airlines to market downturns. Southwest Airlines has proven this fact on numerous occasions in the US. Zorn cites several reasons for the resilience of LFAs in times of recession: first, a lower overall and more variable cost structure; second, lower breakeven load factor; and third, business and leisure traveller migration from expensive airlines to LFAs. The financiers substantiate this fact. For instance, Schoder Salomon Smith Barney value LFAs as growth stocks while the traditional airlines are treated as cyclical.

Occasionally market downturns can be particularly sudden and cataclysmic. In September 2001, the terrorist attacks on New York and Washington D.C. had a particularly negative impact on the airline industry. Market confidence, already weakened by a nascent recession in the US and parts of Europe, plummeted in the wake of these attacks and their follow-on. Safety fears meant that air traffic numbers declined sharply. Global airlines such as British Airways and American Airlines declared large-scale jobs cuts and sought financial assistance from their respective governments. Already weakened by sustained losses, flag carriers like Swissair and the affiliated Sabena were pushed into or to the brink of bankruptcy.

This industry turmoil prompted the question: 'how were LFAs affected by the fallout from the US attacks and related traffic slump and were they better able to weather the market storm than their traditional competitors?' All of the evidence in Europe – and in the US – indicates that the leading LFAs fared significantly better than their full fare rivals in the wake of the terrorist attacks on the US. Nonetheless, a significant variance did emerge between US and European low price carriers. In the US, LFAs were not as fortunate as their European counterparts. Location (all operations being within the US) combined with the post-attack industry shutdown imposed by the Federal Aviation Administration (FAA), meant that all American airlines were adversely affected by the airline industry crisis that developed after 11 September 2001. In early October 2001, the low fare leader and fourth largest airline in the US, Southwest Airlines, announced that the company flew 2.6 billion revenue passenger miles (RPMs) in September 2001, a 21.6 per cent decrease from the 3.3 billion RPMs flown in September 2000. Available seat miles (ASMs) decreased 3.6 per cent to 4.8 billion from the September 2000 level of 5 billion. Also, the load factor for the month was 53.4 per cent, compared to 65.7 per cent for the same period in 2000. Expressed in an even more obvious manner, Southwest's load factor averaged 66.8 per cent for the period from 1-10 September and 45.4 per cent for the period from 14-30 September. Bookings for the week ended 23 September were approximately 60 per cent below normal targets. However, bookings for the week ended 30 September improved and were only 10-15 per cent below normal targets. The airline acknowledged explicitly that its September 2001 traffic results were severely affected by the 11 September terrorist attacks on the US.[4] Unlike the other major US airlines, Southwest avoided schedule reduction and staff redundancies in the wake of the terrorist attacks on the Twin Trade Towers and the Pentagon. However, it was forced to defer the delivery of 11 new Boeing 737-700, citing as the reason the slowdown in air traffic after the September attacks.[5]

JetBlue Airways delayed the start of two new services in light of declining demand after the terrorist attacks (Sobie 2001a). However, unlike its full fare competitors, JetBlue said that it has no plans to furlough any employees or delay deliveries of new Airbus A320 aircraft.

Sun Country fared much worse. Already beset by second quarter 2001 operating losses of almost $12 million, the Minnesota-based low fare carrier was forced to trim its capacity by 26 per cent in late September 2001 (Sobie 2001b). This involved dropping four services and downsizing its workforce by 20 per cent. Speaking in late September 2001, a Sun Country spokeswoman said that the carrier would terminate service from its Minneapolis hub to Boston, Chicago O'Hare, San Diego and Seattle and reduce frequencies on some of its 25 remaining services. The airline was also considering returning some of its 12 Boeing 727s but had no plans to delay delivery of new Boeing 737s. President and CEO David Banmiller stated that:

The tragic events of September 11th and reduced passenger loads continue to impact the entire industry's profitability...To protect the long-term viability of Sun

Country Airlines, we had to make some difficult decisions related to our schedule and appropriate staffing levels.[6]

With the reductions, Sun Country became the seventh low fares US carrier to cut its schedule and the sixth to plan staff layoffs. Several other low-fares carriers, including AirTran Airways and Frontier Airlines, avoided laying off some groups (such as pilots) through wage concessions. In addition to AirTran and Frontier, other US LFAs that slashed jobs and schedules in the wake of the September 2001 terrorist attacks include: American TransAir, National Airlines, Spirit Airlines and Vanguard Airlines.

Despite these low fare sector travails, leading budget airlines emerged from the crisis in a stronger market position relative to their full fare rivals. A prominent and inclusive measure of this disparity is the comparative market capitalisations[7] of leading LFAs and major full service carriers. Morrell points out that for airlines with stock market quotations, the market capitalisation shows investors' valuation of the airline as a whole on a daily basis, including an assessment of intangible assets (such as slot allocation), management strength and business prospects (1997, p. 79). The durability of LFA market capitalisations post-US attacks was significant. Broadly speaking, there were three main reasons for this divergence. First, leading LFAs on both sides of the Atlantic had strong balance sheets and very little – if any – debt. Second, consumers are more price sensitive in times of recession and more likely to fly with a LFA than a full service carrier. Third, airlines that outsource much of their activities (as LFAs do) stand to gain during industry downturns, as they can usually avail of better prices from their subcontractors. Moreover, they are not forced to lay off a large number of employees within their own organisations. Two weeks after the World Trade Centre explosions, despite its problems, Southwest Airlines had the strongest market capitalisation of all the US airlines (Figure 10.1). The Texas-based low price leader was in fact worth more than the five largest US carriers combined ($10.8 billion versus $8.56 billion).

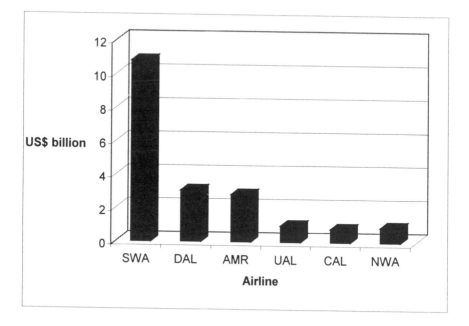

**Figure 10.1 Market capitalisations of the major US airlines post-
September 11, 2001**

Source: data derived from New York Stock Exchange statistics, 26 September 2001.

* Southwest (SWA), Delta (DAL), American (AMR), United (UAL), Continental (CAL),
Northwest (NWA).

These figures can obviously change rapidly and the data point offered here
is random. However, it does provide an indication of how the market can
value a leading LFA relative to major carriers during a time of industry crisis
and economic uncertainty. Furthermore, with virtually no debt, the highest
net worth in the industry[8] and operating margins of 16-17 per cent (compared
with an industry average of 3-5 per cent), Southwest Airlines was in a
considerably stronger market position than all other large US airlines. Shares
in Southwest outperformed all of its rivals after the calamities of 11
September 2001, beating the American Stock Exchange's Airline Index by
about 50 per cent. In the weeks after the attacks Southwest stock was up 76
cents – 5.4 per cent – to \$14.74 on the New York Stock Exchange.[9] By
comparison, other majors fared badly on the stock exchange after 11
September. Within two weeks of the bombings, Continental Airlines shares
fell 67 per cent, making it among the cheapest stocks in the sector.[10] Before
the attacks, Continental was the only major hub-based airline to post a profit

year-to-date. Similarly, American Airlines stock value fell by 37 per cent during the same period.

In September 2001, airline analysts and the air transport industry as a whole were in agreement that the US hijackings would reduce domestic and international passenger demand in Europe (Wagland 2001b). In a warning to investors, Schroder Salomon Smith Barney stated that, 'the terrorist attacks in New York and Washington on 11 September 2001 are likely to have a catastrophic effect on European airline profitability'. Schroders estimated that air travel would fall by as much as 20 per cent initially, using the Gulf War 1990/01 as a reference point. In the first quarter after the war traffic dropped 23 per cent, followed by a drop in traffic by 6 per cent year-on-year for the subsequent three quarters.

This was certainly the case for traditional, full fare carriers. However, a different story emerged in the low fare sector. This was acknowledged by market analysts such as Schroders, who saw Europe's low-fare carriers as the only ones to remain in profit:

> We expected all major European airlines to report net losses for the current fiscal year and most likely extending into next year as well. Only short-haul, low-fares airlines are likely to remain profitable through the current situation.[11]

The overall situation for Europe's LFAs was considerably more upbeat than in the US. All three leading LFAs – Ryanair, easyJet and Go – launched ticket price promotions to maintain sales, eschewed all forms of state aid and remained on target to increase their passenger numbers and profit margins.[12] A statement in late September 2001 from Barbara Cassani, Go's CEO, stated that Go was well positioned to weather the storm and had no plans to make job cuts.[13] She went on to argue that LFAs would be much less affected than traditional airlines and that with no exposure to the North Atlantic and much lower fixed costs, LFAs could manage their businesses more flexibly to remain profitable. Although Go's sales did drop by 20 per cent in the immediate aftermath of the US attacks, they recovered within two weeks. As with other LFAs on both sides of the Atlantic, Go embarked on a massive low price 'seat sale' in late September to encourage people back on to airplanes. In early October 2001, easyJet announced that it flew 680,383 passengers in September 2001, an increase from 534,913 in September 2000. The month's load factor also increased slightly, rising from 83.03 per cent in September 2000 to 83.16 per cent one year later.

In the wake of the attacks on the US, Ryanair emerged with the second highest market valuation of all Europe's airlines, preceded only by the German aviation giant, Lufthansa. For instance, just over two weeks after the attacks, Ryanair had a NASDAQ market capitalisation of $2.68 billion. By comparison, Europe's largest airline, British Airways, was listed with a market capitalisation of only $2.65 billion.[14] Other large, full service European carriers fared even worse. For instance, the Dutch flag carrier, KLM, had a market capitalisation of just over $400 million in late September 2001.[15] Ryanair management declared that the company had no real decline in business as a consequence of the terrorist attacks on the US.[16] Out of a total schedule of 1,800 flights during the week after the 11 September attacks, the company was obliged to cancel 16 and only half of those cancellations were due to the cumulative impact of additional airport security measures at airports in the early part of the week. Overall, during the week after the atrocities, bookings were down 10 per cent on normal. These subsequently returned to normal levels, and the carrier quickly recovered the week of slippage with a number of seat promotions. Advance bookings and loads remained strong, and therefore the immediate consequences of the US events on Ryanair were not significant.[17] The carrier expressed confidence that it could weather the market storm following the US attacks much better than the national flag carriers due to a lower cost base and greater operational efficiencies, together with a lack of aircraft debt and substantial cash resources (all of Ryanair's airplanes are owned by the company and the airline had cash resources of IE£700 million in late 2001). As with Southwest, Ryanair's cash resources ensured that it did not have to lay off any of its workers and allowed the company to embark on its largest ever seat sale in direct response to the post 11 September drop in demand.

Europe's LFAs took maximum advantage of the problems afflicting their full fare rivals in the wake of the September 2001 US attacks. For example, following the 2 October 2001 announcement that the entire Swissair fleet was grounded, easyJet offered to fly stranded passengers on services between London Luton and London Gatwick to Geneva, London Luton to Zurich, and Geneva to Barcelona and Nice for just £20 one way.[18] These special fares were made available upon production of a valid Swissair ticket at the airport sales desks and were valid until 5 October. Ryanair also refused to be pessimistic, moving ahead with plans to expand its fleet through the acquisition of up to 50 more aircraft. The belief within the company was that not only could they survive an economic downturn but they could in fact benefit from it. This is because recession means that people become more price conscious for both business and leisure travel – albeit that this growth may be generated at lower fares and yields. Also, taking advantage of an aircraft surplus and downturn in aircraft prices, Ryanair can increase its fleet at a relatively low cost during time of crisis for its traditional competitors.

Sustaining advantage through the low fare business model

Based on the 2000 financial year, *Airline Business* magazine's profitability analysis of the world's top 150 airline groups added further evidence to our argument that efficient LFAs are the undisputed success story of the world airline business and the role models for future profitability and growth in the industry. Ryanair emerged as the airline with the highest operating margin in the world in 2000 (23.4 per cent), followed by Southwest Airlines with 18.1 per cent. Of the top 25, six were LFAs and less than half were large, full fare carriers. The remainder were efficient niche players like EVA Air of Taiwan and successful regional airlines such as Mesa Air Group in the US. In the same study, easyJet had the fastest traffic growth of the top 150 ranked airlines in the world. European low fare rivals Go and Ryanair were also among the ten carriers with the fastest traffic growth.

A key feature of successful LFA business models is a willingness to make hard choices and strategic trade-offs (Porter 1996) in order to maintain or develop a successful market position. This requires a focus on profitability and cash generation, rather than on gaining immediate market share. Put another way, it involves avoiding lucrative markets if entry entails a significant rise in operating costs. Companies such as Southwest and Ryanair have been willing to forego dense, often high yield routes that might distort their cost reduction models.

There are certain essential features of the low fare model that should not be deviated from if a company wants to ensure profitability and survival. These are first, offer only a point-to-point service (eliminates time wastage caused by baggage and passenger transfers); second, operate a single aircraft type (saves on maintenance and crew training costs); third, maximise aircraft utilisation through reducing gate turnaround times; fourth, charge for all frills such as food and drink (conserves money directly but also indirectly through lower aircraft cleaning costs); fifth, do not offer a frequent flyer loyalty programme (removes associated management and implementation expenses); and sixth, be ticketless (reduces staff costs) and sell directly whenever possible (saves on travel agent commission). Other variables are important but it may not be necessary to adhere to them precisely. For instance, easyJet and Buzz both serve a number of more expensive primary airports. They do so in order to attract business passengers who often purchase tickets close to or on the date of departure and therefore in a higher yield category. This results in higher operating costs but usually greater per passenger yield too.

Low price can increase a firm's customer base but, unless the firm maintains *the* lowest prices in the industry, it will not guarantee customer loyalty. Even with the lowest prices, a firm can lose market share if it fails to respond to changing customer needs and demands. To compete on price *and* turn a profit requires an airline to be extremely strict on cost. The consistent and enduring success of firms like Ryanair and Southwest indicate that this is feasible. Low operating costs and cheap ticket prices are essential to LFA success. However, the success of any airline also depends on providing a safe and reliable product. Safety standards for European airlines are applied universally and carefully regulated. Reliability is not so readily assured. The essential feature of a reliable airline product are on-time departures and arrivals, low cancellation rates, minimal lost or damaged baggage and helpful and informed customer service staff who are readily available when problems occur. In this respect, differences do emerge between Europe's LFAs, with interpretations of service reliability varying between airlines. Achieving operational cost reductions through diminished service standards can weaken an airline's brand image and loyalty and undermine its long-term market competitiveness. Cost reduction is therefore a necessary modus operandi for LFAs but should not be achieved at the expense of an unreliable service product.

During the airline industry crisis of late 2001, the high market capitalisations of low fare leaders Southwest and Ryanair – relative to their larger, full fare peers – was further proof that LFAs had come of age. The market capitalisations of low fare leaders held steady in the wake of the US terrorist attacks, while the major carriers on both sides of the Atlantic were decimated. This situation may not endure but it is illustrative of the market power and durability of the LFA model.

Update 2002

Change in the airline industry is rapid and ongoing. Events have therefore moved on since this book was completed in November 2001. Some changes were anticipated in the text but others were unforeseen. One of the most unexpected occurrences was the announcement in early 2002 by BMI British Midland that they were entering the LFA market in Europe. The low fare offshoot was named 'bmibaby' and was launched in March 2002 from East Midlands Airport in the UK. The choice of base was a strategic response to Go's decision to make the airport – BMI's historical base – its third UK hub. The new airline's strategy was premised on the standard principles of the LFA model: point-to-point services, no free food, one-way, low price Internet fares and a standardised fleet of Boeing 737 aircraft. Initially, bmibaby's fleet consisted of two Boeing 737-300s transferred from the parent company. Routes chosen from East Midlands included Palma, Barcelona,

Nice, Malaga, Faro and Murcia – destinations already served by Go from its London Stansted and Bristol hubs. Other destinations – such as Dublin and Prague – anticipated new routes offered by Go from East Midlands. The direct competitive challenge posed by bmibaby to Go was obvious and deliberate. Go's chief executive, Barbara Cassani, dismissed BMI's move as one of an:

> airline in disarray...this tactic was tried many times in the US and failed every time'.[19]

Ryanair chief executive, Michael O'Leary reacted similarly, describing the BMI move as 'a late, kneejerk reaction' and Ray Webster, easyJet chief executive commented that a low cost carrier could not be created from a high cost operation.[20] Although it is too early to methodically assess bmibaby's performance and prospects, past experiences in the US and Europe tend to support the views of the rival LFA chief executives. Late entry into an already crowded UK low fare market is challenging, particularly in the absence of a unique value proposition. The service and customer expectation baggage of direct and explicit association with a full fare airline can prove fatal, as companies such as Continental Airlines found out in the US during the early 1990s.

Further European LFA launches occurred or appeared imminent during 2002. As with bmibaby, at the time of writing it was too soon to analyse most of these or to comment conclusively on their likely market success or failure. However, the basic tenets and measures of the low fare business model, combined with historical precedent, apply in all cases.

British Airway's German subsidiary, Deutsche BA, outlined plans to move towards a low fare model and to rebrand itself simply as 'DBA'. In spite of this, the company appeared hesitant as to how far it would take the low fare model. CEO Adrian Hunt declared that the airline would not move to a no frills strategy and that it would retain an emphasis on high quality service.[21] As we noted in earlier chapters, such a market straddling position could prove detrimental for DBA. DBA management respond to critics by arguing that their role model is US carrier JetBlue, rather than Ryanair or Southwest. This means striving to achieve cost efficiencies on aircraft configuration and utilisation for instance, whilst at the same time offering passengers high quality catering (for an extra charge) and comfortable seating.

French carrier Air Lib (successor to AOM and Air Liberte) remarketed five of its domestic routes in March 2002 under a low fare brand called Airlib Express. This strategic shift followed the collapse of its former shareholder, SAirGroup and signalled the company's effort to define its market niche and differentiate its product offering from that of the market dominant Air France. Senior management[22] also acknowledged the need to improve the airline's cost structure and increase productivity. Using a fleet of 162 seater MD-83 aircraft, Airlib Express commenced services from Paris Orly Airport to popular destinations in the south of France. Initial price offerings were low (starting at €29 one-way), with no restrictions and a simple fare structure. Although tickets would be sold via existing travel agent networks, management stated their intention to move increasingly towards direct sales – particularly via the Internet.

In Sweden, low fare start-up Goodjet was set to launch initial services in mid-2002 from Gothenburg Landvetter Airport to Paris Beauvais and Nice. Financed by a group of Gothenburg business people, Goodjet would be Scandinavia's first dedicated budget airline. Commencing operations with a Boeing 737-300 aircraft and one-way fares of SKr 475 (US$45), Goodjet explicitly models itself on existing low fare carriers and aims to attract both business and leisure travellers.[23]

Elsewhere in Scandinavia, Danish airline Sterling announced in early 2002 that it too would reorientate itself towards the low fare market. The carrier serves mostly Mediterranean destinations from Copenhagen and Stockholm.[24] As with Deutsche BA, Sterling appears unwilling to fully adopt the low fare model. Thus, although the airline intends to switch from the 189 seat Boeing 737-800 to the low fare standard 148 or 149 seat 737-700 or 737-300 and to simplify its fare structure, management is reluctant to abandon service frills such as complimentary in-flight catering.

Central Europe also witnessed the emergence of an embryonic LFA. Slovakian start-up SkyEurope Airlines commenced operations in February 2002. The carrier began with a domestic service from the Slovak capital Bratislava to the city of Kosice, followed by an international service from Bratislava to Zurich.[25] Although operating a mixed fleet of EMB-120s and Boeing 737-300s (not yet acquired at the time of writing), the infant airline's management profess to follow the low fare business model.

Other notable developments occurred in Australia and in Canada. In Australia, Virgin Blue ended months of speculation in February 2002 when management declared that both its financial needs and the future needs of customers and employees would be best served by it remaining independent.[26] This terminated any prospects of a merger or other linkage between Virgin Blue and Ansett. In March 2002, Virgin Blue, announced that it was raising A$260 million (US$140 million) through the sale of a 50 per cent equity stake to the Australian transport group Patrick Corporation. The deal served an important strategic purpose: by officially becoming an Australian carrier rather than a British one, Virgin Blue gained access to the

New Zealand and wider Oceanic market. Moreover, the deal relieved pressure on the airline to raise cash through a public share offering.[27] Virgin Blue management declared that the investment would allow the airline to grow to a 50 aircraft fleet and a 50 per cent market share within five years.[28] The company further declared their intention to launch international services to New Zealand and a number of Pacific Island states such as Fiji. These strategic objectives would prove challenging for an airline struggling against the colossus that is Qantas. In early 2002, the Australian market leader controlled 85 per cent of the market. Although profitable and on the assent, Virgin Blue controlled just under 15 per cent, following the closure of Ansett in March 2002.

In Canada, the second largest airline, Canada 3000, was declared bankrupt in late 2001. Reasons for the company's demise vary but it would appear that it was ultimately a problem of liquidity. Leasing its entire fleet and losing C$700,000 per day, Canada 3000 ran out of cash.[29] This was compounded by the airline's 'too fast, too soon' expansion strategy. The acquisition of first CanJet and then Royal Airlines during the first half of 2001 proved extremely expensive for the young company. Canadian airline industry commentators[30] argued that both acquisitions were overpriced. Furthermore, absorbing CanJet and Royal proved more difficult than anticipated. In addition, Canada 3000's switch from charter to primarily scheduled services was not as straightforward as expected. Finally, Canada 3000's market positioning was always problematic. Sandwiched between full service Air Canada and low fare WestJet, Canada 3000 found it difficult to establish a clear and defensible market space. The market entry of Air Canada's low fare offshoot, Tango, overlapping many of Canada 3000's routes, signalled further losses for Canada's hapless second carrier. The demise of Canada 3000 raised competitive problems in Canada, as Air Canada subsequently surged to 80 per cent of the domestic market. Other immediate beneficiaries included charter airlines such as Skyservice. WestJet availed of the opportunity to expand further into eastern Canada but at a cautious and deliberate pace. At the time of writing, it appeared probable that one or more new entrants, hoping to secure the leases of Canada 3000 aircraft, would fill the vacuum in scheduled services. Former senior management at Canada 3000 such as the ex-president, Angus Kinnear, appeared likely to found new, low fare, airlines based in eastern Canada.

LFAs have also begun to take-off in Southeast Asia. Carriers claiming to be modelled on leading American and European budget airlines have emerged in Thailand (PBAir and Air Andaman) and in Cambodia (Siem Reap Air). In December 2001, Air Asia was relaunched in Malaysia as a trendy, no frills operation. The airline's president, Tony Fernandes comments:

We'll always remain true to the gospel of Ryanair and Southwest.[31]

Cost reduction is embedded in the company's culture, with no free in-flight services and multi-tasking by flight crews to save money and to improve turnaround times (flight attendants are required to disembark passengers and to clean the aircraft at the same time). Cost savings allow Air Asia to consistently offer lower fares than its main rival, Malaysia Airlines.

In the Philippines, Cebu Pacific Airways now claims to have 30 per cent of the domestic market and models itself on the low fare pioneer, Southwest Airlines.[32] The airline keeps costs down by selling a large percentage of its tickets online and operating out of uncongested secondary airports where turnaround times are lower. Domestic market saturation is forcing Cebu Pacific to grow internationally and this may spell trouble ahead for the Philippine carrier. In launching services from Manila to Hong Kong for instance, Cebu Pacific has entered into direct competition with large flag carriers such as Cathay Pacific. The company has also acquired larger, more expensive aircraft for such routes and has added business class service. Such moves contravene fundamental principles of the low fare model outlined in earlier chapters and risk undermining the success of airlines such as Cebu Pacific.

The corporate restructuring plan announced by British Airways (BA) in March 2002 lent further support to the success and durability of the LFA model. In reorganising their European operations and their second hub – London Gatwick – based network in particular, the global behemoth explicitly borrowed from the practices and principles of its low cost rivals. BA management announced that fleet and aircraft configurations would be radically simplified at Gatwick, with the Boeing 737 being used exclusively for short-haul routes. The stated objective was to raise utilisation by 10 per cent. A simpler pricing structure was also promised, with a more straightforward approach to revenue management – along the lines of that used by easyJet.[33] Within Europe, the low fare model – or select aspects of it – had clearly triumphed over established full fare airline business practices. However, questions remain as to how rigorously the model should be applied and to what extent variants of the Southwest/Ryanair archetype will thrive in the long term. For instance, both easyJet and Go are considering moving away from the standardised fleet principle. This runs contrary to the second essential feature of the low fare business model ('operate a single aircraft type'), outlined earlier in this chapter. Both airlines indicated in early 2002 that they were considering acquiring Airbus aircraft for fleet expansion. The reconfiguration of the A319 from 145 to 150 seats makes it a viable alternative to the 149 seat Boeing 737-300/700. easyJet CEO Ray Webster argues that commonality of fleet is an important part of the easyJet business model but that it is now appropriate to consider all options.[34] In the US, JetBlue has never used Boeing 737s – widely accepted as the most cost efficient and suitably sized aircraft for budget carriers. JetBlue does operate a standardised fleet but one consisting only of Airbus 320s (see Chapter 8). These issues leave us to ponder the question of how far an airline can stretch or digress from the fundamental principles and practices of the low fare business model and still remain competitively viable and financially robust.

Notes

1   Such as Alexandra Lennane, writing in Sunday Business, 17 June 2001, p. 16.
2   The Airline Business World Airline Ranking, September 2001, p. 80.
3   The Economist 'uncharted airspace', 22 September 2001, p. 73.
4   This was confirmed in a Southwest press release of 3 October 2001, www.iflyswa.com
5   Taken from Yahoo!.Finance, 'Southwest Airlines defers 11 Boeing deliveries', 26 September 2001.
6   Cited in Ionides 2001.
7   Morrell defines market capitalisation as the 'market share price per share multiplied by the number of shares outstanding' (1997, p. 61).
8   In mid-September 2001, Southwest had $3.8 billion worth of hard assets to borrow against. This compared to $3 billion for American, $2.8 billion for Delta, $2.3 billion for United and $200 million for Continental. Northwest and US Airways had negative net worths of -$606 million and -$1.8 billion respectively.
9   This data is derived from a Reuters report dated 28 September 2001.
10 Stacey L. Bradford writing in Yahoo! Finance, 25 September 2001.
11 Schroders report cited in Maria Wagland, 2001.
12 Joanna Walters 'More job losses a certainty as passengers desert skies', The Observer, 7 October 2001, p. 8.
13 Go press release, 24 September 2001, www.gofly.com
14 British Airways is approximately ten times larger than Ryanair, measured in fleet size and cities served.
15 Data derived from New York Stock Exchange statistics listed on the Yahoo! Finance website as of 26 September 2001.
16 This was stated by Sean Coyle, Commercial Director at Ryanair, in a communication to this author on 20 September 2001.
17 Information derived from a Ryanair press statement made by CEO Michael O'Leary, 18 September 2001. This can be found at www.ryanair.com
18 This was stated in a press release on easyJet's website, 2 October 2001.
19 Barbara Cassani quoted in 'BMI launches cheap offshoot', *Flight International*, 15 January 2002.
20 Ibid.
21 Hunt cited in David Kaminski-Morrow 'Deutsche BA details new low-fare concept', *Air Transport Intelligence news*, 15 March 2002.
22 Air Lib president, Jean Charles Corbet, quoted in Maria Wagland 'Air Lib hits French domestic market with low-cost unit', *Air Transport Intelligence news*, 6 March 2002.

23   David Morrow 'Swedish start-up Goodjet seek to open budget market', *Air Transport Intelligence news*, 31 January 2002.
24   David Morrow 'Sterling intends fleet switch in move to low-fare ops', *Air Transport Intelligence news*, 28 January 2002.
25   David Morrow 'Spain's Swift Air behind Slovak start-up SkyEurope', *Air Transport Intelligence news*, 25 January 2002.
26   Official Virgin Blue statement, quoted in David Fulbrook 'Virgin Blue declines tie up with Tesna', *Air Transport Intelligence news*, 22 February 2002.
27   David Fulbrook 'Virgin Blue eyes half of Australian market', *Air Transport Intelligence news*, 13 March 2002.
28   'Patrick buys into Virgin Blue', *Flight International*, 19 March 2002.
29   David Knibb 'Canada 3000 collapse raises questions', *Airline Business*, January 2002.
30   Comment from an Air Canada source in a correspondence with this author, November 2001.
31   Quoted in Frederik Balfour 'Small is beautiful', *BusinesWeek*, February 25 2002, p. 29.
32   Ibid.
33   Kevin O'Toole and Mark Pilling 'Climbing the mountain', *Airline Business*, March 2002.
34   Ray Webster quoted in Graham Dunn 'EasyJet considers A319 for further expansion', *Air Transport Intelligence news*, 7 January 2002.

Appendix

Vreats

Comparison of Train- and Air Fares in the European Union

Trip specifications:
Leaving Friday 2nd of March 2001 (Afternoon)
Returning Sunday 4th of March 2001 (Evening)
All fares quoted are standard 2nd class and Economy class fares that meet the above trip specifications

Route	Mode	Carrier	Airport1	Average Travel Time	No. of Transfers /Layover	Fare (one w	Fare (round-trip)
Brussels - Frankfurt	Train			05:49	1	66.99EUR2	127.76EUR2
Brussels - Frankfurt	Airplane	Lufthansa	BRU - FRA	01:05	0		144EUR7
Brussels - Frankfurt	Airplane	Sabena	BRU - FRA	01:03	0		220.3EUR8
Brussels - Berlin	Train			07:11	1	129.37EUR1	225.53EUR2
Brussels - Berlin	Airplane	Lufthansa	BRU - TXL	01:25	0		137EUR7
Brussels - Berlin	Airplane	Sabena	BRU - TXL	no direct flights			
Brussels - Milan	Train			12:09	0		218.64EUR14
Brussels - Milan	Airplane	Alitalia	BRU - MXP	01:35	0		324EUR9
Brussels - Milan	Airplane	Sabena	BRU - MXP	01:30	0		200.52EUR8
Brussels - Rome	Train			19:05	1		278.14EUR14
Brussels - Rome	Airplane	Alitalia	BRU - FCO	02:05	0/1		793.978EUR9
Brussels - Rome	Airplane	Sabena	BRU - FCO	02:13	0		236.59EUR8
Frankfurt - Vienna	Train			07:31	0	98.03EUR3	196.06EUR
Frankfurt - Vienna	Airplane	Lufthansa	FRA - VIE	01:30	0		390.69EUR7
Frankfurt - Vienna	Airplane	Austrian Airlines	FRA - VIE	01:30	0		253.02EUR7
Frankfurt - Luxembourg	Train			03:35	1	45.82EUR4	91.64EUR
Frankfurt - Luxembourg	Airplane	Lufthansa	FRA - LUX	no direct flights			
Frankfurt - Luxembourg	Airplane	Luxair	FRA - LUX	00:45	0		262.04EUR7

Route	Mode	Carrier	Airport1	Average Travel Time	No. of Trans- fers /Layover	Fare (one w	Fare (round-trip)
Frankfurt - Paris	Train			06:12		73.34EUR6	146.68EUR
Frankfurt - Paris	Train			06:20	3	80.3EUR5	160.6EUR
Frankfurt - Paris	Airplane	Lufthansa	FRA - CDG	01:20	0		255.75EUR7
Frankfurt - Paris	Airplane	Air France	FRA - CDG	01:20	0		171.85EUR10
Madrid - Lisbon	Train				0	46.28EUR1	95.56EUR
Madrid - Lisbon	Airplane	Tap	MAD - LIS	01:05	0		154.08EUR11
Madrid - Lisbon	Airplane	Iberia	MAD - LIS	01:10	0		210EUR12
Madrid - Paris	Train				0		183.93EUR15
Madrid - Paris	Airplane	Air France	MAD - CDG	02:03	0		382.2EUR10
Madrid - Paris	Airplane	Iberia	MAD - ORY	01:53	0		190EUR12
Paris - Amsterdam	Train	Thalys		04:11	0	76.69EUR	141.94EUR6
Paris - Amsterdam	Airplane	Air France	CDG - AMS	01:13	0		204.06EUR10
Paris - Amsterdam	Airplane	KLM	CDG - AMS	01:10	0		204.08EUR13
Paris - Rome	Train			14:34		102.76EUR	223.82EUR6
Paris - Rome	Airplane	Air France	CDG - FCO	02:05	0		1035.70EUR10
Paris - Rome	Airplane	Alitalia	CDG - FCO	02:05	0/1		810.707EUR9
Paris - Bruxelles	Train	Thalys		01:23	0	57.78EUR	107.18EUR6
Paris - Bruxelles	Airplane	Air France	CDG - BRU	01:03	0		179.17EUR10
Paris - Bruxelles	Airplane	Sabena	CDG - BRU	00:58	0		179.19EUR8
Paris - Milan	Train			07:50	1		185.07EUR6
Paris - Milan	Airplane	Air France	CDG - MXP	01:30	0		514.93EUR10
Paris - Milan	Airplane	Alitalia	CDG - MXP	01:33	0		762.675EUR9
Paris - Luxembourg	Train			03:59	1	42.08EUR	84.16EUR6
Paris - Luxembourg	Airplane	Air France		no flights from 2nd to 9th March			

Route	Mode	Carrier	Airport1	Average Travel Time	No. of Trans- fers /Layover	Fare (one w	Fare (round-trip)
Paris - Luxembourg	Airplane	Luxair	CDG - LUX	00:58	0		435.19EUR7
Luxembourg - Brussels	Train			02:41	0		46.11EUR14
Luxembourg - Brussels	Airplane	Sabena	LUX - BRU	00:50	0		253.10EUR8
Luxembourg - Brussels	Airplane	Luxair		no direct flights			

Legend

1	FRA	Frankfurt International
	LUX	Luxembourg Findel
	BRU	Brussels
	AMS	Amsterdam - Schiphol International
	MXP	Milan - Malpensa
	CDG	Paris - Charles de Gaulle
	FCO	Rome - Leonardo da Vinci-Fiumicino
	MAD	Madrid - Barajas
	ORY	Paris - Orly
	LIS	Lisbon
	VIE	Vienna - Schwechat
	TXL	Berlin - Tegel
2		Fare obtained from the Websites of Belgian and German Railways
3		Fare obtained from the Websites of Austrian and German Railways
4		Fare obtained from the Website of German Railways (DB) and the Information Service of Luxembourgish Railways (CFL)
5		Fare obtained from the Websites of German and French Railways
6		Fare obtained from the Website of French Railways (SNCF)
7		Fare obtained from the Lufthansa Website
8		Fare obtained from the Sabena Website
9		Fare obtained from the Alitalia Website
10		Fare obtained from the Air France Website
11		Fare obtained from the Tap-Air Portugal Website
12		Fare obtained from the Iberia Website
13		Fare obtained from the KLM Website
14		Fare obtained from the Website of Belgian Railways (SNCB)
15		Fare obtained from the Website of Spanish Railways (Renfe)

Bibliography

Adams, M. (2001), 'Discount airlines see better odds as others slash flights', *USA Today*, 26 October, pp. 3A-B.

Aer Lingus *Annual Report and Consolidated Accounts*, for year ended 31 December 1996.

Airline Business (1996), 'Mixed Fortunes', May.

Airline Business (1997), 'A Picture of Health', May.

Airline Business (2001), 'The airline rankings: financial analysis, September 2001, pp. 62-92.

Air Transport Users Council (1998), *Annual Report 1997/98*, London: AUC.

Air UK Group Limited Financial Statements (1995), for year ended 31 December.

Airclaims (1997), *Airline Finance and Traffic*, Airclaims Publications, London.

AirTran Holdings Inc. (2001), *Annual Report 2000*, Atlanta, Georgia.

Ames, B.C. and Hlavacek, J. D. (1990), 'Vital truths about managing your costs', *Harvard Business Review*, January-February, pp. 140-7.

Ashton-Davies, T. (1996), 'Focus on customer service at all costs', *Professional Manager*, July, pp. 12-13.

Association of European Airlines (1995), *EU external aviation relations: AEA policy statement*, Brussels.

Association of European Airlines Yearbook (2000), Brussels.

Aviation Week and Space Technology (2000), 'European regionals seek routes to profit', 9 October.

Baker, C. (2000a), 'An anxious era', *Airline Business*, November, pp. 75-7.

Baker, C. (2000b), 'KLM uk sets off for low cost growth', *Airline Business*, February, p. 19.

Baker, C. (2001), 'Buzz still waits for fleet upgrade as it cuts service', *Airline Business*, September, p. 24.

Banfe, Charles F. (1992), *Airline Management*, Prentice Hall, Englewood Cliffs, New Jersey.

Barkin, T.I. Hertzell, O.S. and Young, S.J. (1995a), 'Facing low-cost competitors: lessons from US airlines', *The McKinsey Quarterly*, No.4, pp. 86-99.

Barrett, S.D. (1987), *Flying high: airline prices and European regulation*, Avebury, Aldershot.

Barrett, S.D. (1997), 'The implications of the Ireland-UK airline deregulation for an EU internal market', *Journal of Air Transport Management*, 3:2.

Bendell, T. Boulter, L. and Kelly, J. (1993), *Benchmarking for competitive advantage*, Pitman, London.

Berechman, J. and de Wit, J. (1996), 'An analysis of the effects of the European aviation deregulation on an airline's network structure and choice of a primary West European hub airport', *Journal of Transport Economics and Policy*, September, pp. 251-68.

Berry, L.L., Parasuraman, A. and Zeithaml, V.A. (1994), 'Improving service quality in America: lessons learned', *The Academy of Management Executive*, vol.VII, no.2.

Bhide, A. (1992), 'Bootstrap finance: the art of start-ups', *Harvard Business Review*, November-December, pp. 109-17.

Birns, H. (2001),'Comair launches frills-free carrier to entice non-flyers', *Flight International*, 14 August.

Bloomberg New Bulletin, 8th and 13th August 1996.

Bowen, B. and Headley, D. (2001), *The national airline quality rating: results 2001*, paper and report presented at the Aviation Management Education and Research Conference, The Molson Business School, Montreal, Canada, 16-17 July 2001.

British Airport Authority (1996), *Heathrow: a celebration of 50 years*, London: BAA.

British Midland (1996), *Clearing the flight path for competition*, BM, Castle Donington.

British Midland (1997), *Unfinished Business: a report on competition, choice and value for money in European air travel*, Charles Barker Publishing, London.

Burghouwt, G. and Hakfoort, J. (2000), The European aviation network, 1990-98, *Air Transport Research Group conference*, 3-4 July, Amsterdam.

Button, K. and Swann, D. (1989), European Community airlines – deregulation and its problems, *Journal of Common Market Studies*, XXVII, 4 June, pp. 259-82.

Button, K. (ed.) (1991), *Airline deregulation*, London: David Fulton Publishers.

Buzzell, R.D. and Gale, B.T. (1987), *The PIMS principle*, Free Press, London.

Capell, K., Tromben, C. and Echikson, W. (2001), 'Renegade Ryanair', *Business Week*, 14 May, pp. 38-43.

Chan, K. W. and Mauborgne, R. (1997), 'Value innovation: the strategic logic of high growth', *Harvard Business Review*, January-February, pp. 103-12.

Cini, M. and McGowan, L. (1998), *Competition Policy in the European Union*, Basingstoke: Macmillan.

Civil Aviation Authority (1995), *The single European aviation market: progress so far*, London: CAA.

Civil Aviation Authority (1995-7), *UK airlines: monthly operating and traffic statistics*, CAA, London.

Civil Aviation Authority (1998), *The single European aviation market: the first five years*, CAP 685, London: CAA.

Collins, J.C. and Porras, J.I. (1996), 'Building your company's vision', *Harvard Business Review*, September-October, pp. 65-77.

Comité des Sages (1994), *Expanding Horizons*, a report by the Comité des Sages for Air Transport to the European Commission, Brussels, January 1994.

Commission of the European Communities (CEC) (1984), *Civil Aviation Memorandum No.2: progress towards the development of a Community air transport policy*, COM(84) 72 final.

Commission of the European Communities (1992), *Report by the Commission to the Council and the European Parliament on the evaluation of aid schemes established in favour of community air carriers*, Doc. SEC (92), 431 final, 19 March.

Commission of the European Communities (1992), *Air transport relations with third countries*, COM(92) 434 final, Brussels, 21 October 1992.

Commission of the European Communities (1994), *The way forward for civil aviation in Europe*, COM(94) 218 final, Brussels, 1 June.

Commission of the European Communities (1999), *The aviation single market is a real achievement to be consolidated, while worldwide challenges are ahead of Europe* , IP/99/339, Brussels, 21 May.

Commission of the European Communities (2001), *Updating and development of economic and fares data regarding the European air travel industry*, Directorate General Energy and Transport, Contract No B99-B2704010-SI2.1738/P C2 98 002, Brussels, July.

Council Regulation (EEC) No 95/93 of 18 January 1993 on common rules for the allocation of slots at Community airports, *Official Journal L 014, 22/1/1993*, pp. 0001-0006.

Council Directive 96/67/EC of 15 October 1996 on access to the groundhandling market at Community airports, *Official Journal L 272, 25/10/1996*, pp. 0036-0045.

Couvret, P. (1996), 'Back to your routes', *Airline Business*, November, pp. 60-3.

Cram, L. (1993), 'Calling the tune without paying the piper? Social policy regulation: the role of the Commission in European Community social policy', *Policy and Politics*, Vol.21, No.2, pp. 135-46.

Cram, L. (1994), 'The European Commission as a multi-organization: social policy and IT policy in the EU', *Journal of European Public Policy*, Vol.1, No.2, pp. 195-217.

Dambey, D. (2001), 'Member states support EU restrictions on aid for stricken airlines', *The Financial Times*, 17 October.

Dobson, A.P. (1995), *Flying in the Face of Competition*, Avebury, Aldershot.

Doganis, R. (1991), *Flying Off Course*, London: Harper Collins Academic, 2nd ed.

Doganis, R. (1994), 'The impact of liberalization on European airline strategies and operations', *Journal of Air Transport Management*, 1:1, pp. 15-25.

Dcganis, R. (2001), 'Survival lessons', *Airline Business*, January, pp. 62-5.

Done, K. (2001), 'British carriers eye some more markets', *The Financial Times*, 11 May.

Donnelly, S.B. (2001), 'Blue Skies', *Time Magazine*.

Dresner, M, Lin, J-S.C. and Windle, R. (1996), 'The impact of low-cost carriers on airport and route competition', *Journal of Transport Economics and Policy*, Vol. xxx, no.3, pp. 309-28.

Dunn, G. (2001a), 'Transavia adds Malaga to Basiq Air destinations', *Air Transport Intelligence News*, 15 May.

Dunn, G. (2001b), 'SAA cuts fares to counter upstart Kulula', *Air Transport Intelligence News*, 13 July.

Economic and Social Committee of the European Communities (1985), *EEC Air Transport Policy*, report of the section for transport, Brussels, October 1985.

Feldman, J.M. (1996), 'Booting up competition', *Air Transport World*, October, pp. 89-90.

Feldman, D. (1998), 'Winning strategies for airports – a look at developments in Europe', *Airline Business*.

Feldman, J.M. (2000), 'IT, culture and Southwest', *Air Transport World*, No.5, pp. 45-9.

Field, D. (2001), 'Regionals – top 100 ranking', *Airline Business*, May, pp. 62-4.

Field, D. (2001b), 'Back in the limelight', *Airline Business*, August, pp. 42-4.

Flint, P. (2000), 'Back on schedule', *Air Transport World*, No.11, pp. 47-51.

Flores, J. (2001), 'Amazonian Blues', *Flight International*, 4 September.

Freiberg, K. and Freiberg, J. (2001), *NUTS! Southwest Airlines craze recipe for business and personal success*, TEXERE Publishing: New York/London.

Fullbrook, D. (2001), 'Japan's Skymark reports smaller first-half loss', *Air Transport Intelligence news*, 18 June.

Garda, R.A. and Marn, M.V. (1993), 'Price wars', *The McKinsey Quarterly*, No. 3, pp. 87-100.

Garvin, D.A. (1993), 'Building a learning organization', *Harvard Business Review*, July-August, pp. 78-91.

Go (1999), 'Room for all: a report on the low cost airline sector from Go', company press release.

Goodbody Stockbrokers (1998), *Ryanair: preparing for fleet expansion*, Equity Research, 20 August.

Graham, B. (1997), 'Regional airline services in the liberalized European Union single aviation market', *Journal of Air Transport Management*, 3:4, pp. 227-38.

Gudmundsson, S.V. (1998), 'New-entrant airlines' life cycle analysis: growth, decline and collapse', *Journal of Air Transport Management*, 4, pp. 217-28.

Gudmundsson, S.V. (1999), 'Airline alliances: consumer and policy issues', *European Business Journal*, 11:3, pp. 139-45.

Guild, S. (1995), 'Not so easy', *Airline Business*, June, pp. 68-73.

Guillebaud, D. (1998), 'Survey on travel and tourism', *The Economist*, 10 January.

Hanlon, P. (1996), *Global Airlines: competition in a transnational industry*, Oxford: Butterworth Heinemann.

Haas, E.B. (1958), *The Uniting of Europe: political, social, and economic forces, 1950-1957*, London: Stevens & Sons.

Hamel, G. and Prahalad, C. K. (1993), 'Strategy as stretch and leverage', *Harvard Business Review*, March-April, pp. 75-84.

Hamel, G. (1996), 'Strategy as Revolution', *Harvard Business Review*, July-August, pp. 69-82.

Hinthorne, T. (1996), 'Predatory capitalism, pragmatism, and legal positivism in the airline industry', *Strategic Management Journal*, vol.17, no.4, pp. 251-70.

Holiday – Which? Magazine (2001), *Which airline?*, Spring, pp. 80-3.

Holloway, S. (1997), *Straight and Level: practical airline economics*, Ashgate Publishing, Aldershot.

International Chamber of Commerce, policy statement (1995), 'State Aid to Airlines', *Commission on Airlines*, 13 June.

Ionides, N. (2000a), 'Third Japanese new-start Fair Inc launches services', *Air Transport Intelligence News*, 8 August.

Ionides, N. (2000b), 'Spoiling for choice', *Airline Business*, October.

Ionides, N. (2001a), 'Virgin Blue eyes ten Ansett aircraft, plans new routes', *Air Transport Intelligence News*, 14 September.

Ionides, N. (2001b), 'Sun Country to cut 20% of workforce', *Air Transport Intelligence News*, 2 October.

Irish Department of Transport, Energy and Communications (1997), *Statement of Strategy*, February.

Janić, M. (1997), 'Liberalisation of European aviation: analysis and modelling of the airline behaviour', *Journal of Air Transport Management*, vol.3, no.4, pp. 167-80.

J.D. Power and Associates/Frequent Flyer Magazine (1997), 'Domestic Airline Customer Satisfaction Study', www.jdpower.com.

Jeziorski, A. (2000), 'Low key liberalisation', *Flight International*, 14 March.

Johnson, K. and Scholes, G. (1997), *Exploring corporate strategy*, Prentice Hall, London.

Jones, D. (1996), 'Baby boomers', *Airfinance Journal*, December, pp. 22-5.

Kay, J. (1993), *Foundations of corporate success*, Oxford University Press, Oxford.

Kassim, H. (1995), 'Air transport champions: still carrying the flag', In J. Hayward (ed.) *Industrial enterprise and European integration*, Oxford: Oxford University Press.

Keohane, R.O. and Hoffman, S. (1991), 'Institutional Change in Europe in the 1980s', in R.O. Keohane and S. Hoffman (eds.) *The New European Community*. Colorado: Westview Press.

Killian, M. (2001), 'The twin-engined Cockatoo', *Airliner World*, August, pp. 52-9.

Kim, W.C. and Mauborgne, R. (1997), 'Value innovation: the strategic logic of high growth', *Harvard Business Review*, January-February, 103-12.

Kinnock, N. (1998), opening remarks for 'Meeting the global challenge: the outlook for civil aviation in the EU' (organised by Forum Europe), Brussels, 27 January.

Knibb, D. (2000a), 'WestJet eyes move to number one', *Airline Business*, April, p. 16.

Knibb, D. (2000b), 'Australian test match', *Airline Business*, August, pp. 76-9.

Knibb, D. (2001a), 'Air Canada takes action to counter business slump', *Airline Business*, September, p. 20.

Knibb, D. (2001b), 'Canadian challengers', *Airline Business*, September, pp. 101-4.

Lawton, T.C. (1999), 'Governing the skies: conditions for the Europeanization of airline policy', *Journal of Public Policy*, vol.19 no.1, pp. 91-112.

Lawton, T.C. (1999), 'The limits of price leadership: needs-based position strategies and the long-term competitiveness of Europe's low fare airlines', *Long Range Planning*, vol.32, No.6, pp. 573-86.

Lawton, T.C. (2000), 'Flying lessons: learning from Ryanair's cost reduction culture', *The Journal of Air Transportation World Wide*, Vol.5, No.1, pp. 89-106.

Lawton, T.C. (2001), 'Missing the Target: assessing the role of government in bridging the European equity gap and enhancing economic growth', *Venture Capital: International Journal of Entrepreneurial Finance*, Vol.4, No.1, pp. 7-23.

Lennane, A. (2000), 'Super models', *Airfinance Journal*, February, issue 225, pp. 28-31.

Lookturn Ltd. (1997), *Air transport progress '97*, London.

Lyle, C. (1995) 'Agent blues...', *Airline Business*, November, pp. 56-60.

Lynch, R. (1997), *Corporate strategy*, Pitman, London.

Mason, K. (2000a), 'The propensity of business travellers to use low cost airlines', *Journal of Transport Geography*, 8:2, pp. 107-19.

Mason, K. (2000b), 'Marketing low cost airline services to business travellers', paper presented at the 4th Air Transport Research Group Conference, Amsterdam, 2-5 July.

Mazey, S. (1996), 'The development of the European idea' in J. Richardson (ed.) *European Union: power and policy making*, London: Routledge.

McKinsey & Co. (1995), 'A new game plan for Europe', *The Avmark Aviation Economist*, April.

McMillan, B. (2000), "Japan's 'Big Three' keep up pressure on Skymark", *Air Transport Intelligence News*, 23 August.

McWhirter, A. (2000), 'Plain saving: no frills but no big bills either', *Business Traveller*, June, pp. 24-7.

Mintzberg, R., Quinn, J. B., and Ghoshal, S. (1998), *The strategy process*, Prentice Hall, Hemel Hempstead.

Moravcsik, A. (1991), 'Negotiating the Single European Act: national interests and conventional statecraft in the European Community', *International Organization*, Vol.45, 1, 651-88.

Morgan Stanley (1997), 'European Transport: Airlines (Ryanair: Flying Celtic Tiger)', *Investment Research UK and* Europe, 2 May.

Morrell, P.S. (1997), *Airline Finance*, Ashgate Publishing, Aldershot.

Morrell, P. (1998), 'Air transport liberalization in Europe: the progress so far', *Journal of Air Transportation World Wide*, 3:1, pp. 42-60.

Morrell, P. and Lu, H-Y. C (2000), 'Ahead of the game', *Airline Business*, February, pp. 80-3.

Nuutnen, H. (1996a), 'US low cost new entrants: pre- and post-ValueJet', *The Avmark Aviation Economist*, June, pp. 4-10.

Nuutinen, H. (1996b), 'US low cost airlines: the barriers to entry go up again', *The Avmark Aviation Economist*, November, pp. 4-11.

Oliver, N. and Wilkinson, R. (1989), 'Strategic fit: the real lesson from Japan', *University of Wales Review of Economics and Business*, 4.

O'Toole, K. (2000a), 'The new European', *Airline Business*, March, pp. 32-5.

O'Toole, K. (2000b), 'Regional reflections', *Airline Business*, May, pp. 39-43.

Phelan, P. (2000), 'Impulse confirms June statement for cut-price 717 services', *Flight International*, 18-24 April.

Porter, M.E. (1985), *Competitive Advantage*, Free Press, London.

Porter, M.E. (1996), 'What is Strategy?', *Harvard Business Review*, November-December, pp. 61-78.

PricewaterhouseCoopers (2000), *Study of certain aspects of Council Regulation 95/93 on common rules for the allocation of slots at Community airports*, final report to the European Commission, 20 May.

Quinn, J.B. and Hilmer, F.G. (1995), 'Strategic Outsourcing', *The McKinsey Quarterly*, No.1, 1995, pp. 49-70.

Randall, J. (2001), 'BA gets back on course now Go has finally gone', *Sunday Business*, 17 June, p. 18.

Redmile, Annie (2000), 'Passenger priorities', *Airline Business*, March, pp. 70-2.

Rhoades, D.L. and Waguespack Jr., B. (2000a), 'Service quality in the U.S. airline industry: variations in performance within airlines and between airlines and the industry', *Journal of Air Transportation World Wide*, vol.5 no.1, pp. 60-77.

Rhoades, D.L. and Waguespack Jr., B. (2000b) 'Judging a book by its cover: the relationship between service and safety quality in US national and regional airlines', *Journal of Air Transport Management*, 6, pp. 87-94.

Richardson, J.J. and Lindley, R. (eds), (1995), Journal of European Public Policy special issue, *The Single Market and global economic integration*, 2, 3.

Robertson, T.S. (1995), 'Corporate graffiti', *Business Strategy Review*, vol.6, no.1, pp. 27-44.

Rubython, T. (1999), 'BA's brightest star', *EuroBusiness*, vol.1, no.1, June, pp. 36-40.

Ryanair plc. Annual reports, internal company documentation, marketing documentation, press releases.

Ryanair Holdings plc (1998/1999/2000/2001) *Annual Report and Financial Statements*, Dublin.

Sampson, A. (1984), *Empires of the sky (the politics, contests and cartels of world airlines)*, London: Hodder and Stoughton.

Scharpf, F. (1994), Community and autonomy: multi-level policy-making in the European Union, *Journal of European Public Policy*, Vol.1, No.2, pp.219-42.

Schultz, A.C. and Schultz, E.P. (2000), 'The case of Morris Air: a successful startup', *Journal of Air Transportation World Wide*, vol.5 no.2, pp. 87-109.

Seristö, H. and Vepsäläinen, A.P.J. (1997), 'Airline cost drivers: cost implications of fleet, routes, and personnel policies', *Journal of Air Transport Management*, vol.3, no.1, pp. 11-22.

Shaw, S. (1985), *Airline Marketing and Management*, Pitman, London.

Skapinker, M. (1997), 'Why the air is thick with budget fares', *The Financial Times*, September 3.

Shifrin, C. (2000), 'Out of the blue', *Airline Business*, March, pp. 42-3.

Shifrin, C. (2001), 'JetBlue creates mini-hub in LA', *Airline Business*, July, p. 15.

Sobie, B. (2001a), 'AirTran Airways to trade on NY stock exchange', *Air Transport Intelligence News*, 7 August.

Sobie, B. (2001b), 'Former WestJet chief to run Air Canada's low fare carrier', *Air Transport Intelligence News*, 21 August.

Sobie, B. (2001c), 'Frontier lowers profit estimate for 3Q', *Air Transport Intelligence News*, 5 September.

Sobie, B. (2001d), 'JetBlue trims schedule but avoids layoffs and delivery delays', *Air Transport Intelligence News*, 20 September.

Sobie, B. (2001e), 'Sun Country trims capacity and plans job cuts', *Air Transport Intelligence News*, 25 September.

Sochor, E. (1991), 'The Politics of International Aviation', London: Macmillan.

Solon, D. (2000), 'Corporate strategy: JetBlue Airways Corporation', *The Avmark Aviation Economist*, November, pp. 4-7.

Stalk, G., Evans, P. and Shulman L.E. (1992), 'Competing On Capabilities: the new rules of corporate strategy', *Harvard Business Review*, March-April, pp.57-69.

Sull, D. (1999), 'easyJet's $500 million gamble', *European Management Journal*, vol.17, No.1, pp. 20-32.

Sweeney, C. (2001), 'State-aid to Aer Lingus ruled out', *The Sunday Independent* (Ireland), 7 October, p. 17.

Sweeney, C. (2001), 'She holds the skies in her own two hands', *The Sunday Independent* (Ireland), 7 October, p. 18.

The Economist (1998), *Dream factories: a survey of travel and tourism*, 10 January.

The Economist (2001), 'The Sky's the Limit: a survey of air travel', 10 March, p.6.

The Economist (2001), 'unchartered airspace', 3 October.

The Financial Times (1996), 'Airlines may have breached Brussels terms', 23 February.

The Robinson-Humphrey Company, Inc. (1997), *Ryanair: the growth airline of Europe*, equities research, basic report, Atlanta, Georgia.

Thomas, I. (2000a), 'Branson unsettles Australia', *Air Transport World*, February, pp. 32-9.

Thomas, I. (2000b), 'Better late than never', *Air Transport World*, November, pp. 74-7.

Uittenbogaart, Peter (1997), 'Airline competition on the route between Amsterdam and London', *Journal of Air Transport Management*, 3:4, pp. 217-25.

UK Department of Transport (1997), *EC aviation liberalisation information pack*, London: Aviation Group.

United States Department of Transportation (1996), *The low cost airline service revolution*, DOT: Washington D.C.

United States Department of Transportation (1996), 'New lost cost airlines benefit consumers', press release, Office of the Assistant Secretary for Public Affairs, April 23, Washington D.C.

United States Department of Transportation (2001), *Air travel consumer report*, August, Washington D.C.: Office of Aviation Enforcement and Proceedings.

United States Securities and Exchange Commission (2001), *Vanguard Airlines Inc., quarterly report for the period ended June 30, 2001*, Commission File Number 0-27034, Washington D.C.

Van den Polder, R. (1994), 'Lobbying for the European airline industry', in R.H. Pedler and M.P.C.M. Van Schendelen (eds), *Lobbying the European Union*, Aldershot: Dartmouth.

Wagland, M. (2001a), 'Cile delays Aerocontinente Chile's relaunch', *Air Transport Intelligence News*, 12 September.

Wagland, M. (2001b), 'Schroder adds to dire warnings on airline financial health', *Air Transport Intelligence News*, 14 September.

Walker, K. (2000), 'World's Apart', *Airline Business*, July, p. 28.

Walters, J. (2001), 'more job losses a certainty as passengers desert skies', *The Observer*, 7 October, p. 8.

Williams, G. (1993), *The airline industry and the impact of deregulation*, Aldershot: Ashgate.

Williams, J.R. (1998), *Renewable advantage: crafting strategy through economic time*, The Free Press: New York.

Wheatcroft, S. and Lipman, G. (1986), *Air transport in a competitive European market*, EIU Special Report No. 1060.

Wright, V. (1995), 'Conclusion', in J. Hayward (ed.), *Industrial enterprise and European integration*, Oxford: Oxford University Press.

Zellner, W. (1999), 'Bringing new air to New York', *Business Week*, May 10.

Zorn, B. (2001), 'Comparing low cost markets in the USA, UK and Europe', aviation presentation, Amsterdam, 27 February.

Index